Social change  'ife
in J·

Manchester University Press

Social change and everyday life in Ireland 1850–1922

Caitriona Clear

Manchester University Press
Manchester and New York
distributed exclusively in the USA by Palgrave

Published by Manchester University Press
Oxford Road, Manchester M13 9NR, UK
and Room 400, 175 Fifth Avenue, New York,
NY 10010, USA
www.manchesteruniversitypress.co.uk

Distributed exclusively in the USA by
Palgrave, 175 Fifth Avenue, New York,
NY 10010, USA

Distributed exclusively in Canada by
UBC Press, University of British Columbia,
2029 West Mall,
Vancouver, BC, Canada V6T 1Z2

British Library Cataloguing-in-Publication Data
A catalogue record for this book is available from the British Library

Library of Congress Cataloging-in-Publication Data applied for

ISBN   978 07190 7438 7 *paperback*

First published 2007

First reprinted 2009

Printed by Lightning Source

Contents

Acknowledgements

So many people had a hand in the production of this book that my only difficulty in writing these acknowledgments is finding synonyms for the words 'thanks' and 'helpful'! The comments of undergraduate, postgraduate and diploma students on material I gave them to read over the years often spurred me towards the re-evaluation of some historical 'truth' I had been teaching for some time. Thanks to these most important people, without whom I would not have a job in the first place. Thanks to Professor Steven Ellis and to NUI, Galway for giving me a sabbatical year in 2005, when I put a shape on a very rough manuscript. The biggest thanks is to Pádraig Lenihan: not only did he line, insulate, floor, door, window and wire the garden shed in which I did most of this writing, he also encouraged me all the way. James Hardiman Library, NUI, Galway is a good place to work – Marie Boran, Gerry D'arcy, Josephine Finn, Evelyn Flanagan, Kieran Hoare, Gaby Honan, Margaret Hughes, Mary O'Leary, have my sincere thanks. The library stewards, led by Michael O'Connor, were always helpful and pleasant, while college porters John Devaney, Joseph Devaney, Peter Faherty and Matt Reck went way beyond the call of duty in their kindness, courtesy and humour at all times.

I did much of this research over the years in the National Library of Ireland; my thanks go to its wonderful staff. Peter Murray of the Crawford Gallery, Cork, gave me permission for the lovely cover illustration. The National Archives and the old Public Record Office at the Four Courts, and the old State Paper Office in Dublin Castle, have all been great places to do research – my thanks to their members of staff too.

On the actual book, Niall O Ciosáin read one chapter and made very useful comments. I also either discussed the book (in whole or in part, recently or long ago) with, or received valuable documents, information, insights and encouragement from, the following people, in roughly alphabetical order: Tom Bartlett, Marie Boran, Nicholas Canny, Mary Cawley, Mary Clancy, Kathleen Clear, Paddy Clear, Eileen Clear, Mary Clear (Dublin), the late Sr Gertrude Clear (Boston), Mary Coll, Maura Cronin, Mary Cullen, John Cunningham, Geraldine Curtin, Larry de Cléir, Síle de Cléir, Mary Daly, Leonore Davidoff, Phil Faherty, Tony Fahey, the late Jenny Finlay, Máire Flannery, John Gibbons, Michael Gorman, Alan Hayes, Sinéad Jackson, Sr Conleth Kelly, Claudia Kinmonth, Margaret Larkin, Mary Lawless, Maureen Langan-Egan, Pádraig Lenihan, Gráinne Lenihan, Paddy Lenihan, Bríd Lenihan, John Logan, Maria Luddy, Marie Mannion, Eithne McCormack, Margaret MacCurtain, Dympna McLoughlin, the late Gearóid MacNiocaill, Gerard Moran, Thomas Murtagh, Diarmuid O Cearbhaill, Liam O'Connor, Margaret O hOgartaigh, the late Joe O'Halloran, Tony O'Leary, Ciaran O Murchadha, the late T.P.O'Neill, Gearóid O Tuathaigh, Lionel Pilkington, Jacinta Prunty, the late Agnes Ryan, Patricia Ryan, Pauline Scully, Ide Sionóid, Jim Smith, Penny Summerfield, the late Sr Eileen (Baptist) Synnott, Sr Carmel Synnott, Elizabeth Tilley.

I was very lucky to have inspiring history teachers in the Presentation Convent, Sexton Street, Limerick – a Sr Patricia (a visiting Sister of Mercy who taught us in 1972–73 and whose surname I never learned, a brilliant teacher), Sr Maria Assumpta (who taught Latin but with a great eye for Roman history), Tony Costello and Dave Shee. In the European University Institute in Florence, where I began some of the vagrancy research in 1984–85: Fiona Hayes, Damian Collins, Richard Dunphy, Vincent Eicher, Norbert Hentz, Eve Lerman, Susanna Terstal, Martin van Gelderen, Henk Voskamp, Stuart Woolf and others were very enlightening, and I derived great benefit from the seminar series at the Institute.

At Manchester University Press Alison Welsby and Jonathan Bevan have been courteous, pleasant and prompt at all times, but the anonymous reader of the manuscript deserves my deepest gratitude for pointing out some embarrassing inaccuracies, curbing some flights of fancy and poking at some flabbiness in the narrative. *Go raibh míle maith agaibh go léir!* Mistakes, misinterpretations and misrepresentations are all my own.

And an acknowledgment finally to Donncha, Manus, Cora and Síle Lenihan whose only contact with my history persona are my constant mutterings about when I was their age . . .

Chronology of Irish politics, 1800–1922

1800   Act of Union, removing College Green Parliament
            from Dublin; all Irish MPs sit in Westminster.
1829   Catholic Emancipation, led by Daniel O'Connell.
            Catholics, some of whom had the parliamentary vote
            since 1793, are eligible to be elected to Parliament.
1830s–40s   The ultimately unsuccessful movement for Repeal of
            the Union, led by Daniel O'Connell.
1845–49   The Great Famine: approximately 1 million die,
            1 million emigrate.
1858   Formation of the Irish Republican Brotherhood
            (Fenians) with close links to Irish emigrants in
            America. Failed rising in 1867. Strong influence on
            Irish nationalism down to 1916.
1867   Franchise extended all over UK and Ireland, to include
            a greater number of working-class and labouring men
            than before.
1869   Disestablishment of the Church of Ireland. William
            Gladstone becomes Prime Minister: 'my mission is to
            pacify Ireland'.
1870   Land Act gives tenants grants to purchase holdings and
            gives legal basis to 'Ulster custom' (free sale of holdings
            and security of tenure) where it exists.
1873   The Home Rule Party is set up, under Isaac Butt,
            looking for restoration of the College Green Parlia-
            ment and independence within the empire for Ireland.
1875   Introduction of the secret ballot.
1879–82   A combination of bad weather, low prices and
            worldwide depression give rise to agrarian dissatisfac-
            tion, expressed in the formation in 1879 of the Irish

Land League. Charles Stewart Parnell assumes leadership of the Home Rule Party, of which he had been a member, in 1880. Land Act 1881 gives further concessions to tenants, and is extended after much agitation in 1882. Land League is wound down and replaced by the Irish National League, an organization of the Home Rule Party.

1885   Male franchise extended even further.

1885–86   Gladstone announces his conversion to the cause of Home Rule. The Home Rule Party allies itself with the Liberal Party. Almost half of the House of Commons supports Home Rule, though the First Home Rule Bill fails. Ulster Unionist Party is founded.

1886–91   Plan of Campaign – ongoing non-violent resistance to rent on 203 estates throughout the country, backed by some Home Rule politicians – Matthew Harris, Tim Harington, Tim Healy, William Redmond, Willliam O'Brien, David Sheehy – and many journalists. Failure, but a propaganda victory.

1885–1908 Successive Land Acts, mainly under Conservative governments, eventually make Irish tenants owner–occupiers and compel the landlords to sell their lands. Part of 'Constructive Unionism'.

1880s–1922 'Constructive Unionism': Congested Districts Board 1891 pours much money and expertise into the 'congested' and very poor areas of the west. Department of Agriculture and Technical Instruction, under Horace Plunkett, is set up to improve agricultural performance and profits. Farmers are encouraged to form co-operatives. Travelling classes and other educational initiatives and incentives established. Dissemination of information about public health and welfare.

1890–91   Home Rule Party splits over Parnell divorce case; death of Parnell.

1884–93   Gaelic Athletic Association, Gaelic League: revival of interest in Irish games and Irish language. Hugely popular organizations throughout the country, fostering parish and county identities, in the case of sport, and eventually, by the early twentieth century, getting Irish taught in Ireland's schools.

1894	Irish Trades Union Congress formed, with a membership of trade unions representing mainly skilled workers, but an important step for labour movement.
1898	Local Government Act: setting up of county councils, urban district councils. Women's representation increased at local level (part of Constructive Unionism).
1900	Home Rule Party reunites under John Redmond, goes from strength to strength, and Home Rule is passed by the Houses of Commons and Lords by 1911. Cumann na nGaedheal is formed under Arthur Griffith, a party of non-violent and non-parliamentary nationalism which accepted women as equal members. Maud Gonne founds Inghinidhe na hEireann (Daughters of Ireland.)
1908	Formation of the Irish Transport and General Workers' Union, under James Larkin. Also, most vocal and active suffrage movement, Irish Women's Franchise League.
1885–1912	Unionists all over Ireland, but particularly in Ulster, organize against Home Rule for political, religious and economic reasons.
1912	Labour Party founded (full title: Irish Trades Union Congress and Labour Party). Solemn League and Covenant and formation of Ulster Volunteers, a militia of support to the Edward Carson-led Ulster Unionists.
1913	Dublin Lock Out; members of the ITGWU locked out of their workplaces. Failure, but propaganda victory. Formation of the Irish Citizen Army under Captain Jack White.
1914	Irish Volunteers – with female auxiliary Cumann na mBan – formed by Eoin MacNeill. First World War breaks out in August. Majority of Volunteers follow John Redmond's advice to fight with Britain. Minority calling themselves Irish Volunteers 'serve neither King nor Kaiser, but Ireland'.
1916	Easter Rising in Dublin – Irish Volunteers, Irish Citizen Army and Irish Republican Brotherhood. Signatories to the Proclamation, which embodies a social-democratic, nationalist vision, are court-martialled and executed – Patrick Pearse, James Connolly,

Thomas Clarke, Thomas MacDonagh, Eamonn Ceannt, Sean MacDiarmada, Joseph Plunkett – as are other garrison leaders (except Eamon de Valera, an American citizen, and Constance Markievicz). Rising crushed, but executions produce wave of popular sympathy for insurgents and for nationalism in general. Arthur Griffith's Sinn Fein becomes the political mouthpiece of the Irish Volunteers and an alternative to the Home Rule movement.

1918   Wave of support for non-parliamentary nationalism following anti-conscription campaign 1917–18. Sinn Fein election victory 1918. Parliamentary franchise extended to include all men over 21 and all women over 30. First woman ever elected to House of Commons is Sinn Fein's Constance Markievicz, but does not take her seat because she is a member of the first Dáil.

1919   First Dáil set up Dublin (elected in 1918, abstaining from Westminster.)

1919–21 War for Independence. Britain sends 'Black and Tans' and 'Auxiliaries' as paramilitary police force. Second Dáil elected.

1920   Government of Ireland Act establishing Northern Ireland as part of the United Kingdom.

1921–22 Truce. Treaty establishing Free State accepted by majority in Dáil Eireann and Treaty candidates successful in general election.

1922   Saorstát Eireann/Irish Free State consisting of twenty-six counties, while status of the north to be decided by Boundary Commission. Women over 21 get citizenship in Free State on equal terms with men – in Northern Ireland and UK, they have to wait until 1928.

Religion: an explanatory note[1]

Because of Ireland's historical background – the penal laws against Catholics implemented from the late seventeenth century and the novelty of Catholic participation in local and national government – Irish society was extremely self-conscious about religious identity. Schools and other institutions reflected this self-consciousness: any institutions which had their origins in voluntary initiative were run on denominational lines. Catholic nuns were working in at least half of all workhouse hospitals by 1900, and these women – who vastly outnumbered Catholic priests and brothers – were the primary evangelists.[2]

This was a time of increasingly intensive church-centred practice for all denominations. Many devotional practices from Rome and the Continent were introduced into Catholicism, and there was a greater emphasis on mass attendance. Protestant denominations experienced many revivals, especially in Ulster. The north-east of the country had a concentration of Protestants, although Belfast became progressively more Catholic over this period. Elsewhere, while many (though by no means all) major landowners and 'gentry' were Protestants, there were also concentrations of lower-middle-class and working-class Protestants in all the major cities and, outside the nine counties of Ulster, clusters of Protestant farmers and labourers throughout the country, especially in Wicklow, Wexford, Cork, Limerick, north Tipperary, King's County, Carlow, Kilkenny and Kildare.

People of the Jewish faith, mainly immigrants from Eastern Europe, began to make up a noticeable minority in the bigger cities towards the end of the nineteenth century. They never settled in rural Ireland.

Notes

1 For a discussion of writings in the English language on Irish religious history, see S. J. Connolly, 'The moving statue and the turtle dove: approaches to the history of Irish religion', *Irish Economic and Social History*, Vol. 31 (2004), pp. 1–22; see also Risteard O Glaisne, *Módhaigh: scéal Eaglaise, scéal Pobail* (Baile Atha Cliath 1998); Louis Hyman, *Jews in Ireland: from earliest times to the year 1910* (Shannon 1972); and Dermot Keogh, *Jews in Twentieth-Century Ireland* (Cork 1998).

2 Tony Fahey, 'Nuns in the Catholic Church in Ireland in the nineteenth century', in Mary Cullen (ed.), *Girls Don't Do Honours: Irish women in education in the nineteenth and twentieth centuries* (Dublin 1987), pp. 7–30; and Caitriona Clear, *Nuns in Nineteenth-Century Ireland* (Dublin 1987).

Introduction

Good social history sees people's lives 'from the inside out', in Henry Glassie's words,[1] evaluating their working lives and social and personal relationships from their standpoint. People do not go about in a permanent state of consciousness of the wider historical trends in which they are playing a part. As well-informed a man as Dr Charles Cameron, leading public health exponent, could scoff, in 1874, at the idea that the Irish population count was falling: 'It is absurd to believe that the births of Dublin, or any part of Ireland, but slightly exceed the deaths . . . The prolificness of the Irish has become almost a proverb.'[2] People made decisions – to train, to emigrate, to leave home, to stay at home, to marry, to stay single – based on the knowledge they had at the time. The historian must appreciate this before judging the quality of life at any given time.

The historian must also juggle the need to portray life as it was, and the need to chart change and the reasons for it. History is not a series of photographs; it is a moving picture. But to over-use 'eventually' and 'in the long term' is to wriggle out of describing life as it was experienced at various times. Life in Ireland in the seventy years covered by this book was more than an inexorable acceleration towards (and an explanation of) post-independence Ireland, north and south. The trick is to make sparing use of historical hindsight, and to bear in mind Alison Light's comment about growing up in post-war England:

> [W]e didn't think of ourselves as a class – someone might be 'hard-up' or 'badly-off' or 'stuck-up'; it would be many years before being 'working class' became my 'background'. For us there was only the foreground and we were living in the thick of it.[3]

In this book I look at that foreground and at those who inhabited it.

This is a history of how people worked, where they lived, what they ate, wore, sickened and died (or recovered) from, rather than a history of how they saw themselves, each other and their place in the world. In her book on the Victorian house, Judith Flanders cheerfully admits that she is more interested in S-bends than in sex.[4] I am more interested in material life than in *méntalités*. Here, I summarise much useful information about life in Ireland in the period 1850–1922, incorporate some original research, suggest new lines of inquiry and dispute some historical orthodoxies that have grown up over the years.

An undergraduate course entitled 'Gender, work and family in Ireland 1850–1922' was the spur for this book. Finding a suitable textbook was difficult. Existing social histories of Ireland either did not incorporate the research of recent decades or focused more on economics than on social issues. While those works remain essential reading for the student,[5] some kind of summary is sorely needed. Putting multiple copies of books on desk reserve in the library and spending a lot of time at the photocopier, I consoled myself with the thought that there is no need for a textbook as such. Doesn't a text imply an approved and agreed-on narrative, with subject areas and cut-off points? Wouldn't such a narrative exclude as much as it included? However it was not easy to get students to discuss different historical viewpoints on various phenomena without their (and my!) knowing what had actually happened. There is no point in comparing Akenson's view of emigration with that of Miller[6] without knowing, first of all, how many emigrated and when. It is impossible to debate changes in the quality of life without first pinning down what ailments people were dying of and what facilities existed to help or hinder their battle with disease and hardship. What began as a series of handouts setting out the basic facts evolved into a story I had to write. And somewhere along the way, from the newspapers, Census records, Parliamentary Papers, Poor Law records, local history journals, popular autobiographies and other sources I consulted (some of them for the second or third time), Ireland between 1850 and 1922 stopped being a dress-rehearsal for the twentieth century and started to emerge as a place full of all kinds of people with varying degrees of control over their lives. The questions the social historian always wants to ask are: 'Did life get better or worse? Were people happier or unhappier?' Yet before I tried to answer these big questions – to which there are no easy answers – I had to get to know the texture of everyday life. That is why I refer to individual experience whenever possible.

Although Irish language sources are used extensively in this book, the decline of the Irish language is too big a subject for it; so too is religion, though I include a short explanatory note. Politics, local or national, and pressure groups – nationalist, Unionist, trade unionist or feminist – have also been left out, though a chronology of political events has been included. Only passing attention is paid to wealthy landowners and upper–middle-class people in towns and cities, for their diet, clothing, accommodation and health did not differ much from those of wealthy British people at this time, and there are plenty of books about them.[7] I would not presume to call myself a historical voice for the voiceless, but I have tried in this book to look at people whose lives have not been looked at very often before. This is a summary and a survey; if my only achievement is to identify gaps in the research, I am well pleased. Enterprising students can pick up on suggestions for further research scattered throughout the text.

Notes

1   Though this is not a cultural history, I have, like many other scholars, derived great benefit from the humane and inspiring anthropological work of Henry Glassie. This statement is taken from *Passing the Time in Ballymenone: culture and history of an Ulster community* (Indiana, IN 1982), p. 86.

2   Charles A. Cameron, *A Manual of Hygiene, Public and Private, and Compendium of Sanitary Laws* (Dublin 1874), p. 35.

3   Alison Light, 'The word made flesh', *History Workshop Journal*, Vol. 46 (autumn 1998), pp. 177–86.

4   Judith Flanders, *The Victorian House* (London 1993), pp. 2–3.

5   J. J. Lee, *The Modernisation of Irish Society 1848–1918* (Dublin 1973); L. M. Cullen, *An Economic History of Ireland from 1660* (Dublin 1972); L. M. Cullen (ed.), *The Formation of the Irish Economy* (Cork 1969); and Cormac O Gráda, *Ireland: a new economic history 1780–1939* (Oxford 1994).

6   D. H. Akenson, *The Irish Diaspora: a primer* (Belfast, 1996); Kerby A. Miller, *Emigrants and Exiles: Ireland and the Irish exodus to North America* (Oxford 1985).

7   Peter Somerville-Large's *The Irish Country House: a social history* (London 1995) is good on Irish landowners and the relatively prosperous urbanites of this period.

1

Agriculture

As far as major trends and changes in Irish agriculture after 1850 are concerned, the bog (so to speak) has been so skilfully, ably and comprehensively stripped that it would be an insult to the hard-working historians who performed this back-breaking task to clamp their sods of evidence in different patterns to make them look somehow new. What follows is a brief summary of their findings, but the bulk of the chapter is a discussion of change and continuity in everyday farm-work in Ireland between 1850 and 1922 for men, women and farm labourers.

Summary of existing research

The most obvious change in Irish agriculture over this period was the gradual transfer, between 1870 and 1909, of ownership from landlords to tenants. The most vigorous phase of the popular countrywide movement led by the Land League, known as the Land War, 1879–82, was succeeded by the less high-profile but arguably more effective (because more irritating and consistent) Plan of Campaign, 1885–91. Successive Conservative governments, meanwhile, gave more and more concessions to Irish tenant farmers. Owner–occuiership was established by the Conservatives in 1903 and was fully completed by the Liberals in 1909. Donnelly and Turner agree that the change from tillage to pasture-farming can be dated to the early 1860s, and that bigger farmers had built up enough prosperity and confidence by the 1870s to unite and challenge the British government and the landlords by 1879 – though Moody, Vaughan, Solow, Clark, Donnelly and Bew differ as to the crucial precipitating factor in the land movement. Other important changes in agriculture over these years were an increase in the average size of holdings, or farms, the overall swing from tillage-farming (crops) to pasture-farming (beasts), the decline in the number of agricultural labourers and assisting relatives on farms and the commercialization of farming. Farmers' contact with the town – the fair, the market and the shop – became more important. [1] The policies of constructive unionism in the 1890s led to a distinct improvement in Irish agricultural practice, produce and profits; Horace Plunkett's Irish Agricultural Organization Society (1894), the Department of Agriculture and Technical Instruction and other initiatives around the turn of the century raised the standards for breeding, dairying and other farming activities. The First World War created a big demand for Irish agricultural produce at home and abroad. [2] Before this, farmers' standard of living had risen, but the rise was uneven. Smaller farmers, in the west in particular, managed to survive only through seasonal migration to Britain or to other parts of Ireland, remittances from emigrants abroad and whatever supplementary work they could pick up locally. [3]

Fields, crops and beasts: mainly men's work

The switch from tillage to pasture was never total. All farmers kept some fields of potatoes (for the family and for sale) and oats, wheat or barley. Even in parts of the country where pasture would seem to be the only possible option – the relatively barren land in Glengowla, between Oughterard and Maamcross, Co. Galway, for instance – farmers had a few fields in oats and, of course, potatoes: an acre of potatoes and an acre-and-a-half of oats, in Corr na Mona, according to Padraig O Suilleabháin; while every farmer in Glengowla would sow barley as well as oats and potatoes, according to Sean MacAodhagáin, referring to farming from the 1860s onwards. [4]

Early winter marked the end of the agricultural year. It was at this time of year that the big tillage farmers of Ulster and Leinster polished their shoes and went into town to sell their corn [5] and that pasture farmers stored their hay and turf, dug their potatoes and threshed their corn, usually oats. In some parts of the country – north Cork, Kilkenny and Wexford – cattle were stalled for the winter, but in Ireland's comparatively mild climate it was not always necessary to stable beasts for the winter months. [6] The size of a herd was also a determining factor: a makeshift byre against the side of the house could serve for one or two beasts – in small farmer Connell Boyle's house in Donegal in 1898, the main entrance to the house was through a byre. There were also cowhouses in the south-west by the 1880s.[7] Cows were still kept 'tied down there at the end of the kitchen' on one farm on the Sligo–Roscommon border in the 1860s, but not by the early twentieth century. The Public Health Act of 1874 made it illegal for animals to share accommodation with humans; this would have been impossible to enforce, but there was an enhanced public health awareness among the general public.[8] Bigger herds left out all winter were foddered daily and looked after in extremes of temperature. Sheep were seldom stalled. Some farmers ploughed in early winter, before the frosts set in, and corn was sometimes sown at this time, according to an older system of ploughing.[9]

Deep winter was the quiet time: fences and agricultural implements were maintained and mended; ditches and drains were dug; potatoes were pitted. The quiet did not last long, however. In January turnips were 'snagged' – very hard work, often in brutal conditions. Early in February fields were prepared for potatoes, oats and other crops, and for hay. Potatoes were sown before St Patrick's Day, but before this could happen, as soon as possible after Christmas manure (made, variously, of animal droppings, seaweed, kelp, turf mould and old animal bedding) was spread on the fields. Artificial fertilisers came into use towards the end of the nineteenth century, for bigger tillage farmers in the north and east in particular. Once manured, the fields were left for two or three weeks, and then the sod was turned. This could be done with a plough on bigger farms, but on small farms a spade or loy was used, and the task could take up to three weeks.

Potatoes were sown in ridges, later in drills. Drills were more modern, but ridges made sense in the kind of uneven ground which many Irish farmers worked. Sowing the seed potatoes – *sciolláins* – had to be done carefully, three across, according to one account, leaving a foot between each row, making sure they were buried deeply but not too deeply. Once the potatoes were in, the corn was sown. It was considered lucky, in places as far apart as Fermanagh and Kerry, to sow the corn on Good Friday.[10] Again, the level of intensity of this work depended on the tools available. Where farms were small – as in the west – or labour was cheap and plentiful – south Tipperary and east Cork – setting or sowing crops was done with the spade or the loy. Setting oats involved, as well as ploughing, rolling and 'hacking', or harrowing, to ensure that the seed was not buried too deep. Bigger farms had ploughs, of either wood or iron.

Ploughing with horses could take three people – one to guide the plough, one to throw the seed (often an elderly man with experience) and one to guide the horses.[11]

There were over half-a-million horses in Ireland by 1901. The small, sturdy, Kerry bog pony and the Connemara pony are the most celebrated, but the native breed of heavy horse, the Irish draught, was a hardy all-purpose animal, highly valued in rural and urban settings.[12] Horses, being sensitive creatures, are upset by shouting and sudden movements, and the story was told that one year no crops grew on the spot where a farmer had cursed his horses. Expensive to buy, horses were also costly to feed: a ploughing horse needed 7 *máums* (two palms together) of oats three times a day; if a team of 3 horses were ploughing, this adds up to 63 *máums* a day – easily a 4-stone bag.[13] Horses were considered men's business – however women may have been involved (albeit in the background) in the buying and selling of cattle and other beasts, they never went to horse-fairs.[14] Many farmers relied on the ass, mule or jennet for work and transport; the number of these humble creatures rose from about 100,000 in 1851 to nearly 250,000 in 1911, the growth most marked after 1881.[15] Pasture farming also boosted the number of dogs, needed to round up cattle and sheep.

New hayseed was sown after setting the corn, but that hay would not mature until the summer after next; meanwhile second hay, grown from the remains of the previous year, would be growing. Cows, geese and other animals had to be kept away from the hayfield – this was work which devolved to the younger members of the family.

In April and May, turnips, cabbage, beet and onions (the soot from the spring-cleaned chimney was very good for these) were sown.[16] The trenches of the potato field were dug and the earth thrown up over the top of the ridges ('the first earth'). This was done again a month later or whenever the stalks appeared. From about the 1870s, in June and July the potatoes were sprayed with 'bluestone' – copper sulphate – to protect them from blight.

In late winter and early spring, cows calved, sheep lambed, pigs had their litters. Sheep usually managed on their own, but the farmer had to be vigilant for frost and snow, and delicate or orphaned lambs were bottle-fed by the fire. Cows did not need as much intervention as they do today, because the calves of cattle breeds at the time were smaller and easier to deliver. On dairy farms calves were weaned straight after the 'beestings' (colostrum, or pre-milk) and fed artificially thereafter; cattle being kept for stock fed their own calves. Throughout most of Munster the sight of a cow suckling her young was very unusual; on small farms in Connacht, where calves were reared for stock, it was more common.[17] Sows, by all accounts good-natured and intelligent animals, were so large that they had to be watched for the first few nights in case they accidentally trampled their young. 'Staying up with the *bonavs*' was a great treat for children in some parts of the country, the sow and her brood being brought in near the fire for the duration.[18] Milking and the feeding of calves were usually women's work, and I discuss them in the next section. Meanwhile throughout the winter and early spring stock in the fields were fed with hay, turnips and other root crops grown especially for them.

Fuel was always a labour-intensive matter for farmers. Wood, which simply had to be chopped and stacked, was easiest of all, but making or 'dancing' the *culm* (a fuel derived from coal-dust mixed with other materials) which was burned in some of the mining districts – the Leitrim–Roscommon border, Ballingarry, Co. Tipperary, Castlecomer, Co. Kilkenny – was hard work and could take up to a week.[19] Turf, the fuel of most Irish rural people, took even longer. Work began with the first burst of fine summer weather in May. Cutters ate lightly: too heavy a breakfast or mid-day meal would make them *trom agus tartmhar* (heavy and thirsty), even sick; soda bread and buttermilk or a drink made out of oatmeal and water (said to be excellent for quenching thirst) were brought to them in the middle of the day. A team of 3–12 men (neighbours, labourers or family members), depending on the size of the job, would go to the bog. Once the turf was stripped (i.e. the 'scraw', or top covering of grass, removed), one man would dig, throwing the sods to another who would lay them out flat in a semicircle to dry. Turns would be taken at the heaviest work. Some days later, the turf was turned over and after about a week it was 'footed', or clamped, in a dolmen shape, so that the wind would dry it. The turf would be drawn home by donkey-and-cart at the end of August. Wet summers destroyed or reduced the turf crop.[20] Baseline inspectors for the Congested Districts Board in the 1890s, Breathnach tells us, took particular note of how hard people worked on the bog.[21]

Wet weather could also destroy the hay. Like the bog, this was often worked on the *meitheal* system, where neighbours helped each other out, expecting to be helped in their turn (though the arrangement was not always reciprocal, and a widow or elderly farmer would often be helped without expectation of such repayment). Adult offspring who had moved away often came home for this, their annual holiday. First the hay was cut using a sickle, though by the 1880s the larger scythe had taken over. Mechanical mowers were available by the 1890s, but most farmers used the scythe. The hay was then left out to dry in 'blows'; then it was turned and raked, and made into small cocks – a fine, calm day was needed for making hay-cocks. In late autumn the hay was drawn home and stored in barns or sheds. It took thirty-two handwritten copy-book pages for one Kerry farmer to describe the entire hay-making and hay-saving process, as he recalled it from his youth in the 1870s.[22]

Early summer was the time when sheep were sheared and their wool sold. Each sheep yielded 3lbs weight of wool per year which, according to one Galway farmer, would have sold for a shilling a pound in the late nineteenth century.[23] With their dual value for wool and mutton, sheep were worth the considerable trouble it took to herd them up the sides of rocky mountains and along the edges of bogs, and to protect lambs in the freezing conditions of late winter.

This was a period of technological advance for farming. Although tractors did not come into general use until at the earliest the 1920s, at the other end of the technological scale, the wooden and, later, the iron plough were common in the 1860s and 1870s. The plough would not always be effective on uplands or certain kinds of ground, and in impoverished parts of Mayo and Galway there were no ploughs in the 1890s – there were, however, significant regional differences. Traditions associated with ploughs in other parts of the country suggest some familiarity with these implements.[24] The ass-and-car was not always practicable: on one farm in Castlegregory, Co. Kerry, before the Congested Districts Board put in a small road in 1918, the hay had to be carried home from the meadow on men's shoulders, fastened with a rope and some kind of *lúb*.[25] Still, farmers' new-found purchasing power and the spread of retailing meant that improved implements were more accessible. According to Feehan, the number of farmers with hay-rakes doubled between 1886 and 1895 (from 3,525 to 7,184). The popular 'tumbling paddy' steel-toothed rake cost £3, putting it within the reach of the smallest farmer; Pierce's safer wheeled rakes cost £10.[26] Farmers also invested in small implements like flails, root-cutters, sprayers, harrows and winnowing trays.[27]

Oats and barley were the first to be harvested in mid-August, the reapers being followed by the binders. Binding was done quickly and deftly, often by women, as in this account from Cork relating to the late nineteenth century:

> The best binder I ever knew used to throw the sheaf over her shoulder back when she had it bound and whip the binder for the next sheaf out of it by catching the necessary number of straws out of the head of it as it fell away from her.[28]

A number of bound sheaves were then 'stooked' – stacked in a pile. In one part of Wexford, the reapers rose at 3 a.m. and worked till 8 a.m., stopping during the day because it was too hot, and starting again around 6 p.m.[29] But outside of the sunny south-east, reaping and binding seems to have gone on all day. The weather might break at any time, so speed was necessary. The horse-drawn reaper – which would only pay for itself on the larger tillage farms – certainly reduced the need for workers; there were over 14,000 of these machines in the country in 1895. Large tillage farmers often hired labourers from some distance away. Much of Wexford's crop was brought in by 'Kilkennys' earning a shilling a day in the 1880s and 1890;[30] the advantages of this for the farmer will be discussed in the section on labourers.

After the harvest came the threshing, and for this task a clear frosty day in early winter was ideal. Threshing with a flail was hard, though not heavy, work, involving a light, rhythmical movement by one, two or three men in a barn, a clean farmyard or otherwise at the side of the road. Mat the Thresher in Kickham's *Knocknagow* is well-respected because of his skill at this difficult task.[31] Smaller farmers did their own threshing or had a servant boy do it in the barn. By the end of the century, the larger farms hired threshing machines; there were 8,546 of these in Ireland in 1895.[32] Like the mechanical reapers, they were only practicable on very large tillage farms, and therefore were most popular in the north and east. The horse- or steam-powered threshing machine needed 8–10 people to work it.

The potato, the last of the crops, was harvested before *Samhain*, or the feast of All Saints, on 1 November. Irish workers went to pick potatoes in other countries, notably Scotland, and also in other parts of Ireland, but all farms had their own potato fields as well. Digging potatoes was very hard work. Once dug, the potatoes had to be pitted, to preserve them; then, after Christmas, they had to be cut with a thin sharp knife for the seed (*scioltán* or *sciollán*), and put in bags to dry. This was very hard work, often done by the women.[33] In fact, in the absence of men, all the tasks relating to the potato crop would be done by women in addition to their own – considerable – areas of responsibility.

Yards and young: mainly women's work

Ailliliú na gamhna, na gamhna geala bána
Na gamhna maidin shamhraidh ag damhsa ar na bánta.[34]
(O how lovely are the bright white calves dancing in the fields of a summer's morning.) (Traditional song, Kerry)

The singer is female, and the song celebrates the calves from which she makes her living; although there were male herds, girls and women had particular responsibility for the young of livestock. Although women worked whenever and wherever they were needed on the farm, this and looking after milk, butter and eggs, and caring for farmyard animals like pigs and poultry, were their primary tasks. All this was done in addition to the everyday maintenance work (cleaning, cooking, washing, drying, looking after the very old and the very young) carried out or managed by women of the house in all walks of life.

It was the woman's job on the farm to light the fire, first thing in the morning, to boil the animal feed. Sometimes she would have to get up in the night to take off one saucepan of pigs' potatoes and put on another, like Ellen Landy's mother in Mullinahone, Co. Tipperary, in the early twentieth century.[35] Farmyard animals had to have food specially prepared – they did not subsist on scraps. The money a woman earned from these activities gave her a level of economic independence, but she worked hard for it.[36] Bourke argues that the rise of the creameries took away some of women's traditional dairy earnings on large farms in the 1890s, but this would have been compensated for by the rise in the numbers of poultry:[37] the numbers of poultry rose from 747,00 in 1851 to 1.8 million in 1911.

In some parts of the country, women thought it bad luck to tell anyone exactly how many hens they had.[38] However, on small farms in the Plain of Galway in the 1870s and 1880s the women would have *cúpla sgór* (about 40) hens, 8–10 ducks and the same number of geese. Hens were often kept in the house at night, in an enclosure of some kind, to protect them from the cold and from foxes. Ducks, being hardier, had a small 'house' outside (as did hens, also, in some cases). Geese were able to look after themselves in winter conditions,[39] but had to be minded or they would wander off into neighbours' fields and eat there. The gander did duty as watchdog – to 'see somebody past the gander' was to walk to the gate with them. In the early twentieth century Florence Irwin encountered a very old gander in rural Ulster named General Gordon.[40]

Whether the women milked on their own or were helped by the men depended on the size of the herd; milking was not necessarily 'women's work'. The milk was put into pans on shelves for the cream to rise to the top, and this would then be churned, usually twice a week, to make butter. The milk that was left over – the buttermilk – was consumed by the family or used in bread-making.[41] Butter-making was extremely labour-intensive work. The cream was churned either with a dash or a handle churn. Careful washing and scalding was always carried out, even before the reforms of the 1890s;[42] dirty vessels turn butter rancid and inedible. Once 'gathered', the butter was taken out of the churn, 'washed' with spring water several times, and then shaped into 'firkins' to be sold or consumed by the family.

Animals, on which so much depended, were vulnerable to a variety of diseases.[43] Pragmatism rather than sentiment dictated that they were *led*, not *driven*. Horses received unusually respectful treatment, and cows, whose offspring and milk were crucial to a family's survival, had often to be coaxed, even sung to, to give milk. Holy medals were sometimes hung on byres and cowhouses. That cows, like horses, were named (according to physical characteristics – Starry or Whitey – or after the person from whom they were bought, e.g. Hogan) shows that they were individuated. Apart from names, all animals had their special calls – *Tiuc, tiuc* ('Chuck, chuck') for hens, *Hurrish* for the sow, *Ban, ban* for the other pigs, *Feeaun, feeaun* for the ducks, *Wirrha, wirrha* for the bull. In Co. Galway ducks were called with *Faoit*, geese with *Beadaí* and *Hup, hup* to encourage horses and asses; *sook, sook* to call calves was common throughout Ireland, as was *sop, sop* for cows.[44] Cats were vital to keep down rats and mice in the hay and grain sheds, and from that, and keeping the milking area mopped up, they made a handy living for themselves.[45]

Women's work on the farm kept them on their feet from dawn until long after dusk, all year round. Only on very large farms, like that of the O'Briens in Co. Limerick in the 1870s, were the daughters of the house free to read books in the garden at harvest time; on most other farms, large and small, if not in the fields, they would have been preparing and taking out the mid-day meal and organizing a big supper for the workers the end of the day, in addition to their farmyard duties. And even on the Lough Gur farm, with its hired labourers and dairymaids, Mrs O'Brien, the woman of the house, was up and ready to receive the milk into the dairy at 7 a.m.[46] The market during Christmas week, at which she sold her precious turkeys, geese and ducks, marked the fulfilment of the country-woman's work.[47]

The adage that a woman's work is never done applies in particular to these farming women, especially if they had young families to care for, or incapacitated old people. A 78-year-old man slipped from the past into the present tense when he gave evidence to the Folklore Commission in 1943:

> *Tá go leor leor oibre le déanamh ag an mbean nach dtugann an fear faoi deara.*[48]
> (The woman has lots and lots of work to do that the man doesn't notice.)

Paid help on the farm

Day-labourers, temporary migrants and servant boys and girls would undertake all of the tasks mentioned above, in field, bog and farmyard. The number of agricultural labourers in Ireland fell rapidly after 1850, though historians have yet to agree whether this was because of a rejection of labourers by farmers or a rejection by labourers of long hours for low pay.[49] The larger farms were increasingly unwilling to sub-let smallholdings to day-labourers in exchange for work, but labourers were also unwilling to work for little or no wages. 'Herds' on large pasture farms in the west often had smallholdings and *collops*, according to Cunningham, an arrangement whereby one or two of their beasts grazed with those of the employer.[50] Some farmers might have arrangements going on for generations with a particular family in the locality. Most agricultural labourers (except for servant girls) were male, but women – much cheaper to hire than men – worked on the harvest, binding, and as herds when they were needed.

William O'Brien's United Irish League in the early twentieth century with its 'cattle drives' against 'graziers' shows the popular resentment, particularly in Meath, Kildare and Tipperary, of large farms which employed little or no labour.[51] Although the Irish Agricultural Labourers' Union, set up in Kanturk in 1873, was shortlived, it established branches as far apart as Westmeath, Dublin and Clare, as well as in Limerick and Kerry. The organization's limited geographical appeal and the willingness of the leadership to throw in their lot with the bigger land movement spelt its downfall.[52] The Irish Land and Labour Assocation, founded at Limerick Junction, Co. Tipperary, in 1894, was one of Ireland's first trade unions for unskilled workers,[53] and agricultural labourers swelled the ranks of the Irish Transport and General Workers' Union in the years leading up to 1914. In 1919–22 there were 'soviets' (Russian-style worker occupation and control of creameries and food-processing plants) in Bruree, Knocklong and other towns and villages in Munster – short-lived though they were – which were indicative of a rural radicalism springing from long-articulated and well-developed labourer discontent.[54]

Historians infer a rejection *of* labourers *by* farmers from the fall in the number of agricultural labourers after 1850, one even going so far as to refer to the 'declining status' of labourers.[55] But had labourers' status ever been high? The decline in their number after 1850 could have been due partly to many labourers' definitive rejection of a low-paid, miserable, life of subsistence. Education narrowed the cultural distance between farmer and labourer, and the latter's expectations of a better standard of living rose. By the 1860s labourers were emigrating in their thousands, while those who remained in Ireland were demanding better housing and higher wages. Rates of pay for agricultural labourers as for everyone else, did indeed improve between 1851 and 1911, but the numbers receiving wages were much smaller at the latter date. Can this diminished workforce be blamed entirely on farmers? The big grazier – resented because of his wealth, lack of neighbourly engagement and underemployment of local people – was in a minority; the average struggling 40-acre farmer cannot be blamed for labourer unemployment or underemployment. Medium-sized pasture farmers were not prosperous enough to employ more than one or two day-labourers all year round at fair wages. It is odd that tillage farmers were not the focus of resentment, because in Wexford, Down and other tillage regions they often hired gangs from outside the locality. West Kerry people would go to Waterford, but some workers were from neighbouring areas. In Tipperary and Kilkenny working-class townswomen in the early twentieth century hired themselves out as day-labourers to the tillage farmers in the vicinity for a shilling a day and a bag of potatoes. These women may not even have described themselves to the Census as agricultural labourers.[56] Workers from outside the locality were cheaper; they came and they went; and, crucially, the farmer did not have to look at their hungry faces at slack times of the year. Crop farming needs large numbers of workers for intensive short bursts during the year; apart from saving the hay and the turf, pasture farming needs, as Turner and Donnelly point out,[57] the all-round commitment of a lesser number of workers. Only 14 per cent of all farmers in 1911 – the highest proportion in this period – held farms of over 50 acres. Even in the rich, high-tillage counties of Kilkenny and Wexford farms of over 50 acres never made up more than 22 per cent of all farms; in high-tillage Derry and Tyrone they made up less than 12 per cent of all farms.[58] (See table A1, Appendix.)

If the occupation of independent labourer was dying out, that of servant was still going strong until about 1940. Boys and girls started in their early teens, sometimes going to hiring fairs, sometimes to local farmers known to their parents. Food and living accommodation varied in quality though they rarely approximated to those of the farmer. Even on the generous O'Brien farm in Co. Limerick, the maids and men, in the 1860s, broke their fast in the kitchen with maizemeal stirabout, milk and potatoes, while their master and mistress ate, respectively, two duck eggs and a hen's egg in the parlour.[59] Maura Laverty, writing autobiographically about the second decade of the twentieth century, gives an insight into mistress–servant relationships in and around her native town of Rathangan in rural Kildare:

> Gran . . . had a habit common to most women in our part of the country of avoiding any servile term when referring to her employees. She would never say, 'Judy Ryan works for me' but 'I have Judy Ryan living with me'.[60]

Laverty implies that the people of her locality were unusual, but there is similar evidence from small farmers in south-west Kerry, where the servant boy or girl was often to be found in service in childless households, and no great distinctions seem to have been maintained.[61] Ultimately, working conditions depended on the personal morality of the master and mistress rather than on farm size or region. O'Dowd tells many stories about badly fed, poorly housed and mistreated servant boys and girls, and she cites at least one ballad, *The Galbally Farmer*, written in the late nineteenth century by P. W Joyce, a professional song-writer, about the ill-treatment of a servant boy.[62] The fact that these stories exist, not only in the folklore (many of them, incidentally, told by farmers) but in the wider entertainment culture, shows a strong public awareness of this phenomenon.

Though they are often remembered as part of the family – the Hayes family's 'workman' in Limerick in the 1890s had as much right as the parents to chastise the children, a right he exercised[63] – labourers had little to look forward to in their everyday lives or their future. Pat Williams from Bargy, south Wexford, who started his working life in 1864 at the age of 10, recalled that at quiet times of the year men would work all week for the tillage farmer for an ounce of tobacco. Ned Buckley from east Cork recalled young labourers cheering each other on to finish the ridge at sowing, and jeering the man they 'broke' – the one who couldn't keep up and so had to leave the field.[64] This competitiveness – which probably enlivened a tedious job – played right into the farmers' hands.

Women farmers

Although women carried out most kinds of agricultural work, they were not described as farmers (either to the Census or among themselves) unless they were the heads of farm households. The proportion of women farmers rose from 6.8 per cent in 1861 to 14.7 per cent in 1911 (table A2, Appendix); most were widows, a result of the tendency of middle-aged men to marry women younger than themselves, though some were single, having inherited and never married. Most women farmers were over 45, accounting for 72 per cent of all female farmers in Kildare and over 81 per cent in Carlow, Donegal, Fermanagh and Down, in 1891.[65]

While the male farmer predominated everywhere, he was somewhat more likely to have female working neighbours in prosperous agricultural areas characterized by large holdings than in poorer agricultural areas characterized by small holdings. Leinster and Munster had more female farmers than any other part of the country, in 1861, 1891 and 1911, and in Munster these women were mainly concentrated in Tipperary, Limerick and Waterford. Counties where female farmers nudged towards a fifth of all farmers were not only prosperous but were, in the main, pasture farming strongholds. Tyrone, Londonderry, Down and Antrim, where tillage held its own between 1881 and 1911, also held some of the lowest percentages of female farmers in the country – except for Down in 1891. Is there a connection between female farmers and the spread of pasture farming? On a day-to-day level, pasture was easier for women to manage. Women rarely ploughed, and while they reaped and bound they did not command others to do so. Care of livestock was women's work, and the only labourers (if any) needed were a herdsman or two, some help with calving and lambing and a trusted retainer (or a son or son-in-law) to sell beasts at the fair. Employees–labourers would have been few in number, and kept on all year round. Women may have found this kind of labour relationship easier to manage than gangs of local boys and men.

In Monaghan, Armagh and Louth, small farming areas, each with a high proportion of female farmers, there were considerable supplements to tillage farming – pig- and poultry-breeding in Monaghan and Louth and apple- and flax-growing (or employment in textile-related tasks) in Armagh. Pigs and poultry were traditionally seen as in women's care, while textile producers employed large numbers of women. Fruit-tree produce was one of the ancillary agricultural activities for women encouraged by the policy of constructive unionism.

It is possible that the title 'farmer' as recorded on the Census form was simply a nod to the claims of old age. Widow Hanoria Larkin, 85 in 1901, was the farmer and head of the house she shared, on a 40-acre holding in Gortaniskey, Lusmagh, King's County, with her 45-year-old son James (occupation: 'farmer's son'), his wife Ellen ('farmer's daughter-in-law') and their children, ranging from young teenagers to toddlers.[66] This was probably the situation in which most female farmers found themselves. Whether Hanoria's authority was real or nominal, nobody thought it odd to describe her as the farmer and head of the house, in an era when the 'lady' was defined by both her lack of an occupation and her subordination to male relatives.

This discussion has centred on women who described themselves to the Census as farmers, and indeed, this self-identification is as important as the work they did for what it tells us about women's position and status on the farm. There were also, of course, *de facto* women farmers (described in the Census as 'engaged in home duties') who worked alongside the men in field and farmyard day after day, and in the west in particular took over the entire work of the holding in the summer and autumn when the men seasonally migrated to Britain.

Conclusion

The image of the stout and secure farmer with priests for sons and daughters safely dowered has replaced that of the starved, squeezed peasant hanging precariously onto his patch of land. Both extremes existed, and one or another has been given priority according to historiographical fashion. But there were many farmers in between Mr O'Brien of Lough Gur, with his two duck eggs in the parlour for breakfast, and the Mayo smallholders who never saw a plough, and spent half the year in Scotland. Even in fertile Queen's County, Westmeath and Meath, even in Golden Vale Limerick, farms of 50 acres and over made up less than a quarter of all holdings throughout the period. In Ireland as a whole during these years, farms of 30 acres and under made up well over two-thirds of all holdings (table A1, Appendix). A farmer with 30–50 acres could be 'snug' but he could not afford to be smug, depending as he did on the weather and agricultural prices to keep food on the table and settle bills at the shop. Wet summers and autumns were catastrophic; wet winters meant flooding, loss of livestock and impossible foddering. The bad years of 1859–64, the worldwide depression and bad weather contributing to the political crisis of 1879–81, the droughts in the mid-1880s leading to a collapse of prices for dairy produce, all represented considerable hardship.

Even under relatively good conditions, the farming family worked unceasingly the whole year round. Machines, where they existed, did not operate by remote control; they were worked outdoors, in all extremes of weather, battling against nature, racing against time. With the exception of a tiny minority of gentleman–graziers, everyday pasture farming involved far more than Plunkett's derisive 'opening and shutting of gates'. O Gráda comments that observers often mistook farmers' seasonal idleness (which alternated with frenetic work) for laziness.[67]

The farmer held on to his or her newfound prosperity by not paying too much in wages. If there are winners and losers in any history, then the servant boy was certainly the loser in the period 1850–1922. His poor treatment was lamented in song and story as early as the 1890s, but it was not until the 1940s, when the servant boys threw down their shovels and made for the boat, that farmers began to offer better wages and conditions. The farmers' imperviousness to criticism in the wider culture suggests a self-confidence born of a certainty that the supply of servants would never run out. But upper-middle-class people had a similar certainty and complacency about the domestic servants they exploited and underpaid until at least 1940.[68] It is unfair to hold farmers to a higher standard of morality.

And if labourers were losers, it is not clear that all farmers were winners. The farm on which John Hayes was born, in 1887, in Moher, near Murroe in Co. Limerick, is an example of the insecurity of even the reasonably sized farm. Forty-nine acres, much of it stony and boggy, made up this farm, which required continuous labour to stay drained. Evicted by Lord Cloncurry in 1882, the family lived in a Land League hut until 1893, during which years 4 of the 6 children born before 1882 died, and another child besides John was born and died. Six years after their land had been restored to them they were able to send John, their youngest, to a fee-paying school in Limerick city (he later won a scholarship to the seminary) and to employ a labourer. The historian who stumbles on the Hayes family around 1905, with a labourer on their farm and a son well on the way to the priesthood, might be tempted to regard them as both snug and smug, but their security and status were paid for in privation and grief.[69] Although the Hayes' child mortality was unusually high for country people at the time, the family's overall experience illustrates the see-sawing from catastrophe to comfort that was the lot of one medium-sized farmer in a good and fertile region of Ireland.

Notes

1   Information on Irish agriculture in these years comes from the following works: R. D. Crotty, *Irish Agricultural Production: volume and structure* (Cork 1966); J. S. Donnelly Jr, *The Land and People of Nineteenth-Century Cork* (London 1975), and 'The Irish agricultural depression 1859–64', *Irish Economic and Social History*, Vol. 3 (1976), pp. 33–54;

20   *Ireland, 1850–1922*

P. J. Drudy (ed.), *Irish Studies*, Vol. 2: *Land, politics and people* (Cambridge 1982); S. Clark & J. S. Donnelly Jr (eds), *Irish Peasants: violence and political unrest 1780–1914* (Madison, WI 1983); Michael Turner, *After the Famine: Irish agriculture 1850–1914* (Cambridge 1996); C. O Gráda, 'Seasonal migration and post-Famine adjustment in the West of Ireland', *Studia Hibernica*, 13 (1973), pp. 48–76; *Ireland: A New Economic History, 1780–1939* (Oxford 1994), and 'Of bullocks and men: agricultural change after the Famine', in C. O Gráda, *Ireland Before and After the Famine* (Manchester 1988), pp. 128–52; John Feehan, *Farming in Ireland: history, heritage and environment* (Dublin 2003); Anne O'Dowd, *Spalpeens and Tattie Hokers: the history and folklore of Irish seasonal migration* (Dublin, 1991); David S. Jones, 'The cleavage between graziers and peasants in the land struggle', in Clark and Donnelly (eds), *Irish Peasants*, pp. 374–417; John W. Boyle, 'A marginal figure: the Irish rural labourer', in ibid., pp. 311–37; D. Fitzpatrick, 'The disappearance of the Irish agricultural labourer', *Irish Economic and Social History*, 7 (1980), pp. 66–92; Daniel Bradley, *Farm Labourers: Irish struggle 1900–1976* (Belfast 1988); John Cunningham, *Labour in the West of Ireland: working life and struggle, 1890–1914* (Belfast 1995); Liam O'Donnell, *The Days of the Servant Boy* (Cork 1997); Richard Breen, 'Farm servanthood in Ireland 1900–1940', *Economic History Review*, 36 (1983), pp. 87–102; Pádraig Lane, 'The organization of rural labourers 1870–1890', *Cork Historical and Archeological Society Journal*, Vol. 100 (1995), pp. 149–60; Laurence Geary, *The Plan of Campaign* (Cork 1988); W. E. Vaughan, *Landlord and Tenant in Ireland 1850–1914* (Dublin 1984); Samuel Clark, *Social Origins of the Irish Land War* (Princeton, NJ 1979).

2 Andrew Gailey, *Ireland and the Death of Kindness: the experience of constructive unionism 1885–1903* (Cork 1987); National Co-operative Council, *Plunkett: a symposium on co-operation* (Dublin 1954).

3 O Gráda, 'Seasonal migration'.

4 Irish Folklore Commission (IFC), MS 865, Feirmeoireachta, 16/2/43, pp. 297–355, and MS 586, 15/11/38.

5 IFC, MS 54, Pat Williams, Ballymutty, Wexford, 30/3/35, pp. 271–3.

6 Crotty, *Irish Agricultural Production*, pp. 67–8.

7 Frank Sweeney, *The Murder of Connell Boyle, Co. Donegal 1898* (Dublin 2002), p. 4; IFC, MS 616, John O'Donoghue, Kilgarvan, Co. Kerry, 18/4/38.

8 Evidence from Annie Flynn, born 1907 in Keshcarrigan, in Michael J. Conry, *Dancing the Culm: burning culm as a domestic and industrial fuel in Ireland* (Carlow 2001), p. 264; and see chapter 6 in this book, on public health.

9 Feehan, *Farming in Ireland*, pp. 93–120.

10 IFC, MS 558, Mrs Maguire (92), Derryvullen, Fermanagh, 12/8/38, p. 419; MS 853, Mary Kennedy (78), Anascaul, Co. Kerry, 10/12/42, p. 223.
11 IFC, MS 514, Sean O Murchadha (76), Duhallow, Co. Cork, 6/11/37, pp. 155–65; MS 742, Ned Buckley (77), 8/2/41, pp. 196–211.
12 See Mervyn Watson, 'The role of the horse on Irish farms', in Trefor Owen (ed.), *From Corrib to Cultra: folklife essays in honour of Alan Gailey* (Belfast 2000), pp. 122–35.
13 IFC, MS 853, Mary Kennedy, Anascaul, Co. Kerry, Evidence collected 10/12/42, p. 223; MS 853, Michael O'Sullivan, grew up in Castlegregory, Co. Kerry, 14/12/42, pp. 228–36.
14 IFC, MS 853, Charles Bateman (72), Kilcolman, Co. Cork, November 1942, p. 411.
15 *Agricultural Statistics for the Year 1881*, table 13; and *Irish Agricultural Statistics 1901*, table 13.
16 IFC, MS 586, pp. 76–7.
17 I grew up in the counties of Tipperary, Limerick and Clare in the 1960s and 1970s and never once saw a calf feeding from its mother.
18 IFC, MS 616, John O'Donoghue, Kilgarvan, Co. Kerry, 18/4/39, pp. 7–9.
19 For an explanation of this, and for a rich insight into Irish social history, see Conry, *Dancing the Culm*.
20 Accounts of work on the bog are sprinkled throughout the folklore manuscripts; some of the most complete are in IFC, MSS 844, Padraig O Gallchobhair, Rann na Feirste, pp. 178–89, and 557, Seamus O Muircheartaigh (83), 8/7/38, pp. 1–67.
21 Ciara Breathnach, *The Congested Districts Board of Ireland 1891–1923: poverty and development in the West of Ireland* (Dublin 2005), p. 42.
22 IFC, MS 853, Pat Daly (71), Annascaul, 15/12/42, pp. 245–77.
23 IFC, MS 865, Padraic O Suilleabhain, Corr na Mona, pp. 76–7.
24 Kevin Danaher, *In Ireland Long Ago* (Cork 1964), pp. 69–74; IFC, MS 853, Mary Kennedy (78), Anascaul, 10/12/42, p. 223.
25 IFC, MS 557, Séamas O Muircheartaigh (83), 8/7/38.
26 Feehan, *Farming in Ireland*, pp. 248–59.
27 Timothy P. O'Neill, 'Tools and things: machinery on Irish farms 1700–1981', in Owen (ed.), *From Corrib to Cultra*, pp. 101–14.
28 IFC, MS 742, Ned Buckley, Knocknagree, Co. Cork, 8/2/41.
29 Diarmuid O Muirithe & Deirdre Nuttall (eds), *Folklore of County Wexford* (Dublin 1999), pp. 122–31.
30 IFC, MS 54, South Wexford, p. 271.
31 Charles Kickham, *Knocknagow; or the Homes of Tipperary* (London 1870).
32 Feehan, *Farming in Ireland*, pp. 248–66.

33 IFC, MS 557, Seamus O Muircheartaigh, Co. Kerry, 8/7/38, pp. 1–67.
34 'Aililiú na gamhna', traditional Kerry song, reproduced in Seán Og & Mánus O Baoill, *Ceolta Gael* (Cork 1975), p. 8.
35 Conry, *Dancing the Culm*, p. 180.
36 Feehan, *Farming in Ireland*, pp. 248–69; Central Statistics Office, *Farming Since the Famine: Irish farming statistics 1847–1996* (Cork 1997).
37 Joanna Bourke, *Husbandry to Housewifery: women, housework and economic change 1890–1914* (Oxford 1993). For a discussion of gender, authority and poultry, in the west in particular, which takes issue with Bourke, see Breathnach, *The Congested Districts Board of Ireland*, pp. 54–5.
38 IFC, MS 616, O'Donoghue, pp. 5–25.
39 IFC, MS 865, Pádraic O Suilleabháin, pp. 518–84.
40 Florence Irwin, *The Cookin' Woman: Irish country recipes* (Belfast 1986 [1949]), p. 5.
41 Ibid., also MS 616, John O'Donoghue, pp. 1–50; Regina Sexton, *A Little History of Irish Food* (Dublin 1998), pp. 92–3; Leslie Clarkson and Margaret Crawford, *Feast and Famine: a history of food and nutrition in Ireland 1500–1920* (Oxford 2001), pp. 88–110.
42 O Gráda, 'Of bullocks', p. 138, argues quite convincingly that nobody would have bought rancid butter, so some level of cleanliness must always have been observed.
43 See, for various terms and cures, Michael L.Doherty, 'The folklore of cattle diseases: a veterinary perspective', *Béaloideas: Journal of the Irish Folklore Society*, 69 (2001), pp. 41–75.
44 IFC, MS 616, O'Donoghue, pp. 20–1; MS 865, O Suilleabháin, pp. 523–5; O Muirithe & Nuttall, *Folklore of County Wexford*, pp. 129–30.
45 IFC, MS 865, O Súilleabháin, p. 518.
46 Mary Carbery, *The Farm by Lough Gur* (London 1937, Cork 1973) pp. 260–1, p. 22.
47 Maura Laverty, *Never No More: the story of a lost village* (London 1942), p. 159.
48 IFC, MS 865, O Súilleabhain, pp. 330–5.
49 Fitzpatrick, 'Disappearance of the Irish agricultural labourer'; Boyle, 'A marginal figure'; Bradley, *Farm Labourers*; Cunningham, *Labour in the West*; O'Donnell, *The Servant Boy*; Breen, 'Farm servanthood'.
50 Cunningham, *Labour in the West*, pp. 46–8.
51 See Jones, 'Cleavage'.
52 Lane, 'Rural labourers'.
53 Cunningham, *Labour in the West*, p. 117; Emmet O'Connor, *A Labour History of Ireland 1824–1960* (Dublin 1992), pp. 53, 62.
54 Cunningham, *Labour in the West*, pp. 94–116; David Lee, 'The Munster soviets and the fall of the house of Cleeve', in D. Jacobs and D. Lee (eds),

Made in Limerick: a history of industries, trade and commerce (Limerick 2003), pp. 287–306.

55 Kerby A. Miller, *Emigrants and Exiles: Ireland and the Irish exodus to North America* (Oxford 1988), pp. 409–12, and generally.

56 See Conry, *Dancing the Culm*, pp. 163–77, pp. 193, 199, and generally.

57 Turner, *After the Famine*; Donnelly, *Land and People*.

58 *Census of Ireland*, 1911, General report, table 148, showing the number of agricultural holdings by size, 2 April 1911.

59 O'Dowd, *Spalpeens*; Bradley, *Farm Labourers*; on labourers' conditions, see Carbery, *The Farm by Lough Gur*, pp. 20–3.

60 Laverty, *Never No More*, p. 111.

61 IFC, MS 616, John O'Donoghue, pp. 57–8.

62 O'Dowd, *Spalpeens*, pp. 129–62, 220–99.

63 Stephen Rynne, *Fr John Hayes, Founder of Muintir na Tire* (Dublin 1960), pp. 28–9.

64 IFC, MS 54, 29/3/35, pp. 271–80: MS 742, 8/7/41, pp. 196–211.

65 *Census of Ireland*, 1861–1911, Occupational tables.

66 National Archives, Dublin, Census of Ireland, MS 1901, for Lusmagh, King's County. Hanoria Larkin was the author's great-great-grandmother. Thanks to Margaret Larkin, Lusmagh, Co. Offaly, for the photocopy of the relevant Census MS.

67 O Gráda, 'Of bullocks'.

68 Mona Hearn, *Below Stairs: domestic service remembered in Dublin and beyond 1880–1922* (Dublin 1993); Caitriona Clear, *Women of the House: women's household work in Ireland 1922–1961* (Dublin 2000).

69 Rynne, *Fr John Hayes*, pp. 12–40.

2

Non-agricultural work

Introduction

There was some development of non-agricultural employment in Ireland between 1851 and 1922, but this does not mean that there was work for everyone. Emigration masked the true extent of unemployment, millions of people moving from the country and sending home money to those who could not survive on the wages paid for the work they described themselves as doing to the census. Any discussion of 'gains' must bear this firmly in mind.

There was, however, an increase in the *numbers* of people employed in professional and white-collar work, in local government and civil service work, in commercial and distributive work, in transport and communications, and in some kinds of industrial work, despite the fact that the population in 1911 was only two-thirds of what it had been in 1851 (see table A3, Appendix). While Ireland did not have countrywide factory employment it did exhibit other signs of a modern industrial economy – a well-developed transport system and a thriving commercial and financial sector. The number and variety of retail outlets grew, while the developing network of state-funded institutions from National School to lunatic asylum provided employment too.

The definition of *work* changed between 1850 and 1922. The hand-to-mouth subsistence work to which many people claimed attachment in 1851 gradually ceased to be considered real employment. Homeless pedlars, prostitutes, beggars and others of precarious income gradually disappear from the Census occupational tables only to turn up again in the vagrancy statistics, the tables of those 'known to the police' and the records of institutions.

Industry: manufacturing

Although industry in this period was dominated by Belfast and Derry, it was not dead in the rest of the country. Numbers employed in production rose between 1850 and 1911, and not just in Ulster.[1] O Gráda shows that the number of woollen mills in the country rose from 11 in 1850 to 114 in 1902, almost all of them outside Ulster, while Bielenberg's study of Cork gives a variety of industries employing thousands of people. Food-processing and brewing remained buoyant all over the country – the output from brewing trebled between 1850 and 1914, and 40 per cent of this output was exported. Over 8,000 people were 'ministering to food' in Dublin city in 1891, and while some of them were working in commercial outlets, most were in factories. The main breweries were Guinness in Dublin, Smithwick in Kilkenny, Murphy and Beamish & Crawford in Cork. In Limerick from the 1850s to the 1890s, 2,000 people were employed in Tait's Clothing Company, said to be the largest military-clothing firm in the world. Blarney Woollen Mills employed 300 people in the 1860s, 600 by the 1880s, while Co. Cork had 2,000–3,000 people working in wool and worsted at the end of the nineteenth century. There were seven flour mills in Cork city alone.[2] The Malcomson cotton factory in Portlaw, Co. Waterford, employed over 1,000 people from 1825 to 1876 in a purpose-built village.[3] Co. Limerick had 39 butter-blending factories in 1891, Cork 18.[4] Industries were often comparatively short-lived: Cunningham cites the Galway Bag Factory, which gave significant employment to 200–300 women in Galway city between 1867 and 1893; Galway Woollen Mills, regarded as a 'replacement industry' for it, was set up in 1895 and wound down in 1911.[5]

Textile and garment production, and shipbuilding were concentrated in the north. The Harland & Wolff shipyard in Belfast dates from the 1850s, the smaller Workman, Clark & Co. from 1880. Flexibility and versatility protected shipbuilding in Belfast from the ups and downs experienced by the industry elsewhere. Spin-off industries of marine engineering and rope-making, and the many trades required to fit up a naval vessel or passenger liner, throve: Harland & Wolff's workforce jumped from 7000 in 1892 to 14,000 in 1914; Workman, Clark & Co. employed about 7000 workers in 1902.[6] Shipbuilding workers brought home a regular and comparatively good wage. Their numbers, however, were small compared to those employed in textile and garment work in the north-east. While the number of female spinners and weavers throughout the country fell by 79 per cent between 1851 and 1911, the latter were concentrated mostly in mills and factories (mostly in the north, but some in Cork), receiving a regular wage, while the former had been struggling for decades to survive. The swift adoption of the powerloom from the 1840s left the Ulster textile industry ripe to reap the benefit of the 'cotton famine' brought on by the American Civil War. Numbers employed in spinning mills rose dramatically between 1858 and 1868, and although the post-war slump brought some unemployment, there were 82,389 people employed in cotton and flax in Belfast, Antrim, Armagh and Down in 1891. This workforce, in contrast to shipbuilding's, was heavily dominated by women, especially in Belfast, where they made up 76.6 per cent of the cotton and flax workforce in 1891, though in Down, 42.3 per cent of those employed were male. Men in weaving and spinning were either sprinkled very lightly in the highly skilled areas or concentrated in the hackling and rough work. The Derry shirt industry employed between 10,000 and 13,000 factory workers (not counting outworkers) in 1897, mostly female. Married women textile and garment workers were often the main breadwinners, with husbands either unemployed or casually employed. The hours were 8 to 8, with an hour for lunch, Monday to Friday, and 6 hours on Saturday, in Derry's shirt factories in 1875. Hours in the spinning mills were similar. The average weekly wage for spinners in 1855 was 5s 6d; it rose to 9s in 1905, and could reach £1 by 1914.[7]

Periodic layoffs were a feature of industrial life everywhere, Ulster included, and workers were not paid during these periods of unemployment. The work was physically hard, sometimes dangerous (shipbuilding in particular) and certainly, in the case of the spinning mills, injurious to health. What was arguably 'good' about the Ulster experience was the chance it gave people to settle down in one place, to marry and to pass work on from one generation to the next. There was little in Belfast or Derry to compare with the dire poverty in Dublin at the end of the nineteenth century.

Trades and services, old and new

While Belfast's industrial workforce was made up of factory and shipyard workers, Dublin's in 1911 was made up of artisans and unskilled labourers.[8] A rise in factory production is always accompanied by a decline in independent tradesmen–artisans, because machines can do the job quicker and more cheaply and because a thriving retail sector, depending on a well-developed transport system, distributes low-cost, mass-produced factory goods to urban and rural areas alike, undercutting the products of local craftsmen and artisans. Weaving almost died out as an independent trade for men; the number of tailors and boot and shoemakers fell by 58 per cent between 1851 and 1911, and many other trades suffered also. In country towns, trades often hung on: Rathvilly, Co. Carlow, inaccessible by rail until the 1880s, had in the 1860s and 1870s, for a population of 350 (and the surrounding countryside), three blacksmiths, a tailor, a carpenter, a shoemaker, a slater, a painter, a stonecutter and a joiner. Nailers, their days numbered already, from nearby Hacketstown and Baltinglass kept the Rathvilly tradesmen supplied.[9] In Cork, while there was a decline in the number of saddlers, weavers and shoemakers over the course of the nineteenth century, the number of carpenters remained stable and the number of coachmakers rose.[10] Ready-made cloth, clothing and shoes cut into the trades in big cities, where shoemakers and tailors were in quite definite decline from 1891 in particular. However, they sometimes survived a little longer in small towns: although there was a marked decline in the variety of trades in the small town (population under 2,000) of Headford, Co. Galway, between 1846 and 1894, tailors, boot and shoemakers, bakers and blacksmiths survived and even increased over those years, showing growing demand for clothing, food and ironmongery, including horseshoes (more draft and transport animals). The tradesmen in the small town (population less than 600) of Cloughjordan, Co.Tipperary, in 1918 were a shoemaker, a harnessmaker, a carpenter, 4 tailors, 2 blacksmiths, one cooper and 2 bakers; a sawmills employed around 20 people.[11] Neither town is a remote rural outpost: Cloughjordan is on the direct Limerick–Dublin railway line, and both it and Headford are within 10 miles of at least two larger towns.

Trades could rise and fall. There were more dressmakers and milliners (seamstresses and shirtmakers are a separate category) per head of the population in 1891 than there had been thirty years earlier. Rising consumption levels in the 1880s and 1890s meant more work for apprentices and skilled workers in the towns and cities. On one day in September 1884 the *Freeman's Journal* advertised sixty-eight vacancies for apprentices to trades of various kinds, and skilled workers like milliners, confectioners, butchers, plumbers, coachpainters, bakers in Dublin and throughout the country. A month later, the same column offered 64 vacancies of this kind – portmanteau-making, trunk-finishing, collar-making, tailors, tailoresses. Twenty-two years later advertisments for this kind of apprentice and skilled worker had almost disappeared. The jobs might still have existed, but vacancies were filled informally, by word of mouth; no expansion had taken place. By 1911 there was a distinct drop in the numbers employed in the clothing trades – Bourke dates this fall from 1901. The availability of finished clothes in an increasing number of shops must be seen as partly responsible. Still, dressmaking and millinery did not suffer as much as tailoring from economic changes: while the number of tailors fell by 43.8 per cent between 1851 and 1911, dressmakers and (female) milliners, by comparison, fell by 27 per cent. Girls and women were entering the paid workforce in greater numbers than ever before, and needed to look not only respectable, but fashionable. Some dressmakers obviously competed well with their local shops, probably by lowering their prices and working ever harder. Kathleen Daly and her sisters had a dressmaking business in Limerick city in the 1890s in which they employed twelve people.[12]

The master craftsman with a small operation survived, but rarely expanded; other artisans became employees of businesses, manufacturers and institutions.[13] Hospitals, workhouses and lunatic asylums employed their own tailors, shoemakers, plumbers and painter-decorators. A business like Guinness's employed coopers and other tradesmen, and department stores employed seamstresses, dressmakers and cabinet-makers. A boy or girl who learned a trade of some kind had a distinct advantage, and although Mary Healy laments that her brother Paddy's childhood was over when, in 1919 at the age of 11, he was offered an apprenticeship in Statham's garage in Kilkenny, he was one of the lucky ones. For girls and women outside the north-east, the opportunities were predictably fewer, though some spinners in Cork in the 1890s could earn 14 shillings a week, and between 15 shillings and £1 in a clothing factory. On the other end of the scale, Katie O'Neill, born in 1887, the third generation of a family of weavers, considered herself privileged to get a job in Lady Desart's weaving factory in Kilkenny in 1905 paying 5s a week.[14]

Sweating

The trades–crafts in the nineteenth century were under attack not only from mass-produced goods in shops but from the rise of 'sweating', especially in tailoring, cabinet-making and shoemaking. Sweating was the subcontraction of various processes – the covering of buttons, the making of collars and of shoelaces – which could be done by people in small workshops (sweat-shops) or in their own homes. Sweated textile work took place mainly in the hinterland of cities and towns with manufacturing bases, and existed alongside the factory system, not instead of it. Derry's famous shirts were not actually made up in the factories: the fronts, cuffs and bodies were bundled up and sent out to be made up by cottage workers. Patrick McGill's autobiographical novels describe this kind of work vividly.[15] Throughout Ulster, according to Neill, garment outwork was family labour, could take up to 16 hours a day and often yielded at most 6 shillings a week. Sometimes carried out by comfortably off women for pocket, or pin, money, the work was more commonly done by poorer women for family survival. Involving 16 to 18–hour days and requiring much care and vigilance to keep materials clean, its only advantage was that it could be fitted in around child-minding and housework.[16]

The building trade also employed many tradesmen – bricklayers, masons, hod-carriers, scaffolders, as well as builders' labourers. While not exactly booming in nineteenth-century Ireland, the trade had its own periodical, the *Irish Builder*, and public institutions of various kinds were being built at the rate of about one a year. Builders' labourers in the 1890s in Cork, according to Cronin, earned 14s a week. This could amount to over £30 a year, but it seldom did, because the work was of its nature finite and uncertain. The best thing that the general labourer could hope for was a job with the local authority mending roads. Debilitating and unhealthy as such work was, it carried some security. Otherwise, there were irregular jobs in transport and general labouring works in ports and towns, around docks and other areas. Stevedores enjoyed a certain amount of security and generational continuity, with the 'button' being handed on from father to son, but dockers' labourers were very insecure.[17]

With the development and expansion of the railway, transport became a significant employer. Carters and cabbies remained important, as public transport within towns and cities did not really emerge until the 1890s.[18] New institutions employed people in domestic, clerical and administrative capacities, as well as those directly dealing with the 'clients'. The police and the prisons offered useful, pensionable jobs for bright, strong boys and girls from medium-sized farms or artisan backgrounds: a 'class matron' (described as a 'superior female turnkey') was earning £30–45 a year in 1849–63, in Grangegorman and Mountjoy.[19] At the prison in Belfast (Co. Antrim) in 1854 a warden could earn £35–45 annually, a 'matron' £30. In many of the district prisons throughout the country, the same surnames of turnkeys and matrons recur over the years, suggesting that these jobs were passed on from father to son and mother to daughter; it was not unknown for a husband and wife to be deputy-governor and matron or turnkey and nurse.[20]

White-collar work in the public service, the Post Office, banks and private businesses was done mainly by males, until the last decade of the nineteenth century, when government and businesses alike discovered that they could get willing, able and respectable women clerk–typists for between a half and two-thirds of the cost of the men.[21] Still, males remained in the majority among bank clerks, legal secretaries and senior clerks in businesses, until well into the twentieth century.

Shop service

WANTED in a respectable Retail Grocery establishment, an humble industrious Lad, one who has served his time in a country town preferred. (*Freeman's Journal*, 19 April 1865)

Ireland experienced great commercial development over the seventy-year period with which this book is concerned.[22] Those employed in small grocery and drapery shops, and in public houses were sometimes apprenticed to the trade itself, but increasingly they kept the job and the pay of an assistant, regardless of how much knowledge of the trade they managed to accumulate. Serving in a shop was a respectable job; when Edward O'Toole finished National School in Co. Carlow, in 1874 at the age of 14, he wanted to 'go to a shop' like his older brothers and many of his friends, but his parents persuaded him to become a monitor and, eventually, a National School teacher.[23] 'Shopgirls' may have been sneered at by some upper-middle class people, but for those who could afford to educate their children only up to age 14, to be working 'in Spaights's' or Moon's or Burgess's was the height of respectability and security.

Before unions put a stop to it in the early twentieth century, shops kept assistants on their feet until 10 or 11 p.m. Switzers', Dublin's famous department store opened at 7.30 a.m. in the 1850s and 1860s, and windows had to be fully dressed by 11 a.m. Shop assistants often 'lived in', particularly in provincial towns where accommodation was hard to find; although Switzers' assistants started to move out to lodgings by the 1880s, the Irish House drapery in Tipperary town had 19 assistants (male and female) and 2 domestics living in on the night of the Census in 1901.[24]

Shopkeepers and dealers

There was scarcely a shop in the Clare town of Kilrush in 1846; in 1861 Coulter on his travels counted 12 shops with plate-glass windows, some 30 feet wide in front and going back 80 feet.[25] Shopkeepers have always had a bad press, depicted as mean, vengeful and grasping in short stories by Padraic O Conaire among others, despised by George Russell,[26] used as a metaphor for grubby materialism by Yeats and viewed by historians as major actors in (and manipulators of) political movements for their own ends.[27] Recent micro-studies by Lambe and Gilligan of two rural shops, one in Tipperary, the other in Meath, describe gathering-places for people of all classes, which often gave credit indefinitely and kept families from starvation. Shopkeepers in Headford, Co. Galway, were always teetering on the brink of bankruptcy and generational continuity was rare. Grocery was a mainly male trade (though there were women grocers), but the number of women drapers rose by 40 per cent between 1891 and 1911. When Mary Ann Treacy married Michael Kelly in 1902, she persuaded him to sell his Kilkenny farm and buy a drapery shop for her in Rathangan, Co. Kildare. The scheming shopkeeper, her beady eyes missing nothing, her large bosom resting on the counter, is a caricature which reflects a reality; male or female, shopkeepers were powerful – withholding or granting credit, knowing everybody's business. But they did not always abuse that power.

Neither did the pawnbroker, though he was in a position to do so. Vital in the family economy of casual labouring people, he was often their only source of ready cash. Most towns had at least one shop with the three brass balls outside it. The number of pawnbrokers rose from 856 in 1861 to 1,013 in 1891, but by 1911 had fallen to

828 – still considerably more per head of the population than in 1861. Pawning, Jim Fitzpatrick points out, meant that those with the least money paid over and over again for their meagre goods.[28]

The professions

National School (i.e. state primary) teaching opened up the professions to many offspring of small farmers and artisans. Until the 1880s much of the training was on the job, which made it accessible to people who could not afford a course of study; later, scholarships were available. Secondary teaching was gradually formalized towards the end of the nineteenth century: the Association of Secondary Teachers of Ireland was set up in 1909, and minimum standards and requirements were laid down in 1918. Teaching was open to both women and men – women's salaries were, at 80 per cent of those of men, comparatively higher than they were in other areas of work, and 55 per cent of National School teachers were women in 1900. A male National School teacher in 1870 at the lowest end of the scale earned £33 a year, a female teacher £30. In that decade, according to Cronin, a skilled workman in Cork city could earn (at least) 28s a week, an annual income that would have been double that of National School teachers, except that the skilled workman's 28s a week hardly ever added up to £67 a year – there were weeks when there was no work at all. The teacher was sure of his or her salary, pensionable from the 1870s. Furthermore, women did not have to resign their jobs on marriage (the infamous marriage bar was brought in only in 1932), and the National School teacher was highly respected, if often overworked.

There were many other kinds of teachers also, for whom little or no training was required. Fee-paying private schools, charitable institutions and private houses employed teachers, governesses and tutors at various rates. Private teaching was the default occupation of genteel women, just as domestic service was for labouring-class women. Governesses, according to Raftery, saw National School teaching as beneath them, although the female National School teacher had a far more secure and lucrative job than the woman who belonged neither upstairs nor downstairs. O'Callaghan Westropp, Madden tells us, paid his governess £30 a year in the 1860s, the same as a female National School teacher on the lowest pay scale. The governess's board and lodging was included, but her job was of its nature finite and there was no pension.

The nineteenth century saw the rise of the hospital as a site for the treatment of the sick, and nursing as a profession developed alongside this. Hospital nursing received a boost when workhouse infirmaries were opened to the general public in 1861 and it became necessary to hire trained nurses – though from 1861 in many Poor Law Unions nuns slipped in to take these jobs. Women from wealthy backgrounds might nurse as nuns or as volunteers in times of war, but women who took up nursing as a career did not usually come from exalted backgrounds. Annie M. P. Smithson went to Edinburgh to train as a nurse in the 1890s. From a Dublin middle-class Protestant family fallen on hard times, she had to cease her education at 15 to help her mother, and nursing was the only respectable vocation open to her. The employment of district nurses by the Poor Law Unions and the founding of Jubilee and Lady Dudley Nurses in the late nineteenth and early twentieth centuries provided opportunities for very hard but fulfilling work with few holidays. The General Nursing Council of Ireland, set up in 1919, established standards of training and examinations, but up to that time every hospital had its own norms and standards for nurse training.

The job category we now describe as 'psychiatric nurse' was inelegantly called 'keeper in lunatic asylum' in 1861, when there were 395 of them. Their numbers rose in subsequent years, and this job kept many small farming families going in the catchment areas of lunatic asylums.[29]

The growth of the 'professions' between 1851 and 1911 was due to the rise in the numbers of nuns, priests, teachers and nurses. The 'learned professions' of law, accountancy and medicine grew little. These were open to young people (only males until the 1880s) whose families could afford to educate them to this standard, though scholarships were sometimes available. The first women doctors graduated in the 1890s. There was no significant growth in the numbers of lawyers and accountants between the Famine and Irish Independence. From 1851, there were new jobs for doctors with the development of the dispensary system, workhouse infirmaries and as a result of the Public Health Act of 1874, but there was no subsequent increase in the number of medical practitioners between 1881 and 1911.

Domestic service

HOUSEMAID or Thorough servant in a small family – a young Woman from the country, who has not been in service before, would go in either of the above capacities, or would take on with anything which she might be found to suit; she can refer to certain ladies in town where she has been for some time past; and to respectable persons in the country as to her character. (*Freeman's Journal*, 8 February 1865)

Although the number of females in domestic service fell far more dramatically between 1851 and 1911 than that of males (respectively, by 44 per cent and 22 per cent), at the latter date women servants made up around 30 per cent of the female workforce – the equivalent figures for France and Belgium in the early twentieth century are, respectively, 10 and 25 per cent.[30] Countrywide, over 80 per cent of Ireland's domestic servants were female. On farms there was some blurring of the distinction between farm servants and farm domestic servants, and what was said about farm servants' working and living conditions in chapter 1 holds good for domestic servants on and off farms – the working conditions depended largely on the morality and sense of responsibility of the employer. The servant was not, however, completely powerless.

Servants' money was poor starting out, but Hearn argues that it was quite good compared to that earned by shop assistants and factory workers.[31] The work was task- rather than time-oriented, but so was most farming and artisan work, and people would have been used to this daily rhythm. Senior domestic servants – cooks, housekeepers, butlers – could earn more than National School teachers, and saving was possible because food and accommodation were provided. The servant, responsible for food and comfort, was in a key position to make her feelings known; she worked at her own pace, took her time 'doing the messages' or posting letters, and was not necessarily under her employer's supervision all the time. A girl – or boy – could look on domestic service as a chance to earn and learn, a temporary stage in life. A butler learnt the wine trade, a groom or coachman could go on to set up a garage or stables, a housekeeper could run a hotel, a good cook was always in demand in private houses, clubs and hotels, a lady's maid was a skilled needlewoman and hairdresser. In towns and cities women servants, in their daily contact with tradesmen supplying the house, had plenty of opportunity to meet potential marriage partners. Upper servants had a high opinion of themselves, with good reason. For a teenage girl or boy with no chance of a trade (an apprenticeship could cost £8, beyond the reach of many parents) but whose parents had the know-how to get them into a good 'training place', domestic service was a ladder. A cook or housekeeper was known as Mrs or Miss to employers and staff alike.

But many people, especially young girls, experienced domestic service as a lonely, uncomfortable, dead-end job, the inferior food and accommodation justified on the grounds that they were better than what they were used to at home. The risk of seduction by an employer is perhaps overstated in literature, but it happened, and the lonely servant was indeed vulnerable to this kind of attention. The more mundane verbal abuse or nagging by the woman of the house could make life difficult for her. Even in a 'good' house, where the mistress and master were reasonably humane, the servant was expected to give up her time off in family crises, and her affection for the family was often manipulated, particularly when there were children involved ('must be fond of children' advertisments usually stated). Authority over her servants was such an integral part of a wealthy woman's identity that when a Mrs Coleman in Dublin brought a petition for divorce against her husband in 1906, one of the instances of mental cruelty she itemized was his countermanding of her orders to servants.[32] No wonder some women preferred the noisy and harsh impersonality of the factory floor or the intense surveillance of the shop to this emotional prison, presided over by often tyrannical members of their own sex.

In Co. Dublin in 1911, female servants were one in 12.9 of the population; in Dublin city one in 24.9, in Cork and Limerick cities 23.9, and in Waterford 21.8. In Belfast the ratio was one in 57.9. Servants were thinnest on the ground wherever there was alternative work for unskilled women, or where the majority of the population were too poor to employ them – in Connacht, particularly in Mayo, and after that, in Belfast and the north-eastern counties.

Though female servants were always in a majority, the percentage of male servants actually rose between 1891 and 1911, not because of any increase in the number of male servants, but because female servants were leaving at a far faster rate than male at this stage. In 1911, Kildare and Meath had the highest percentages of servants who were male (respectively, 25 per cent and 27 per cent), probably because of the number of grooms and coachmen required for the bloodstock industry. In Roscommon, because of its comparatively low number of female servants and high proportion of large houses, 23 per cent of servants were male. Service was a good job for men: O'Callaghan Westropp's butler in East Clare in 1889 earned £24 a year plus his accommodation and food. Coachmen, grooms and gamekeepers often lived in tied houses, and could have a family life.[33]

Institutional service – domestic work in hotels, hospitals, and other institutions – opened up quite a lot in these years. Freelance domestic work – taking in washing, charring, daily work of various kinds – suited married women in particular. Washerwomen were hard hit by commercial laundries in Munster and Leinster between 1861 and 1891 – in Leinster in particular, one washerwoman to every 180 people had shrunk to one to 228 by the later date.

Conclusion

The main industries throughout Ireland, brewing, milling and food-processing, did not generate other industries around them in the same way that steel, pottery, textiles and shipbuilding did. Apprenticeships were expensive and limited in number. Outside the north, industries either employed comparatively few or often died out after two generations; but that crucial 50, 40 or even 30 years enabled people to get married and rear a family, and even if most of the offspring were destined for emigration, to generate some demand for goods and services while they were being reared. Outside Belfast and Derry, urban working-class Ireland limped along, but people might not have seen it like that at the time. Musical and sporting activities in the cities of Cork and Limerick around the turn of the century show a strong self-confidence and sense of identity among young working-class men and women.[34] Even smaller provincial towns saw some increase in employment; in 1901, Fallon tells us, all adults in Clonown, Co. Roscommon, were employed in the townland itself, but by 1911, 5 were working on the railway and 2 others in industries, in nearby Athlone.[35]

Boys or girls from families who could afford to do without their earnings for some crucial teenage years stood a chance of becoming teachers, policemen or nurses, or working up to a position of authority in one of the many new institutions. The gate, however, was very narrow. In all these *new* jobs respectable clothes and demeanour were part of the job description. The actual performance of their work did not demand that factory workers, domestic servants, artisans, dockers, farmers and agricultural workers conform outwardly to a standard of appearance and civility. But a clerk in a government department, local authority or business had to speak politely and have a clean white shirt or blouse; a policeman, warden, workhouse master or mistress, or asylum attendant had to be both authoritative in bearing and deferential to superiors. National School teachers were forbidden to, among other things, lodge in public houses and attend political meetings, and hospital nurses laboured under a system which combined the strictest features of military and religious discipline. These white-collar, professional workers were only one generation away from the uncertain existence of small farms, businesses and trades: the prospect of losing the security of their jobs constrained their freedom of expression considerably.

Girls and women 'gainfully occupied' (according to the Census) made up a far smaller proportion of the female population in 1911 (19.5 per cent) than they had in 1851 (28 per cent). The areas of work which saw the most dramatic fall in female numbers were agricultural labouring (and assisting relatives working on farms), spinning and weaving – low-paid, irregular work. Most women workers were still clustered in low-paid service and sweated work in the early twentieth century, to say nothing of the often undocumented agricultural and casual labour which they carried out. The decades after 1850, however, saw also a huge increase in the number of women holding positions of authority of various kinds: women farmers, shopkeepers, institution administrators, Catholic and Protestant; managers and key workers in orphanages, industrial schools, hospitals, workhouses and small businesses; National School teachers and district nurses. There was an eight-fold increase between 1841 and 1911 in the numbers of those who refused marriage and brought their dowries instead to convents, where they lived in community with other women and nursed, taught or performed domestic work.[36] Although these *authoritative* women represented only a minority of all women (approximately 5 per cent of the female population in 1911[37]), they were competent and prominent in spheres outside the domestic, setting an example for other young women.

38 *Ireland, 1850–1922*

Notes

1 O Gráda, *Ireland*, pp. 273–313.
2 Andy Bielenberg, *Cork's Industrial Revolution 1780–1870: development or decline?* (Cork 1991).
3 Debbie Jacobs, 'Limerick clothing manufacturers and retailers', in Lee and Jacobs (eds), *Made in Limerick*, pp. 23–36; and Frank Prendergast, 'The Decline of Traditional Limerick Industries', in ibid., pp. 2–22; Maura Cronin, 'Work and workers in Cork city and county', in P. O'Flanagan & C. Buttimer (eds), *Cork: history and society* (Dublin 1993), pp. 721–58; Tom Hunt, *Portlaw, Co. Waterford 1825–1876: portrait of an industrial village* (Maynooth 2000); *Census of Ireland, 1891*, General report and county books, occupational tables.
4 Bielenberg, *Cork's Industrial Revolution*, pp. 116–26.
5 O Gráda, *Ireland*, pp. 273–313; John Cunningham, *A Town Tormented by the Sea: Galway 1790–1914* (Dublin 2004), pp. 165–91.
6 All the figures are taken from Peter Ollerenshaw, 'Industry 1820–1914', in L. Kennedy and P. Ollerenshaw (eds), *An Economic History of Ulster 1820–1939* (Manchester University Press 1985), pp. 62–108. Also essential are J. C. Beckett and R. D. Glasscock (eds), *Belfast: origins and growth of an industrial city* (London 1967), especially, E. R. R. Green, 'Early industrial Belfast', pp. 78–87, and Emrys Jones, 'Late Victorian Belfast', pp. 109–119; and J. C. Beckett et al. (eds), *Belfast: the making of the city 1800–1914* (Belfast 1983), especially: Emily Boyle, 'Linenopolis: the rise of the textile industry', pp. 41–56; R. Sweetnam, 'The development of the port', pp. 57–70; and Brenda Collins, 'The Edwardian city', pp. 167–81; also Sybil Gribbon, 'An Irish city: Belfast 1911', in D. Harkness and M. O'Dowd (eds), *The Town in Ireland* (Belfast 1981), pp. 204–20.
7 The numbers are taken from Ollerenshaw, 'Industry 1820–1914'. The classic work on female workers in the linen industry is Betty Messenger, *Picking Up the Linen Threads* (Belfast 1980); other useful works are Brian Lacy, *Siege City: the story of Derry and Londonderry* (Belfast 1990), pp. 195–8; Mats Grieff, 'Marching through the streets singing and shouting: industrial struggle and trade unionism among female linen workers in Belfast and Lurgan 1872–1910', *Saothar: Journal of the Irish Labour History Society*, Vol. 22 (1997), pp. 29–46; P. Holloway & T. Cradden, 'The Irish Trades Union Congress and working women 1894–1914', ibid., Vol. 23 (1998), pp. 47–60; Jonathan Hamill, 'Childcare arrangements within the Belfast linen community', in B. Whelan (ed.), *Women and Paid Work in Ireland 1500–1930* (Dublin 2000), pp. 120–32.
8 A. C. Hepburn, *A Past Apart: studies in the history of Catholic Belfast 1850–1950* (Belfast 1996), p. 70.

9 Edward O'Toole, *Whist for Your Life, That's Treason: recollections of a long life* (Dublin 2003), pp. 7–9; Cullen, *Economic History of Ireland Since 1660, generally.*

10 Maura Murphy, 'The economic and social structure of nineteenth-century Cork', in Harkness and O'Dowd (eds), *The Town in Ireland*, pp. 125–54.

11 Geraldine Candon, *Headford 1840–1922* (Dublin 2004); Michael Hamell, 'Something of Cloughjordan: looking back from 1987 to 1918–27', *Cloughjordan Heritage*, Vol. 2 (1987), pp. 28–33.

12 *Census of Ireland*, 1891–1911, occupational tables; Kathleen Clarke, *Revolutionary Woman: autiobiography of Kathleen Clarke 1878–1972* (Dublin 1991), pp. 1–40.

13 Maura Cronin, *Country, Class or Craft? The politicisation of the skilled artisan in nineteenth-century Cork* (Cork 1994), and 'Work and workers'.

14 Mary Healy, *For the Poor and for the Gentry* (Dublin 1989), p. 5; Cronin, 'Work and workers'; M. Phelan and A. Cantwell, 'Katie O'Neill, weaver and millworker', *Old Kilkenny Review*, Vol. 4, No. 4 (1992), pp. 1057–64.

15 Lacy, 'Derry'; Patrick McGill, *Children of the Dead End* (London 1985 [1914]).

16 Margaret Neill, 'Homeworkers in Ulster 1850–1911', in J. Holmes and D. Urquhart (eds), *Coming into the Light: the work, politics and religion of women in Ulster 1840–1940* (Belfast 1994), pp. 2–32.

17 On builders and their wages, see Fergus D'arcy, 'Wages of labourers in the Dublin building industry', *Saothar*, Vols 14 (1989), pp. 17–34, and 15 (1990), pp. 21–38; on dockers, see Donal Nevin (ed.), *Trade Union Century* (Dublin 1994).

18 Kevin B. Nowlan, *Travel and Transport in Ireland* (Dublin 1983); J. J. Lee, 'The railways in the Irish economy' in L. M. Cullen (ed.), *The Formation of the Irish Economy* (Cork 1969), pp. 77–88; Joseph Leckey, 'The railway servants' strike in Cork 1898', *Saothar*, Vol. 2 (1975–76), pp. 39–44.

19 Bob Cullen, *Thomas L. Synnott: the career of a Dublin Catholic 1830–1870* (Dublin 1997), p. 53 and generally; Rena Lohan, 'Women in Mountjoy Convict Female Prison 1858–63', in B. Whelan (ed.), *Women and Paid Work*, pp. 86–101.

20 *Annual Reports of the Inspectors-General of State Prisons in Ireland, 1854–95.*

21 Any general economic and social history of women will discuss this in greater detail, e.g. D. Simonton, *A History of European Women's Work 1700 to the Present* (London 1998).

22 D. Horgan, *The Victorian Visitor to Ireland: Irish tourism 1840–1910* (Cork 2002).

23 Edward O'Toole, *Whist for Your Life*, pp. 17–18.
24 See note 21 and Cunningham, *Labour in the West*; D. A. Levistone Cooney, 'Switzers of Grafton St.', *Dublin Historical Record*, Vol. 55, No. 2 (autumn 2002), pp. 154–6; Denis Marnane, 'Tipperary town 100 years ago: the evidence of the 1901 Census', *Tipperary Historical Journal*, No. 14 (2001), pp. 1–26; Dan McEvoy, 'My years in the monster house', *Old Kilkenny Review*, No. 49 (1997), pp. 131–8. Spaights's was in Limerick, Moon's was in Galway, Burgess's is still operating in Athlone.
25 Henry Coulter, 'An account of post-Famine Clare 1861', in Brian O Dálaigh (ed.), *The Stranger's Gaze: travels in Co. Clare 1534–1950* (Ennis 1998), pp. 256–60.
26 Liam Kennedy, 'Retail markets in rural Ireland at the end of the nineteenth century', *Irish Economic and Social History*, Vol. 5 (1978), pp. 46–63.
27 E.g. Samuel Clark, *Social Origins*.
28 Miriam Lambe, 'At the cross: a shop in rural Ireland 1880–1911', Denis A. Cronin et al. (eds), *Irish Fairs and Markets: studies in local history* (Dublin 2001), pp. 206–23, and Jim Gilligan, 'Murrays of Dunshaughlin 1896–1910', in ibid., pp. 224–47. On the Kelly–Treacy marriage, I am indebted to Sr Conleth Kelly, Tullow, Co. Carlow, for information; see also O Conaire, *Scothscéalta*, for the story in question; Jim Fitzpatrick, *Three Brass Balls: the story of the Irish pawnshop* (Cork 2001); *Census of Ireland*, General reports, 1861, 1891, 1911, occupational tables.
29 D. H. Akenson, *The Irish Education Experiment* (London 1970); John Coolahan, *Irish Education: its history and structure* (Dublin 1982); Thomas Durcan, *A History of Irish Education Since 1800* (Bala, Wales 1971); T. J. O'Connell, *100 Years of Progress: a history of the INTO 1868–1968* (Dublin 1969); John Logan, 'The dimensions of gender in nineteenth-century schooling', in M. Kelleher and J. Murphy (eds), *Gender Perspectives in Nineteenth-Century Ireland* (Dublin 1997), pp. 36–49; Michael Quane, 'Primary education in Kerry one hundred years ago', *Journal of the Kerry Archeological and Historical Society*, No. 5 (1972), pp. 133–59; Deirdre Raftery, 'The nineteenth-century governess: image and reality', in Whelan (ed.), *Women and Paid Work*, pp. 57–68; Gerard Madden, 'Upstairs, downstairs: some east Clare servants and farm workers 1869–1940', *Sliabh Aughty: East Clare Heritage*, No. 9 (2000), pp. 17–21; see Hearn, *Below Stairs*, p. 90. On nursing, Pauline Scanlan, *The Irish Nurse: a study of nursing in Ireland* (Leitrim 1991); J. Robins, *Nursing and Midwifery in Ireland in the Twentieth Century* (Dublin 2000); Gerard M. Fealy (ed.), *Care to Remember: nursing and midwifery in Ireland* (Cork 2005); Annie M. P. Smithson, *Myself – and Others* (Dublin 1944); M. Luddy, *Women and Philanthropy in*

Nineteenth-Century Ireland (Cambridge 1995); C. Clear, *Nuns in Nineteenth-Century Ireland* (Dublin 1987), pp. 36–68, 100–33. On lunatic asylums, see Mark Finnane, *Insanity and the Insane in Post-Famine Ireland* (London 1982); and *Census of Ireland, 1861, 1891 and 1911*, General reports, occupational tables.

30 *Census of Ireland*, 1851–1911, General reports, occupational tables: on servants in France and Belgium, Simonton, *European Women's Work*, p. 98.

31 Mona Hearn, *Below Stairs*.

32 *Freeman's Journal*, 13 Feburary 1906.

33 Madden, 'Upstairs, downstairs'; *Census of Ireland*, 1851–1911, General reports, occupational tables, provincial and county tables; Mona Hearn, *Below Stairs*, pp. 83–4, and generally.

34 Fintan Lane, 'Music and violence in working-class Cork: the "band nuisance" 1879–82', *Saothar*, Vol. 24 (1999), pp. 17–31; Cronin, *Country, Class or Craft?*, p. 153; John McGrath, 'Sociability and socio-economic conditions in St Mary's Parish, Limerick, 1890–1950', MA thesis, Mary Immaculate College, University of Limerick, 2006.

35 Rosaleen Fallon, *A County Roscommon Wedding, 1892: the marriage of John Hughes and Mary Gavin* (Maynooth 2004), p. 12

36 Clear, *Nuns in Nineteenth-Century Ireland*; and Tony Fahey, 'Nuns in the Catholic Church in Ireland in the nineteenth century', in M. Cullen (ed.), *Girls Don't Do Honours: Irish women in education in the nineteenth and twentieth centuries* (Dublin 1987), pp. 7–30.

37 Counting female farmers, shopkeepers, those in white-collar and professional work including teaching, nursing, the religious life and administrative public service posts of various kinds.

3

Education

Introduction

The French word *éducation* refers to all aspects of a person's upbringing, including the formal acquisition of knowledge. The world of schooling in the nineteenth century cannot be understood without appreciating that going to school made up only part of children' s 'education', and whether this was a small or a large part (or no part at all) depended largely on family priorities. Almost all children (except those in rich families) were trained to help around the house, business, workshop or farm as soon as they could walk and stand still, bringing buckets of water from the well, holding out their arms for wool to be wound around them, minding the baby while the mother worked, or keeping the goose from the corn. By 1922, children who did not go to school were seen as neglected, but their parents may have had very practical, and not always self-serving, reasons for this 'neglect'. In this chapter, 'education' will refer to schooling, but the broader meaning of the word should be borne in mind.[1]

In the years 1850–1922, the National School existed, as did other primary schools not controlled by the State, but secondary schools evolved only slowly into their present form in the early years of the twentieth century. Vocational schools were not set up until 1930, but technical training was given in many National Schools. Only a tiny minority of the population attended university, as not all of the professions demanded a university degree, and primary teacher-training colleges were set up only in the last two decades of the nineteenth century.

In 1911 male and female literacy rates in Ireland were comparatively high and roughly equal, unusual in a largely agricultural,

Catholic country. Attendance at primary school was made compulsory in 1892. There are many comprehensive histories of Irish
schooling,[2] so no more than an outline of the main developments is
attempted here.

The National School

The universal problem of what to do with the children of the poor
was sharpened in Ireland by the fiercely bitter sectarian divisions as
the last of the penal laws against Catholics were dismantled.
Protestant and Catholic free schools run by voluntary organizations
had existed since the eighteenth century, competing with each other
for pupils and for financial resources. The government's response
was to set up the National Board of Education in 1831. A person or
a group (priest, clergyman, nuns, brothers or a voluntary organization) could apply to this Board, based in Dublin, for a capital grant
to set up a school and, thereafter, ongoing funding for teachers'
salaries. Teachers followed a curriculum specified by the Board, with
religious instruction provided during specific hours only. Thus
evolved the modern Irish system of a state-funded, denominational,
primary-school system, as Catholic and Protestant groups applied
for funding for their respective schools. The National Board of
Education did not set up schools all over the country, but provided
funding for those who wished to avail of it. However, once begun,
they had to show how it was done: one 'model' school was set up in
every county and various training schemes were devised.

The National Schools were quite openly state schools. The values
of social deference, respect for one's 'betters', loyalty and obedience
to the State and to officialdom were explicitly promoted in textbooks.
The core curriculum of reading, writing and arithmetic was the same
for both boys and girls, and then there was some gender divergence,
although more advanced subjects like geography and grammar were
available to both sexes. Until 1892, when this choice was taken out
of their hands, it was parents who decided which of their children
to send to school, and for how long. Logan shows that more girls
than boys went to school in agricultural areas, because there was
work for the boys locally; fewer girls went to school in the north-
east and in towns and cities where factory or sweated work was
available to them. However, in cities and towns, nuns, brothers,
priests and Protestant clergy had huge influence in encouraging

female attendance. Mr MacCallum, a National Board inspector, praised the Roman Catholic clergy of Belfast in 1884 for acting as informal attendance officers; 'They visit the schools so often that they know the students by face and name.'[3] Even after compulsory education was introduced, children stayed out of school for months at a time. In Kilkeel, Co. Down, in the second decade of the twentieth century, many boys 'didn't put a foot over the school step' for 5–6 weeks in the autumn, because they would be picking potatoes and blackberries.[4]

The first teacher-training colleges were set up in the 1880s. Up to this time, likely pupils were kept on as 'pupil–teachers' and monitors, after sixth class. An examination in their mid-teens qualified them for a five-month training course in Marlborough Street, Dublin, though there was also a special two-year course for those who could avail themselves of it. The usual route was to stay on at National School as a monitor, to sit a number of examinations to gain a scholarship and then to spend a year at a training college, which was the path taken by Edward O' Toole.[5] The system of 'payment by results', introduced in 1872 and lasting until 1899, is generally believed to have introduced a mechanistic, rote-learning system, but it succeeded in its objective of elevating literacy and numeracy standards.[6] In the early twentieth century, the curriculum was made more attractive and flexible, with an emphasis on nature, physical activity, colour and art. J. S. Doran recalls his infant school, in Co. Down in the early twentieth century, as a 'fairyland': although poorly equipped, it had pictures on the walls, an harmonium, ballframes, plasticine and 'the coloured balls of wool [that we] swung so enthusiastically in our action songs'.[7]

Whatever segregation was applied in the classroom, a child was as likely to walk the road to school with the opposite sex as not – single-sex and mixed schools were about equal in number by 1900. There was also a social mix. The National School, urban and rural, was attended by children of comfortable farmers and shopkeepers,[8] at least until the age of 12 or so when some (though not all) moved on to 'superior schools' or entered apprenticeships. For Anna in Kate O' Brien' s *The Land of Spices*, set in the 1890s, the worst aspect of her father' s bankruptcy is that her brother is going to have to attend the National School with 'vulgar' boys, but most middle-class people were not as sensitive as this.[9] The fact that so many people who could have afforded to pay, sent their children to the National schools is an indication of their quality. Even the worst National schools were subject to periodic inspection and were therefore more likely to be consistently good than most private schools. An 'untrained' teacher need not have been poorly-educated or a bad teacher. And even before its reform in 1899–1900, the course of study was fairly useful. Numbers attending National school rose from 321,209 in 1865 to 492,928 in 1884, a substantial increase, when population decline is taken into account. Granted that children who attended very seldom were kept on the rolls, the opposite was also true; Mr Dewar, inspector in 1884 for the counties Westmeath, Meath, Longford and part of Cavan, noted that the lack of agricultural work in winter drove many children into school who never appeared officially on the rolls at all.

That said, school-buildings were often in poor repair. The first National School in Clonown, Co. Roscommon, in 1859, was built on a graveyard and had no glass in the windows. The practice of having schools near or on graveyards (or adapting buildings already there) was sufficiently common in 1884 for Mr J. MacDonnell, the National Education inspector for the south-east, to condemn it. He particularly disliked the fact that school breaks often coincided with funerals.[10] In the nineteenth century, cemeteries were seen as very unhealthful, and the fact that some schools were held in their proximity indicates a neglectful attitude. Under-resourced schools with poor lighting, and damp and cold interiors were held responsible by some medical authorities in the 1870s for ophthalmia (eye disease);[11] they must also have spread all kinds of respiratory illnesses.

The tradition of the long summer holidays began because children, and often their teachers, were needed on the hay and turf harvests. However, the fact that school re-opened before the big harvest in the autumn was a sore grievance to some big farmers after the introduction of compulsory schooling.

Most Catholic religious congregations overcame their scruples about National Schools; 75 per cent of convent primary schools by 1850 were under the National Board of Education system, despite the religious restrictions. Though some congregations held aloof, most nuns, brothers, parish priests, clergymen and Protestant voluntary groups were glad to get the money and satisfied to comply with the regulations – in impoverished areas, in particular, it was the only way they could survive.[12]

Other schools

There were private primary schools, whether free or fee-paying, hedge schools, which largely died out after 1850, fee-paying or free 'superior' schools, day and boarding, for boys and for girls (industrial schools are dealt with in the section on institutions). The 'hedge' schools got their name when Catholics in the eighteenth century were forbidden by law to run schools and so were forced to carry out schooling wherever they could, in the open air, behind hedges. By the nineteenth century there were still some of these schools in existence, though no longer behind hedges. A man learned in the classics would hire himself out in a neighbourhood to teach the children of a number of local farmers, shopkeepers or anyone who could afford the fee of a few pence a week. The classics and grammar were emphasized; boys were sometimes prepared for entry to another school, sometimes for examinations, accountancy, the seminary, legal clerkships and apprenticeships in the law. Hedge schools died out in the nineteenth century, but can be understood as part of the range of private schooling options available to parents up to that time. Mark Ryan, a farmer's son in Co. Galway, attended a number of hedge schools in his youth in the 1850s, some good, some poor.[13]

Private schools varied widely in quality. One does not have to read Dickens's savage caricature, Dotheboys Hall, in *Nicholas Nickleby*,[14] to appreciate that anxious parents and their unfortunate offspring were wide open to chancers of all kinds. The definition of a 'superior' school was that a foreign language was taught there and, presumably, that substantial fees were paid.[15] There was no state school-leaving examination until the Intermediate, with its Junior, Middle and Senior Grades, was established in 1878. The Post Office, the Home and the Indian Civil Service, the Board of Works and other government departments had entrance examinations. A private tutor nicknamed Criggera Boylan taught 'the Civil Service handwriter' to paying pupils around Crossmaglen, Co. Armagh, in the 1880s and 1890s.[16] University entrance depended on success in the matriculation, and the professions controlled entry in their own ways. The Intermediate, open to both boys and girls, provided an incentive for the setting up of secondary, or high, schools, and a logical consequence was the opening up of university entry to women, which happened in the state universities, the Queen's Colleges, the following year.[17] The more conservative Dublin universities did not accept women as full undergraduates until decades later.[18]

However, only a very small proportion of either men or women attended university. The Intermediate examination provided a clear qualification at age 16 or 17 for those whose parents could afford to keep them at school, and afforded an avenue into many white-collar and professional jobs. Yet the education of teenagers did not always culminate in a school-leaving examination: many (particularly girls) went to school without doing the Intermediate; on the other hand, many studied for the examination without going to school, with the help of a generous National School teacher or private tutor. Nor were all 'superior' schools very expensive: some brothers and nuns charged low fees, or no fees at all, in their schools, while diocesan colleges tried to keep fees at a minimum. Protestant boys and girls in reduced circumstances found places in endowed schools.

Fee-paying secondary schools: boys

There was a rich and varied world of Protestant royal schools, endowed schools, diocesan schools and grammar schools, and Catholic monasteries and diocesan colleges. In general, the people who sent their sons to these schools were those who could afford both to do without their earnings and to pay dearly for their maintenance and tuition. However, boys from backgrounds which were not necessarily wealthy, but had a level of comfort due to a legacy, position in the family or unexpected prosperity, sometimes spent a year or two at these establishments, and occasionally there were scholarships.

In the nineteenth century boys' schools everywhere became more vocationally oriented, and mathematics and the sciences were added to the curriculum. There was a great emphasis on sport and on team identity. The wealthiest people sent their boys either to venerable old Protestant schools like Portora, King' s Hospital and Midleton College or to the newer Catholic Clongowes, Blackrock and Rockwell. The less expensive Catholic diocesan colleges also took day-pupils. Set up in each Catholic diocese and named after the patron saint of the diocese (St Flannan's in Ennis, St Conleth's, Carlow, and so on), these colleges were originally intended as a way of educating candidates for the priesthood – though not all boys who attended them joined the seminary. An tAthair Peadar O Laoghaire, a farmer's son born in 1839, tells of how he managed to attend St Colman' s College in Fermoy:

It was arranged in the college that a boy could attend it without having
to pay the thirty pounds [for a boarding-school fee] . He could take
lodgings in the town and go to the college every day. Then he would
have to pay only six pounds a year for his schooling and maintain
himself as cheaply as he could . . . The boys who lived in the college had
a great advantage over those who were outside in lodgings, as they
had extra tuition every evening.[19]

Town-dwellers had a distinct advantage over country people.
Although scholarships were sometimes available, a boy's parents
would still have to feed him in the holidays and do without his
earnings while he was learning. Thirty pounds in the 1850s was the
top annual salary scale for a male National School teacher, which
shows that such schools would have been out of the range of some
nominally middle-class people. St Jarlath' s in Tuam, Cunningham
tells us, was at the cheaper end of the range, charging £26 a year in
1862, £20 for 'ecclesiastical boarders' – boys who intended going
on for the priesthood (though there was no compulsion on them to
do this). Cheaper or not, of St Jarlath's boys' parents in 1887–91
only two were artisans, the rest being farmers, shopkeepers and
landowners, with a smattering of professionals and white-collar
workers. The introduction of 'County Scholarships' by the Department of Agriculture and Technical Instruction in 1899 made this
level of education more accessible to a wider range of people.[20] The
Christian Brothers' and Presentation Brothers' free secondary schools
for boys opened up white-collar work, the much-coveted 'permanent
and pensionable' jobs and sometimes the professions to people who
could not have afforded school fees.

Fee-paying schools: girls

When education had to be paid for, it was considered more important
to educate the boys than the girls, on the (increasingly mistaken)
assumption that the girls would get married and never use their
education. Like boys, girls often attended fee-paying schools from the
age of 7 or 8 to 17 or 18. As in the case of boys' schools, there was
no clear division between the *primary* and the *secondary* levels. Other
girls came to such schools to be 'finished' after years at National
Schools or at home with governesses.[21] Catholic boarding-schools
were run by some orders of nuns (Mercy, Dominicans, St Louis,
Sacred Heart, Loreto, Ursulines) and the regime was similar in some

respects to that of boys' boarding-schools – strict discipline, physical exercise and the values of self-sacrifice and devotion to duty. Corporal punishment was rare. In the mid-nineteenth century girls' schools were heavily criticised for teaching 'accomplishments', like the piano and painting on velvet, but schools (Catholic and Protestant) taught what parents wanted them to teach. Mathematics' teaching was often poor and the classics were rarely taught until educational reform took hold.

This reform was initiated vigorously by the Protestant mercantile middle class. Margaret Byers founded the Ladies' Collegiate School and Victoria College in Belfast in 1859, teaching the classics and a curriculum similar to that of boys' schools, and inviting lecturers from Queen' s College, Belfast. Alexandra College and School were set up in Dublin in 1866, with a similar curriculum, and it was largely through lobbying by Byers and by Isabella Tod that girls were allowed to sit the new school-leaving Intermediate Examination on equal terms with boys in 1878.[22] Quick to follow their example were the rural and provincial Catholic lower-middle classes. Twelve of the thirteen convent schools where girls sat the Intermediate in 1884 were run by either the Sisters of Mercy or the Loreto nuns, who administered the least expensive pay-schools at that time (the remaining convent was that of the Sisters of St Louis in Monaghan). Only one of these convent schools was in Dublin city and there were none in the cities of Belfast, Limerick, Cork and Galway.[23] The more expensive Catholic boarding-schools run by the Ursulines and Dominicans – later pioneers of women's third-level education – were slower to prepare girls for the Intermediate. The percentage of those taking the Senior Grade of the Intermediate who were girls rose from 15.8 in 1879 to 36 in 1921.[24] This represented considerable progress, though the significance of the 1879 figure should not be overlooked. Immediately an official school-leaving examination was established, girls accounted for between 10 and 20 per cent of those who sat it.

Mary Colum's account of her time in the St Louis Convent in Monaghan in the 1880s gives a flavour of the boarding-school experience in general:

> To try to act like everyone else became my constant preoccupation. We had everything in common. We rose, washed, and dressed in the same moment; said the same prayers in unison; wore the same uniform, did our hair in the prescribed way, plaited down our backs and tied with a silk ribbon. 'Form ranks' or 'get into ranks', that was the order several

times a day whenever we went anywhere in a body. We walked in step
in ranks of two and two going to the refectory, going to the little chapel
... A couple of times a week we had actual military drill by a drill
sergeant ... The supervision was ceaseless; everything we did or even
thought, it seemed to me, was known to the head of the school ...[25]

The relentless supervision, uniformity and almost military control of
the body (one convent school in Limerick employed a drill sergeant
in the early years of the twentieth century[26]) would have been
common in all boys' and girls' boarding-schools. Religious schools,
because of their dedicated, permanent, on-site staff whose whole
purpose in life was their pupils' educational and spiritual advancement, had a distinct edge as far as surveillance was concerned. Kate
O' Brien and Antonia White evoke this world vividly.[27]

Although the Intermediate examination gave a strong focus to
education as early as 1878, 'superior' schooling was far too lucrative
and its practitioners too powerful for there to be ready agreement
to any kind of standardization. Therefore 'secondary schools' were
not really regulated until 1918, when rules and requirements for
secondary teachers were laid down. From that time, all teachers had
to have a university degree and a teaching diploma, and existing
teachers were offered five years' grace to acquire these qualifications.
The Association of Secondary Teachers of Ireland had been
clamouring for such recognition and regulation since its foundation
in 1909.

Conclusion

*Trí bliana a chuir mé isteach ar an scoil, trí blian céasta chonacthas
domh san am sin, ach an té a chuirfeadh ceist anois orm, bheadh
athrach scéil agam le hinse dó.*
(I put in three years at school, which I saw as three tormented years that
time, but if anyone asked me about it now, I would have a different
story to tell him.) Hiúdaí Sheáin, born Donegal, 1853[28]

The most obvious social consequences of mass schooling are aspects
of life we take so much for granted now that we might overlook them.
The school bell was the first sign of time-oriented activity in rural life.
Children had to be presented every school day fit to be seen – not
necessarily shod, but clothed with some semblance of respectability,
faces wiped clean, hair combed. In the days before indoor plumbing,
this meant considerable work. Mothers and fathers after 1892 had

to do without their children's labour, whether their's was agricultural or trade work, or minding the baby while the mother worked. The 'wee mummies' of late nineteenth-century Belfast, Hamill tells us, were barely more than 12, the school-leaving age, and one must surmise that many were even younger before (and perhaps after) compulsory schooling.[29] Children, then as now, brought home from school more than just their lessons: the bothersome headlouse could be eradicated with paraffin or kerosene (the child kept well clear of the fire, which must have been difficult), but respiratory viral infections could be fatal. John Healy's mother, in 1920s Mayo, warned him against sitting beside the 'seldom-feds'.[30] Parents' right to dispose of their children's time and energy was weakened, and because of the denominational nature of schooling in Ireland, the teacher was doubly authoritative, as a representative of both the State and the Church. Most children probably did not know where the authority of one ended and the other began.

Did children reap any benefit from National School? M. Scott Coward's description of Munster children in 1870 gives an impression of enthusiasm at variance with Shakespeare's scholar, 'creeping like snail':

> I used often, as I drove along the country roads, to meet in rain and sunshine, parties of children, bareheaded often, always barefooted, sometimes racing at full speed, whom I have stopped and asked where they were going, and the answer was always either going to school or coming home from school.[31]

A long walk (or run!) in rain and frost to sit all day in a damp, badly heated room cannot have been pleasant, although if they were not at school many children would have been out working in such weather anyway, and at least they got some hours indoors free of heavy manual work. However, on their way to and from school, rural and urban National School attenders had precious intervals of freedom and fun unknown to the drilled ranks of boys and girls in fee-paying boarding-schools.

Did children benefit from the rough equality of the National School system? It certainly gave girls as many and as good chances of advancement as it did boys – and where it did not, that was because of parental priorities rather than the system itself. Girls were taught writing and arithmetic in National School at a time when some educational thinking on the teaching of poor females would have disagreed with such provision. Despite its compulsory needlework and the textbooks' messages about domesticity, the National School was as near a bastion of gender equality as was possible in the nineteenth-century. But was it a model of social equality? John Healy's mother's warning about poor children reminds us that the democracy of the playground was often undermined at home, and many teachers, notoriously, favoured the children who came to school clean, well-dressed and healthy. But children also establish their own hierarchies, and the games played and risks run in the schoolyard and on the road home gave many a labourer's child leadership and status among his peers.

The question of who was the most or least privileged, as far as schooling in general was concerned, might seem simplistic and merely rhetorical. Obviously, the most privileged was the bright son of a wealthy family who went to a 'good' school and entered a profession, or – better still – used his education to enhance his cultural life while managing his property. The least privileged was the shivering child, sore-bottomed on a hard form, ignored at the back of the class unless shouted or sneered at and slapped. In between these two extremes, the story is more complicated, and the 'better' school was not necessarily either the most comfortable environment or the best preparation for life. The boy whose parents saved to send him to a fee-paying boarding-school where he was made to feel socially inferior would have been better off, vocationally and in every way, at an endowed charity school or a Brothers' day-school. For girls, 'superior' schools varied, but the daily example of apparently satisfied husbandless women (religious or lay), devoted to their work, may have persuaded upper-middle-class girls to give up thoughts of marriage or, at the very least, to think of working outside the home. The take-up of secondary education to Intermediate standard was quickest among middle-class Protestants and rural–provincial middle-class Catholics, farmers' and shopkeepers' daughters. Outside of these girls and others fortunate enough to go on to university from the 1880s, the most vocationally advantaged women were those who could stay on at National School, train as teachers and get a job for life which they would not have to relinquish on marriage. Younger members of a family often got more educational opportunities than their elders because parents had become more comfortable and money was coming in from older siblings. This was true of Edward O'Toole and Charles McGlinchey's youngest brother.[32] Sometimes girls were more privileged than boys. When Leitrim-born Susan MacManus and her brother both won King's Scholarships in 1914, she availed herself of it because he had to work the small family farm.[33] Many boys had to leave school early to work and support younger siblings. But they were mostly free of the expectation obtaining in comfortable middle-class households, that they would stay at home to 'help'. This was one area where girls were quite strongly disadvantaged. Annie M. P. Smithson, from a Protestant, middle-class, Dublin family, tells a typical story:

> The spring of 1889 was a busy time for me. I was preparing for the Middle Grade Intermediate Examination, and studying hard. Seldom had I been so happy before . . . as I set off each morning to school.
>
> And then one day the blow fell.
>
> While at morning lessons, a message arrived for me to return home at once . . . On April 3 1889 my dearly loved sister . . . arrived in this weary world . . . I never thought her arrival would put a stop to my studies, I was still afraid that they would be interrupted for a while. But that day in April 1889, when I opened the front gate of the school and walked out into the Meath road [in Bray, Co. Wicklow], that school was never to see me again. Nor any other school . . . So I went back to helping with the children and the house generally. At first I was buoyed up with the thought of returning to school, of being able to sit for the examination. But it was not to be.[34]

Annie – 15 at this stage – managed a few years later to get away from her demanding mother. It was only with the help of an unmarried aunt that she got to Edinburgh to train as a nurse. Still, even before Edinburgh, she had more schooling than Peig Sayers, born in the same year as Annie (1873) into a smallholding, Irish-speaking family in the Dingle peninsula. Peig uncomplainingly left school (which she liked) at 12 to go into service in the town of Dingle. And even Peig, however severe her rupture with education, was more privileged than Hiúdaí Sheáin, a carpenter's son born in Rannafest, Donegal, in 1853. He started school at 10, and left at 13:

> *M'athair a d'iarr orm fanacht sa bhaile. Is cosúil go raibh mo chuidiú de dhíth air.*
>
> (It was my father asked me to stay at home. Likely he needed my help.)

Glad though he was to leave school at the time, he regretted it later, as the statement quoted at the head of this section suggests.[35] Educational gender disabilities were noticeable among those who could afford to pay for schooling, but in the case of small farmers, unskilled labourers and casually employed workers, it is simply impossible to state that either gender was privileged over the other. Family income and priorities were far more decisive factors.

Notes

1 A short selection on general works on the European history of children and the family are as follows: Linda Pollock, *Forgotten Children* (Cambridge 1983); John Gillis, *A World of Their Own Making: myth and ritual in family life* (Oxford 1997); J. Flandrin, *Familles: parenté, maison, sexualité dans l'ancien régime* (Paris 1976); Rafaella Sarti, *Europe at Home 1500–1800* (Yale 2002).

2 Akenson, *Irish Education Experiment*; N. Atkinson, *Irish Education: a history of educational institutions* (Dublin 1969); Durcan, *History of Irish Education Since 1800*; Coolahan, *Irish Education: history and structure*; T. J. O'Connell, *100 Years of Progress*; John Logan, 'Dimensions of gender'; and Cullen (ed.), *Girls Don't Do Honours*. Also important are T. J. McElligott, *Secondary Education in Ireland 1870–1921* (Dublin 1981); J. M. Goldstrom, *The Social Content of Education 1808–1870* (London 1972).

3 Clear, *Nuns in Nineteenth-Century Ireland*, pp. 100–34; *Fifty-First Report of the Commissioners for National Education 1884–1885* [c.4458], Vol. 24, Appendix, pp. 147–9.

4 J. S. Doran, *Turn Up the Lamp: tales of a Mourne childhood* (Belfast 1980), pp. 26–9.

5 O'Toole, *Whist for Your Life*.

6 See Coolahan, *Irish Education: history and Structure*; Durcan, *History of Irish Education Since 1800*; Logan, 'Dimensions of gender'.

7 Doran, *Turn Up the Lamp*, p. 26.

8 See note 2; also Clear, *Nuns in Nineteenth-Century Ireland*, pp. 100–33.

9 Kate O'Brien, *The Land of Spices* (London 1941).

10 'From Kilnamanagh to Coolumper: a history trail along the Shannon', in Clonone Community Centre (ed.), *Clonown: the history, traditions and culture of a south Roscommon community* (Clonone 1989), pp. 120–2; *Report of the Commissioners for National Education 1884–1885*, Appendix, pp. 211, 245.

11 Charles E. Cameron, *A Manual of Hygiene, Public and Private*, p. 209.

12 See works cited in note 2, plus, on religious in education: Barry Coldrey, *Faith and Fatherland: the Christian Brothers 1838–1921* (London 1988); Clear, *Nuns in Nineteenth-Century Ireland*; T. J. Walsh, *Nano Nagle and the Presentation Sisters* (Dublin 1959); Mother Austin Carroll, *Leaves from the Annals of the Sisters of Mercy* (New York 1888);

Desmond Bowen, *The Protestant Crusade in Ireland 1800–1870* (Dublin 1978).

13 The classic account of the hedge schools is Daniel Corkery, *The Hidden Ireland: a study of Gaelic Munster in the eighteenth century* (Dublin 1925); and Mark Ryan, *Fenian Memories* (Dublin 1946); I am grateful to John Cunningham for the latter reference.

14 Charles Dickens, *Nicholas Nickleby* (London 1838).

15 McElligott, *Secondary Education*, p. 4.

16 IFC, MS 1112, Evidence collected from Mary Daly, Co. Louth (grew up in Co. Armagh), 28/8/45, p. 74.

17 For some information on this, see Anne V. O'Connor, 'The revolution in girls' secondary education in Ireland 1860–1910', in Cullen (ed.), *Girls Don't Do Honours*, pp. 31–54.

18 Eibhlín Breathnach, 'Charting new waters: women's experience in higher education 1879–1908', in Cullen (ed.), *Girls Don't Do Honours*, pp. 55–78.

19 An tAthair Peadar O Laoghaire, *Mo Scéal Féin* (Baile Atha Cliath 1900), translated by Sheila O' Sullivan as *My Own Story* (Dublin 1973).

20 John Cunningham, *St Jarlath's College, Tuam 1800–2000* (Tuam 1999), pp. 141–2, 147, 138.

21 McElligott, *Secondary Education*, p. 9, suggests that the demand for middle-class girls' schools resulted from the decline in the number of governesses, but it might have been the other way around.

22 Clear, *Nuns Don't Do Honours*, pp. 100–34; O'Connor, 'The revolution in girls' secondary education'; Anne V. O'Connor and Susan Parkes (eds), *Gladly Learn and Gladly Teach: Alexandra College Dublin 1866–1966* (Dublin nd)

23 The Loreto Order of nuns was founded in Dublin by Frances Ball in 1821; the Sisters of Mercy by Catherine McAuley in 1828. The Sisters of St Louis were a French congregation introduced into Ireland in 1858. The Mullingar Mercy Convent is misleadingly returned as the 'Annunciation' in 1884.

24 *Report of the Intermediate Education Board for Ireland 1884 (1884–85)* [c.4425], Vol. 24; McElligott, Secondary Education, p. 149.

25 Mary Colum, *Life and the Dream* (New York 1928), pp. 1–84.

26 Oral evidence from the late Sr M. Patrick Cussen, Laurel Hill Convent, Limerick.

27 See e.g. Antonia White, *Frost in May* (London 1933, reprinted Virago 1978); O'Brien, *Land of Spices*.

28 Eoghan O Domhnaill, *Scéal Hiúdaí Sheáin* (Baile Atha Cliath 1940), p. 11.

29 Jonathan Hamill, 'Childcare arrangements within the Belfast linen community'.

30 John Healy, *Nineteen Acres* (Achill 1978) p. 23.

31 *Thirty-Seventh Annual Report of the Commissioners of National Education in Ireland 1870–1871* [c.360, c.360.1], Vol. 23, reports from around the country.

32 O'Toole, *Whist for Your Life*; and Charles McGlinchey, *The Last of the Name* (Belfast 1986), p. 142.

33 John McGahern, *Memoir* (London 2005), p. 13; Susan McManus was McGahern's mother.

34 Smithson, *Myself – and Others*, pp. 73–4.

35 Peig Sayers, *Peig* (Baile Atha Cliath 1936).

4

Emigration and migration

They went across the fields at six o'clock this morning, they are in America long ago. (Tipperary boy, 1890s, asked about his sisters[1])

How many and where?

The alarming figures have been so often repeated that we are in danger of taking them for granted: in 1890 there were 3 million Irish people living outside of Ireland and 40 per cent of all Irish-by-birth people in the world were living outside it. Emigration of Irish people had been going on in one form or another since the seventeenth century, but it began to accelerate in the nineteenth. About a million people emigrated from Ireland between 1815 and 1845, 2.5 million between 1846 and 1855, and another 4 million between 1856 and 1914. Because of the difficulty of ascertaining numbers who emigrated permanently to mainland Britain, these figures are probably underestimations.[2] The main authorities on the history of emigration from Ireland and Irish immigrants to Britain and the New World after 1850 all agree that emigration has had a huge impact on Irish society.[3]

Approximately 80 per cent of emigrants between the Famine and Independence/Partition were between the ages of 18 and 30, clustered at the younger rather than the older end of this range. More likely to be single than married, they were about as likely to be female as male. Though Protestants also emigrated in great numbers, Catholics probably predominated in the years 1850–1922.[4] North America was the most popular destination, but a significant minority of emigrants – over 300,000 between 1851 and 1890, and a steady trickle thereafter – went to Australia. An average of 2,000 Irish people a year went to New Zealand between 1871 and 1920. There were also Irish emigrants to South Africa, South America and India, though these made up only a small proportion of the total. About 400,000 of the post-Famine emigrants were assisted to emigrate by the government, Poor Law authorities, individual philanthropists or landlords, although, as Moran reminds us: 'Most Irish migration to North America in the nineteenth century was assisted in one way or another.'[5] This is a reference to chain migration, whereby settled emigrants sent money to help their relatives and friends to emigrate.

Phase 1 1850–c.75

Emigration in the 1850s and 1860s was highest from Antrim, Limerick, Cork, Kerry, Clare and Tipperary, in that order, and although groups from Mayo and Sligo were assisted to emigrate, these two western counties were among the lowest suppliers of emigrants over these years. Those who emigrated on their own initiative were mainly young men and women from small farming and labouring backgrounds. They came from parts of the country where there were plenty of shops and schools, where change and improvement was in the air but work and wages too scarce, and they went mainly to North America and Australia. Passages to Britain were always well within the reach of even the most unskilled labourer, but it was more expensive to get to North America or Australia–New Zealand. At that stage, marginally more men than women emigrated, though the number of single women going away independently of family was high by European standards. These emigrants were not the poorest people – even assisted emigrants had to put up some of their fare and emigration kit themselves – but trends in agriculture were against them. They had sufficient awareness to realize that such improvement was within their grasp too, but not while they remained in Ireland. So they went and settled down; and if they sent some money home, it was mainly to induce others to come out. These emigrants' primary aim was self-improvement rather than buttressing those left behind, and more young families emigrated at this time than later.

Assisted emigration has been overshadowed, yet assisted emigrants made up a significant proportion (10 per cent) of all post-Famine emigrants. Whether the assistance was from the government via an emigration agent or from a philanthropist or landlord, the schemes were highly localized and thus had a big impact on certain areas.

Lord Monteagle assisted over 800 people from west Limerick – mainly Shanagolden and Foynes – to emigrate to Australia between 1838 and 1858. Vere Foster concentrated his efforts on young women in the north of Co. Mayo in the 1850s, and again in the 1880s.[6] Bishop Quinn brought 4,000 people from Donegal to Queensland between 1862 and 1865. The government, anxious to settle people in Canada and Australia, paid fares, provided emigration kit, a hygienic shipboard regime and ships' doctors to make sure the human cargo arrived safely. Their schemes helped either people from the workhouse or landless/small farming families. William and Honor Lloyd, their sons aged 14 (twins) and 7, and their daughters aged 5 and 1, who sailed to Australia in 1851, were a typical family group from the fertile and prosperous East Clare parish of Parteen and Meelick.[7]

Landlord-assisted emigrants were not always so well-provided for. The Fitzwilliam emigration from Coolattin in Wicklow of 6,000 people between 1849 and 1856 was a clearance, with emigrants badly provided for on the journey and at their destination.[8] The notorious Lansdowne emigration of 1850–51 sent almost 4,000 people from south Kerry to New York City in poor clothing in the dead of winter.[9] The 143 emigrants from Derryveagh, in Co. Donegal, to Australia, in 1861 were very well provided for by a philanthropic commmittee, but they had been evicted from their homes in circumstances which led to questions being asked in Parliament.[10] In contrast, Monteagle's emigrants from west Limerick wrote in gratitude to him from Australia with flatteringly worded requests for sisters, brothers, cousins and friends to be sent out.[11] Some even repaid the fare he had lent them. Assisted emigration was often eagerly sought; pauper women knew exactly how to argue their case for inclusion in an emigration scheme.[12]

Phase 2 1880–1922

One would occasionally hear an old man or old woman say haughtily, 'None of my people ever had to go to America, thank God. We always had it.' (Mary Colum, née Maguire, 1884–1957)[13]

After 1880, there was a definite change in the origins, numbers and destinations of emigrants. Emigration assisted by individual philanthropists like Vere Foster, James Hack Tuke, Bishop Ireland and Fr Nugent in the 1880s helped 50,000 people to leave the West of Ireland, but government and landlord schemes were over. The depression of the 1870s had caused emigration to slow, but it accelerated again in the 1880s, when fares to America were lower. A bedrock of emigrants from all over the country was established in the New World by about 1890. Now the chains began to work, as these settled emigrants sent for nieces, nephews, sisters, brothers and cousins. People were still leaving the midlands and Munster, but after 1891 Connacht people began to leave in huge numbers.

Young 'boys' and 'girls' usually travelled in kin or neighbour groups. After the initial settlement, chains were vital. Over 71 per cent of those 'sent for', according to one Australian study, were brothers, sisters or cousins – members of the peer group.[14] We have no way of knowing how many brought out friends, like Peig Sayers' friend Cáit Jim, who sent Peig the fare to America in 1890.[15] The chain migration of the Irish was so common that it was made fun of in an American music-hall song:

> I'm deep in love with Johnny Burke, as the ass is fond of clover,
> And tell him when I have the fare I'll pay his passage over.[16]

Unlike other immigrant groups in the New World, the Irish rarely travelled with, or sent for, their parents. The reason usually given for this was that parents, along with the heir, still had a living on the family holding; only the surplus offspring travelled. This is certainly true of most West of Ireland emigrants from the 1880s, whose contributions were vital to the survival of the family holding. Mary O'Donnell's parting words to the fourth and last daughter she saw off to America in the 1890s were, '[A]nd between ye, let ye send home the slates' (i.e. the money to replace the thatched roof with slates).[17] Yet there was no guarantee that the offspring would 'send home' or even write. In 1898 Mary Carbery visited a lonely, impoverished, old couple in Castlefreke, Co. Cork, who had not heard from their four adult children in America for many years.[18] The mainly Munster, Leinster, Ulster labourer–servant emigrants who set off singly or in family groups in the years 1850–75 were not in most cases leaving viable farms of any size. Did the prevalence of assisted emigration schemes, with their injunctions against helping those over 50, instill a custom that the old couldn't and shouldn't emigrate? Akenson comments that the Irish, wherever they settled, became solid citizens – 'good ordinary Australians'.[19] Were the Irish perhaps too 'good' to the countries to which they went, not burdening them with their 'unproductive' old?

The trend of the emigration of the young, strong and single is the more noteworthy because Irish emigrants were particularly advantaged among European immigrants to the New World. They were mostly (thanks to a potato and buttermilk diet) of strong build, but crucially the emigrants of the 1850s and 1860s were mainly from parts of the country where English had been spoken for at least a generation. Kerby Miller suggests that being monoglot Irish speakers forced many Irish emigrants to the USA to experience emigration as exile rather than opportunity.[20] This could be said of all immigrants to any new country, but there were on balance more English-speakers than Irish-speakers among the emigrants, particularly in the initial post-Famine wave.

Those leaving Ireland after the 1870s (and sometimes before) had information, from contacts already settled, telling them when and when not to come out. This explains the slowing down of emigration to the USA in the late 1870s, a time when jobs were short there, and the temporary rise in emigration to New Zealand in the same decade,[21] when demand was high. It was also important, for the shorter American voyage, to get the time of year right. Thus, Mary Reid, writing from Brooklyn in March 1899, advised her sister Jane, in Antrim, to send Mary's niece Jennie out as soon as possible, 'for the best families all go to the country on the first of July.'[22]

It is very difficult to make out numbers of emigrants to Great Britain over this period. First, Ireland was administratively part of Britain up to 1922, and population movement was not always seen as important to record. Second, temporary migration across the Irish Sea was so common that permanent emigration is difficult both to track and even to define. Does staying for five years constitute temporary or permanent emigration? Third, contrary to what one might expect, given the high profile of Irish immigrants in ghetto-like habitations in large English cities, many Irish people were quite easily assimilated into English life. Nonetheless, some formed quite a distinct ethnic group in Liverpool, Manchester, London and York.[23] Irish applicants for poor relief in England were so numerous in the immediate post-Famine decades that the Irish workhouse authorities were in constant conflict with their British counterparts about apparently Irish paupers who were 'sent home' to the Poor

Law Unions to which they supposedly belonged. Irish Catholic communities were large enough in some cities by the 1880s for the Roman Catholic Church to concentrate priests and nuns in those areas to provide places of worship and schools. Irish Protestants, on the other hand, have been invisible up to recently. Cormac O Gráda estimates that between 1852 and 1910, about a million Irish people went to Britain.[24] How much of this was temporary, how much permanent, how many returned, and went back again, we can never know.

There were other destinations of Irish emigrants on a smaller scale – Africa, South America, India. When William Bulfin was cycling around Westmeath in the 1900s, he was delighted to come across a townland where many of the locals, like himself, had been to Buenos Aires. Several families from Bere Island, Co. Cork, sent emigrants to Argentina, encouraged to do so by an islander who had made good there in the 1880s.[25] Most Irish emigrants to South Africa were white-collar or professional workers; the colony had enough cheap local labour at hand. North and West America and the less urban parts of Australia attracted young, skilled, male emigrants who had a margin of money and the wherewithal to keep themselves while travelling; the Irish in San Francisco in the 1860s were mostly 'adventurers' and entrepreneurs. There was a considerable Irish settlement in Montana. Ireland, like every other country, supplied its share of these people, who could probably have stayed comfortably at home but chose instead to go looking for adventure in foreign parts. They made up only a very small proportion of emigrants, male or female, but they are still part of the diaspora.

There was also missionary emigration, of Irish Catholic women in particular, to convents in North America, India and Australia, 'several thousand' to the USA alone.[26] Nuns, many of them Irish originally, came to Ireland on recruiting drives. As early as 1840 Irish Presentation Sisters established a convent in Madras, India. Sometimes religious emigration was chain migration, as aunts followed nieces (and possibly nephews their uncles) abroad, to the religious life, often travelling as 'civilians' and only 'entering' on arrival. The nine Murphy sisters of Newmarket-on-Fergus, Co. Clare, who entered convents in England, Australia and India between 1885 and 1904, had at least five nieces join them in the religious life in India and Australia between 1914 and 1922.[27]

Men, women, whys and wherefores

Thugas taitneamh don dhuine úd dob fhinne's dob áille snó
Is do chuaigh sé ar bord loinge,' sé Jimmy mo mhíle stór.
(I fell in love with a person of fair and beautiful appearance
And he went off on a ship, Jimmy, my thousand-times love.)
(Traditional)

Reasons for emigrating crowd in on us from all the ballads, songs, stories, personal accounts and historical narratives, but they all point to one conclusion: people emigrated to better themselves and, sometimes, the families they left behind them. Akenson warns us against assumptions about 'push and pull' factors – all we can know is that emigrants took those steps up the gangway and onto the ship. Half the fun of historical writing is speculation, however, and Akenson, quoting David Fitzpatrick, breaks his own rule when it comes to giving reasons for Irish women's emigration overtaking that of men in the 1890s:

> Emigration for tens of thousands of women was not a terrible fate, but a safety net, for 'even the humblest husband or job abroad was better than no husband and no job at home'.[28]

Once Irish women saw that there was no chance of a man at home, they took off to find one abroad? There are three things wrong with this speculation. First, the counties which supplied the most female emigrants in the 1890s – Kerry, Mayo, Sligo, Galway – were those where comparatively young marriages persisted up to 1911. When Peig Sayers, from west Kerry, decided not to emigrate, her alternative was not spinsterhood, but marriage, at 19, to an island-dwelling fisherman. The counties which had the highest proportion of single women aged 35–44 in 1881 and in 1911 – Dublin, Londonderry, Tyrone, Wexford, Queen's, King's, Fermanagh and Meath – also had (then and previously) comparatively low rates of female emigration. Women may have chosen emigration as an alternative to marriage at home, rather than as a last-ditch attempt to get a man. Second, Fitzpatrick and Akenson assume that all women always want to get married. Not all did – the low marriage rate in Ireland in this period, I argue later, was as much women's choice as men's. Third, neither women nor men at that time had the kind of demographic information available to them which would enable decisions based on marriage rates and ages at marriage. Crotty warns us against judging farmers' economic behaviour on the basis of economic information they could not have had.[29] What is true of farming is even more true of courting. Besides, if they were simply going on the trail of a spouse, the 'girls' would have followed the 'boys', and vice versa, and they did not do so. In different years and different regions, there were always more males than females emigrating, or vice versa. Women, like men, went where they could find work, because they knew that earning a living was a prerequisite for any kind of satisfactory life, married or single. Mostly rural women, they had the example of their own mothers: they did not expect an easy life.

Still, almost uniquely among European emigrants to the New World, Irish girls and women left the country independently, in peer groups, without family 'protection'. Were Irish girls thought little of, to be allowed away like this? Robert Kennedy thinks so, and cites Irish females' comparatively high mortality as older children (rather than babies) and young adults in support of his argument that girls were underfed, undervalued, overworked and eventually forced out of the home, because they were more use to the family abroad.[30] However, somebody trusted to send money regularly from thousands of miles away must have had strong bonds with home. If she had not, what was to stop her disappearing in the vast territories of Australia and Canada, or the big cities of North America? Harris suggests that Irish ties to kin and friend were particularly strong, on the evidence of the large number of advertisments taken out by Irish people, looking for their relatives, in newspapers read by Irish Americans.[31] But the reverse could also be true – Irish personal ties were so weak that people were obliged to take out paid advertisments to find brothers, sisters, cousins. Emigrants could, and did, get lost, and a resentful daughter had a golden opportunity to cast off forever those parasites at home, if that was how she saw them. And if she didn't see them as such, if she was forever generous to a greedy family which asked more than it should, who are we to accuse her of 'false consciousness'? Irish girls and women were allowed to emigrate *alone* because they were highly valued as workers and as family members, trusted not only to send money home, but to keep themselves 'out of trouble'. Women and girls, like men and boys, emigrated to make a living. If a marriage partner transpired – and Hasia Diner shows that Irish women in the USA married later than women of other immigrant groups[32] – well and good. However, the fact that so many emigration songs in both languages, with male and female narrators, lament their departure or their leaving behind of sweethearts,[33] indicates that economics took precedence over emotions.

'When they told me I must leave the place': emigration and emotion

> When they told me I must leave the place I tried to keep a cheerful face
> To show my heart great sorrow was a-scorning.
>   But the tears will surely blind me for the friends I leave behind me
>   When I start for Philadelphia in the morning. (Traditional)

Overhearing one Donegal emigrant aboard an Allen liner say to another 'They're cutting the corn in Creeslough the day' inspired Percy French to write one of the most famous songs about Irish emigration.[34] But one would actually have to hear the emigrant's tone to interpret this remark – was it wistful or merely factual? The emotional aspect of emigration is a great unknowable. Miller argues that the post-Famine emigration of rural Irish Catholics, to the USA, was such a wrench and a shock that it was experienced as bitter and reluctant 'exile', and he gathers a persuasive array of personal testimony to prove this. Akenson contends that we simply do not hear from the emigrants who assimilated successfully. The same evidence can be interpreted in a number of ways. For example, the Irish as an immigrant group had an unusually high rate of hospitalization for mental illness, in Australia and in North America.[35] Whether this means that Irish people were more likely to lose their reason due to disorientation and cultural dislocation (homesickness or reluctant exile) or that they were more likely than other immigrant groups to be identified as mentally ill, it indicates considerable pain and suffering in the emigrant experience. But one explanation for the higher rate of asylum committal of Irish people in other countries could be that the Irish were less likely than other immigrants to deal with mental illness within the family and more likely to seek an institutional solution for it. This could indicate weaker kin networks among Irish people than among other immigrants, which could also explain why they did not send for the old people (though they supported them from afar). And what about the low rate of reverse, or return, migration? Italians had a 58 per cent return migration rate, Scandinavians 20 per cent, and Irish people 6–10 per cent.[36] It is easy to understand why so few returned from Australia – the journey took a quarter of a year, and many in the 1850s and 1860s went there with their immediate families. But the majority of emigrants over the entire period went as single people to North America, and the journey took only seven days even in the 1870s. By the 1880s, politicians and public figures thought nothing of going to America twice or even three times a year. There were some return migrants. Many women from Inis Mór, Aran, towards the end of the nineteenth century, went to America to earn their dowries. Some women from Kerry's Blasket Island went to Springfield, Massachusetts, for the same purpose, returning after 7–8 years.[37] The 'returned Yank' was common enough to be caricatured in late nineteenth- and early twentieth-century Ireland, but he or she was usually a visitor:[38] the overall rate of permanent return was low. That there were not many return migrants because there was nothing for them to return to is the simple answer – there was no livelihood, no property. But there was arguably even less for the returning Italian emigrants, except what they brought with them. The low rate of return could imply that Irish people felt no great emotional need to come home.

The words of Phil, the Tipperary boy, quoted at the head of this chapter, about his sisters who left that morning being 'in America long ago' could be literally true today, as it certainly was not then. But as far as he was concerned, once they went across the fields they were gone forever. Mary Healy comments:

> The awful heartbreak of those words . . . has always stayed in my mind, for it implied that they went without anybody to accompany them, and I always wonder did they realize that they would never see Ireland again.[39]

Healy sees loneliness and permanence as the two worst aspects of these girls' departure. We will never know if they saw it that way themselves.

Seasonal migration

> The grass was ripe for cutting, the weather seemed likely to be fine. Everything was ready for the Irishmen, and a rumour came that they had been seen, they were near. (Alison Uttley, referring to England, 1870s[40])

Seasonal migration follows the predictable rhythms of the agricultural year; temporary migration follows short-term work wherever it is to be found, usually in construction and domestic service. In Ireland between 1850 and 1950, seasonal migration for agricultural labour gradually gave way to temporary migration for construction work. The destination was Britain in both cases; the home base in Ireland was maintained and returned to regularly. (Seasonal migration within Ireland is referred to in chapter 1.) The migrants were mostly men, though some women also went from Achill and Donegal.

The intensive cultivation of land in Britain in the late eighteenth century created a demand for cheap agricultural labour. Migration from Ireland reached its peak in the years 1861–65, when about 78,000 'harvestmen' a year bought tickets for the Midland Great Western Railway alone; this does not take into account Donegal people who took the Derry boat to Scotland and others who walked to the ports rather than taking the train. Most of these harvesters originated west of a line from Derry to Cork, though there was always a smattering of migrants from other counties in Ireland too. They travelled in groups or squads, with a ganger, or foreman, sufficiently fluent in English to negotiate terms for them. Sometimes there was a long-standing arrangement from one year to the next with a farmer in a particular locality, who expected them when he saw them in early summer, as did Alison Uttley's father in Oxfordshire. Generation after generation of migrants would go to generation after generation of farmers. The attraction for the farmers is easy to understand – local labour would have been far more expensive, and local labourers might have demanded round-the-year work. The Irishmen came, worked and went. The accommodation and food were primitive, but the money was obviously worth their endeavour.[41]

The departure in early summer meant that there was still some time to go before the harvest, so what did they do in the meantime? Travelling could take up to a week, and once they arrived in June or early July they saved hay or weeded. Given the persistent poverty of many smallholdings in the west which came to harsh light in the 'distress' of the late 1870s, it could be that many harvesters left home early simply to relieve the burden on the family resources for the hungry summer months. *Manger hors de la région* (eating away from home), as in eighteenth-century France,[42] might have been reason enough for the biggest consumers of food (the adult men) to take themselves off in the scarce months, perhaps begging en route. Irish harvesters did not have the name of being beggars; in fact they appeared respectable enough for the railway to bring in a special ticket for them, though the fact that this ticket was known as 'fourth class' gives an idea of their social standing relative to other users of the railway. In the 1850s and 1860s workhouse relieving officers were constantly warned by the Poor Law Commissioners that they should not turn away migrants who were 'honest wayfarers' – 'some of the most fitting objects of public charity' – and the category of 'night-lodger' was developed especially with these migrants in mind.[43] Shanklin, writing on Donegal in the early twentieth century, comments that the women had to stay at home 'while the men were free to migrate', but there was little freedom involved in the hungry hardship the migrants experienced on the journey out or in the back-breaking agricultural work which waited for them.[44] The return journey, with light hearts and maybe a few presents for the family, was a different matter, their pockets full to settle bills at the local shop at home.[45]

Numbers going on seasonal migration from Ireland in general began to fall in the 1870s with the mechanization of many agricultural processes. Migration from Mayo, particularly Achill Island and Donegal, continued strong right up to 1940, and even intensified in the 1920s and 1930s:[46] 30,000, on average, migrated from Ireland every year in the 1880s, though these figures are hard to ascertain – some migrants were not counted, some may have made two trips and were counted twice. In Donegal in 1898, temporary return on family business was so common that an entire murder case hinged around the circumstances of the return of one suspect.[47] In 1885, 75 per cent of migrants were from Connacht; 11.9 per cent of the adult male population of Mayo, it was estimated in 1885, sought employment away from home. In Roscommon the proportion was 3.3 per cent, in Donegal 3 per cent, in Galway 2.2 per cent, Sligo 2.6 per cent, Leitrim 1.7 per cent and Armagh 1 per cent. In no other county did the proportion exceed 1 per cent, though there were 148 migrants from Monaghan and 113 from Louth. Almost all of the Mayo migrants were land-holders.[48] By 1899, the overall numbers had fallen considerably, to 18,912 (though the method of calculation was slightly different) but the proportion from Connacht had risen to over 80 per cent, and Mayo at this stage supplied over half of all Irish migratory labourers.[49]

Seasonal migration for agriculture continued on a small scale until the 1950s. The numbers travelling were augmented by those whose absences had little to do with the agricultural year. These were people who travelled on the rumour or prospect of work in construction, transport and distribution, staying away for anything from 3 to 18 months. There had always been migrants like this – indeed, the word 'navvy' which was often used to describe them has its origins in the 'navigation' or canal-digging work on which they were employed in the early nineteenth century. Temporary (as opposed to seasonal) migration was less likely to be in groups and more likely to be a man on his own or with one other person. The money was better than that for agricultural work, but the work was less regular and the dangers of losing life and limb (or indeed heart) were much greater.[50]

The social effects of seasonal and temporary migration are in some ways similar to those of permanent emigration, in some ways different. First, smallholdings unable to survive in any other way were stabilized by earnings from migration. Second, seasonal migration meant early marriage (no reason to postpone it) and caused population increase in Mayo between 1851 and 1881. In 1911, the pattern of comparatively early marriage still persisted in parts of Mayo and Donegal. Third, earnings from seasonal migration buoyed up the local economy as the money from 'the farmer' or 'the job' in England or Scotland was spent in the local shop.

Conclusion

There were many different kinds of emigrants and migrants from Ireland. Broadly speaking, the emigrants most likely to have broken their ties with Ireland were those who went in family groups, and because many of these left in the 1860s and 1870s, well out of living memory for a long time now, their story, and that of the young, single people who went with them, has faded from our view. But in those 20–25 years, how the human landscape of townlands in Clare, Tipperary, King's County, Antrim, and Limerick must have altered. This emigration contributed to the agricultural prosperity of the years 1850–75 by making more land available to medium-sized and larger farmers, and by having fewer discontented labourers and small-holders putting moral and social pressure on farmers to employ them The people of the west did not, as a rule, emigrate in family groups in the 1880s, 1890s and 1900s. Was it their tradition of seasonal migration, family members going away and coming back, which reinforced this pattern of individuals in each generation departing and sending money home regularly? Permanent emigration, O Gráda shows, took over from widespread seasonal migration after 1880, but it never totally replaced it. But one might have led to the other in ways that we are just beginning to understand from deeper research into the gendered nature of emigration from the west. While seasonal migration was in full swing, women left in charge for half the year or more, with only the elderly and children to help them, saved the hay and the turf, and sometimes the harvest. Harvest yields in the 1850s–1870s were as high as ever they had been. The early winter reunion with husbands must often have resulted (perhaps every second year[51]) in a new baby the following summer or early autumn, at the busiest time of the agricultural year when she had only the elderly and the under-14s to help her. Turf, hay and crops had to be saved, and however small the acreage it was still hard work for a woman who was heavily pregnant or had just given birth. No wonder the daughters of such mothers set boldly off for America from the 1880s onwards. Their mothers' competence inspired them, but the prospect of such single-handed hardship for themselves if they stayed probably gave them the final push. The women of Achill and Donegal, however, continued this single-handed multi-tasking until much later, though they also supplied their share of permanent emigrants.

Although the need to emigrate was one of the factors in the decline of the Irish language, emigrants' remittances facilitated the survival and perpetuation of Irish-speaking communities for several generations. While immediate post-Famine emigration changed eastern and midland – or *prosperous* – Ireland (and parts of Kerry and Wicklow) by removing labourers and cottiers, sometimes whole families at a stroke, permanent emigration after 1880 preserved the cultural and human landscape of the western seaboard – though for dwindling numbers in each generation.

Notes

1 Healy, *For the Poor and for the Gentry*, p. 68
2 These and other summary figures, though gleaned from a variety of historians, are summed up in David Fitzpatrick's indispensable *Irish Emigration 1801–1921: studies in Irish economic and social history* (Dundalk 1984); and Donald Akenson's useful and comprehensive *The Irish Diaspora: a primer* (Toronto 1993).

3 Arnold Schrier, *Ireland and the American Emigration 1850–1900* (Minneapolis 1958); Robert E. Kennedy, *The Irish: emigration, marriage and fertility* (Berkeley, CA 1973); Oliver MacDonagh, *Emigration in the Victorian Age* (Farnborough 1973); Kerby A. Miller, *Emigrants and Exiles*; Akenson, *Irish Diaspora*; David Fitzpatrick, *Irish Emigration*; and *Oceans of Consolation: personal accounts of Irish migration to Australia* (Cork 1994); Patrick O'Farrell, *The Irish in Australia* (Kensington, NSW 1986); Gerard Moran, *Sending Out Ireland's Poor: assisted emigration to North America in the nineteenth century* (Dublin 2004); Gearoid O Tuathaigh, 'The historical pattern of Irish emigration: some labour aspects', in Galway Labour History Group (ed.), *The Emigrant Experience* (Galway 1991), pp. 9–28; Frances Finnegan, *Poverty and Prejudice: a study of Irish immigrants in York* (Cork 1982); R. Swift and S. Gilley (eds), *The Irish in Britain 1815–1939* (London 1989); Angela McCarthy, 'Personal letters and the organization of Irish migration to and from New Zealand 1848–1925', *Irish Historical Studies (IHS)*, Vol. 33, No. 131 (2003), pp. 297–319.

4 Akenson does not agree (see *Irish Diaspora*, generally), but although he argues his case persuasively, it is not very convincing for the post-Famine period anyway.

5 Moran, *Sending Out Ireland's Poor*, p. 13.

6 Christopher O'Mahony and Valerie Thompson, *Poverty to Promise: the Monteagle emigrants 1838–1858* (Darlinghurst, NSW 1994).

7 Donal O Riain and Seamus O Cinnéide, *Stair agus Béaloideas Páirtín agus Míliuc (Meelick and Parteen History and Folklore)* (Limerick 1994), pp. 144–6.

8 Jim Rees, *Surplus People: the Fitzwilliam clearances 1847–1856* (Cork 2000).

9 Sean O Mordha, *Land and Gold: Kenmare and the Lansdowne estate*, RTE documentary, broadcast 9 November 2005.

10 W. E. Vaughan, *Sin, Sheep and Scotsmen: John George Adair and the Derryveagh evictions 1861* (Belfast 1983), pp. 63–4.

11 O'Mahony and Thompson, *Poverty to Promise*, p. 115 and generally.

12 Dympna McLoughlin, 'Superfluous and unwanted deadweight: the emigration of Irish pauper women', in Patrick O'Sullivan (ed.), *Irish Women and Irish Migration* (Leicester 1995), pp. 66–88.

13 Colum, *Life and the Dream*, p. 69.

14 Akenson, *Irish Diaspora*, p. 178; see also O'Farrell, *Irish in Australia*, pp. 85–8.

15 Sayers, *Peig*.

16 'I'm leaving Tipperary' – traditional.

17 John Healy, *Nineteen Acres*, p. 2.

18 Jeremy Sandford (ed.), *Mary Carbery's West Cork Journal 1898–1901* (Dublin 1998), pp. 27–8.
19 Akenson, *Irish Diaspora*, pp. 107–8.
20 Miller, *Emigrants and Exiles*.
21 Akenson, *Irish Diaspora*, pp. 59–90.
22 Brigid McGay, 'Emigrant's letter 19th March 1999', *The Glynns: Journal of the Glens of Antrim Historical Society*, Vol. 25 (1997), pp. 52–3.
23 Swift and Gilley (eds), *The Irish in Britain*; Finnegan, *Poverty and Prejudice*.
24 Cited in Akenson, *Irish Diaspora*, pp. 189–215; on higher Protestant visibility, see ibid. generally.
25 William Bulfin, *Rambles in Eirinn* (Dublin 1907), pp. 411–13; Ted O'Sullivan, *Bere Island: a history* (Dunmanway 1993), p. 39.
26 Suellen Hoy, 'The journey out: the recruitment and emigration of Irish religious women to the United States 1812–1914', *Journal of Women's History* (Indiana), Vol. 6, No. 4 and Vol. 7, No. 1 (winter–spring 1994–95), pp. 65–98; S. Hoy and M. MacCurtain (eds), *From Dublin to New Orleans: the journey of Nora and Alice to America 1889* (Dublin 1994).
27 C. Clear, 'My mother taught me how to pray: the nine Murphys of Newmarket-on-Fergus', *The Other Clare*, Vol. 19 (1995), pp. 64–8.
28 Akenson, *Irish Diaspora*, pp. 38 and 166
29 Crotty, *Irish Agricultural Production*, p. 94.
30 Kennedy, *The Irish*.
31 Ruth Ann Harris, *The Search for Missing Friends: Irish immigrant advertisments placed in the Boston Pilot* (Boston, MA 1989).
32 Hasia Diner, *Erin's Daughters in America* (Maryland 1986).
33 E.g. 'Teddy O'Neill', 'Jimmy mo mhíle stór', 'Paddy's lament', 'The emigrant's lament'.
34 'The emigrant's lament' or 'Dear Danny, I'm taking the pen in my hand', in *Prose, Poems and Parodies of Percy French (1854–1920)* (Dublin 1941), pp. 5–6.
35 Elizabeth Malcolm, 'The house of strident shadows: the asylum, the family and emigration in post-Famine rural Ireland', in Greta Jones and Elizabeth Malcolm (eds), *Medicine, Disease and the State in Ireland 1650–1940* (Cork 1999), pp. 177–94.
36 Fitzpatrick, *Irish Emigration*, pp. 6–7; Akenson, *Irish Diaspora*, p. 14.
37 Maureen Murphy, 'The Fionnuala factor: Irish sibling emigration at the turn of the century', in A. Bradley and M. Valiulis (eds), *Gender and Sexuality in Modern Ireland* (Amherst, MA 1997), pp. 85–101.
38 See, e.g. P. A. Sheehan, *Glenanaar* (London 1916).
39 Healy, *For the Poor and for the Gentry*, p. 68.

40 Alison Uttley, *The Country Child* (London 1963 [1931]), p. 209.

41 For seasonal migration, the main sources are Cormac O Gráda, 'Seasonal Migration', and Sarah Barber, 'Irish migrant agricultural labourers in nineteenth-century Lincolnshire', *Saothar*, Vol. 8 (1982), pp. 10–23; O'Dowd, *Spalpeens*; Gerard Moran, 'A passage to Britain: seasonal migration and social change in the West of Ireland 1870–1890', *Saothar*, Vol. 13 (1987), pp. 22–31; Heather Holmes, 'Organizing the Irish migratory potato workers: the efforts in the early twentieth century', *Rural History*, Vol. 11 (2001), pp. 207–29.

42 See Olwen Hufton, *The Poor of Eighteenth-Century France 1750–1789* (Oxford 1974).

43 See chapter 8 of this book.

44 Eugenia Shanklin, '"Sure and what did we ever do but knit?": women's lives and work in south-west Donegal', *Donegal Annual*, No. 40 (1988), pp. 40–54.

45 Moran, 'Passage to Britain'.

46 Brian Coughlan, *Achill Island Tattie-Hokers in Scotland and the Kirkintilloch Tragedy 1937* (Maynooth 2006), pp. 52–6.

47 Frank Sweeney, *The Murder of Connell Boyle, County Donegal, 1898* (Dublin 2002).

48 *Report on Migratory Irish Agricultural Labourers 1884–5 (1885)* [c.4601], Vol. 85.

49 *Report on Migratory Irish Agricultural Labourers 1899 (1899)* [c.9490], Vol. 106.

50 James E. Handley, *The Navvy in Scotland* (Cork 1970); and Ultan Cowley, *The Men Who Built Britain: a history of the Irish navvy* (Dublin 2001).

51 Every second year, because breast-feeding of the previous summer's baby may have delayed conception the following autumn. At least, this is what one hopes to have been the case! Birth intervals in the west would be a fruitful area of research.

5

Marriage

Téir abhaile 's fan sabhaile mar tá do mhargadh déanta . . .
Tá do mhargadh – níl mo mhargadh – tá do mhargadh déanta . . .
(Go home and stay at home because your match is made . . .
Your match is made – my match is *not* made – your match *is* made
. . .) (*Téir Abhaile*, traditional, Donegal)

Introduction

We are certain of three things about marriage and family in Ireland
in the years 1850–1922. The first is that Irish people in general
married at a lower rate than the European norm; the second is that
they married comparatively late: the average age of brides in 1911
was 29, that of bridegrooms 33. The third is that, once married, Irish
people had what were, by European standards, large families. Over
the past fifty years or so, historians have developed, on the basis of
these three facts, a negative view of post-Famine Irish marriage.
Marriage became, we are told, more mercenary and therefore (for
some reason) hard on women, more likely to involve a bridegroom
a decade or so older than the bride and therefore (again, for some
reason) hard on women, more likely to take place in an extended
family and therefore hard on both men and women – those who were
seen to matter here being younger, reproducing, married couples.
Knuckling under their mothers' authority and unable to select wives
for themselves, men are also pitied.[1] Evidence – literary, statistical,
anthropological, sociological, autobiographical, oral and anecdotal,
some from the nineteenth, some from the twentieth century – is
blended together to form this grey view. The idea of the loveless,
post-Famine, farming marriage has put down such firm roots that

when one historian comes across family lore according to which a couple in rural Ireland in the 1890s fell in love they first time they saw each other, she dismisses it as 'an endeavour to create the idea of romance in situations where there was none' – though she readily accepts similar evidence about other aspects of the partnership.[2]

There are many problems with this gloomy scenario. First, not all Irish people, even Irish farmers, married late, and some parts of the country had much higher rates of marriage than others, right up to 1922. Indeed, the latest and rarest marriers in the entire country were in a prosperous urban area. Second, there was not always a substantial farm or business to pass on to the next generation, and marriage among small farmers, labourers and working-class people in towns and villages does not come into the story at all. Third, reasons for marrying or not marrying are complex and idiosyncratic. The same evidence can be interpreted differently according to people's point of view. Kerby Miller, to show that nineteenth-century Irish women had hard lives, cites Sissy O'Brien's marriage in 1883 to Richard Fogarty, a 'dull, decent man'. But Sissy's memoirs (*The Farm by Lough Gur*) were dictated to and edited by Mary Carbery, the widow of a minor Irish lord, fifty years later, and aimed at an audience hungry for accounts of a simple rural past. This must be taken account when evaluating Richard Fogarty. (And in Sissy's– Mary's laconic account, I did not find him dull or even particularly decent – he kept Sissy hanging on for a few years until she brought him to a proposal by putting out the story that she had another suitor.[3]) Yet many judgements about the apparent lack of emotion of Irish, rural, nineteenth-century marriage are based on even more second-hand and subjective evidence than this. And evidence from the twentieth century is still brought in to explain the nineteenth: as late as 1997, Arensberg and Kimball's study of family life on a small farm in west Clare in the 1930s was described as 'the classic portrait of the post-Famine Irish rural family' and used as background for a discussion of mental illness in nineteenth-century Ireland.[4]

Regional and geographical variations

Married, is it? Sure the men here don't begin to talk to a girl until they're beginning to talk to themselves.[5] (Meath woman to Nellie Gifford, c. 1905)

The worst marriers were on the best land in the country, and the best marriers, on the worst land, Guinnane has established. Although ages at marriage rose and marriage rates fell between 1850 and 1911 all over the country, in 1911 Connacht and Kerry still had the smallest ratio of spinsters to the total number of women over 20, and the lowest percentage of women aged 35–44 who were single (see maps 1 and 2, and accompanying tables, Appendix). Throughout the period, but becoming more sharply accentuated as time went on, the highest percentages of women in their later thirties and early forties who were not married were in Co. Dublin, Meath, Tyrone and Wexford, almost all the Leinster and Ulster counties, and by 1911 Tipperary, Waterford and Limerick.[6] Women most likely to marry young were either on smallholdings in the rural west, or of the labouring class in towns and cities. Irregular but fairly well-paid transport and haulage work in the ports and towns, factory work or freelance service work and work for women on smallholdings, regular annual earnings from seasonal migration, contributed to the decision to marry. But, more importantly, men and women got to know each other over a long period of time: the practice of working in small or large groups together (even single-sex groups) was crucial. In Co. Kilkenny, in 1911, 33 per cent of women aged 35–44 were single, but in the mining area of Castlecomer single women made up only 28 per cent of this age-group (nearer the figure for Dublin city) compared to 37 per cent in the largely rural union of Thomastown. Co. Londonderry had a higher percentage of single women aged 35–44 than Kilkenny, at 36 per cent, yet in Derry city only 30.6 per cent of women in this age-group were single, compared to 36 per cent in the largely rural area of Magherafelt and 37 per cent in Coleraine. In Co. Dublin, unmarried middle-aged women were concentrated not in market-gardening Balrothery or farming Celbridge but in the suburban middle-class boroughs of Rathdown and South Dublin, where in 1881 and in 1911 they made up the largest percentage of their age-cohort in the entire country. In Mayo and Donegal, the sweetheart who was gone for the summer and autumn was home for winter and spring, every year. Donegal had one of the highest percentages in the whole country of middle-aged single women in 1911, at 38 per cent, but in the union which supplied the most seasonal migrants, Dunfanaghy, the percentage was 29, compared with Letterkenny's 47(!) or Millford's 36.

Postponement or avoidance of marriage

Throughout the Western world, from the early nineteenth century, marriage postponement was common among the 'new middle class' of civil servants and clerks. Satirized by Grossmith, Gilbert and Maupassant, and described more affectionately by Dickens, this cautious class had a horror of early and possibly improvident marriage, and thus postponed it, sometimes permanently.[7] Some occupations discouraged, even tried to prevent, marriage – the police forces in Ireland, for example.[8] In most countries these late marriers were made up for by the early-marrying urban and rural working classes, and by the farmers. In Ireland small farmers (the rural equivalent of artisans) came – though slowly and unevenly, as we have seen – to share the demographic behaviour of their 'betters' or they emigrated, and the urban working class, skilled and unskilled, was not big enough to make up the deficit. Furthermore, changes in working life made it increasingly difficult for labourers and female farm servants – the rural working class – to meet, court and marry.

The classic explanation for late marriage/no marriage is that after the Famine farmers stopped sub-dividing land and could therefore pass on the farm only to one of their offspring and provide a dowry, or its equivalent (trade, education), for at best one more; other offspring, deprived of a livelihood, would not marry. A refinement of this argument is that larger farmers had stopped sub-dividing long before the Famine, that only small farmers sub-divided and that the number of those farmers wiped out by the Famine was sufficient to lessen their demographic impact.[9] This is true up to a point. However, the argument that passing on holdings intact from one generation to the next discouraged marriage does not explain the low marriage rates among some of the larger farmers, who could readily provide livelihoods, dowries and, indeed, farms, for all their offspring.

What stopped the large farmers marrying? Was it, as Connell famously argued, the influence and example of the celibate and very powerful Roman Catholic clergy?[10] Irish Catholics were deeply attached to their Church because of persecution and historical circumstance. Yet Protestants were also poor marriers. The heaviest concentration of single women in the entire country in 1881 and in 1911 was in the predominantly Protestant (and urban) south of Co. Dublin. The largely Protestant counties of Antrim, Armagh,

Down and Londonderry had some of the highest percentages of middle-aged single women in all Ireland in 1881 and in 1911. The more Protestant electoral areas of Donegal and north Tipperary had a higher proportion of middle-aged single women than areas in which there was a higher concentration of Catholics.

Was emigration a root cause of high permanent celibacy? At different times, some parts of the country had a higher rate of female emigration and vice versa, so the pool of prospective spouses was diminished. But male and female emigration in the population as a whole was about equal, and there was population movement within Ireland itself. Besides, the counties with the lowest marriage rates were rarely those with the highest emigration. Marriage must often have been delayed while people were waiting to emigrate or for a potential emigrant spouse to send the fare, or return, but this postponement is itself part of a broader reluctance to get married until all emotional and financial requirements were met.

Was one of these requirements a house cleared of all relatives? What can crudely be called 'the mother–mother-in-law factor' has been suggested as a reason for late/no marriage. In many farming marriages the husband was about ten years older than his wife, so she was likely to be left a fairly young and vigorous widow, reluctant to yield her authority in the house to anyone else. Her son, the story goes, would not want to undermine her position by bringing into the house another woman, so he remained single.[11] There are two problems with this apparently neat explanation. First, until nursing homes and sheltered accommodation became a reality the co-resident older parent was simply a fact of life for many people, of all classes and conditions, in all countries, and still is, throughout much of Asia, Africa and South America. It was not exclusive to Ireland, nor was it as *unnatural* as some historians suppose.[12] Why did this co-residence lead (did it lead?) to marriage postponement among the rural–agricultural Irish only? Second, if Irish farming women were such formidable characters, what were their sons like? We cannot have it both ways. Years of living with an authoritative and strong mother would have made the late-marrying, inheriting son patient and 'quiet', or at the very least attuned to the idea of female authority – an attractive marital prospect for the discerning woman, however old he was. This bride, maybe in her late twenties, could well have emerged as the dominant partner and continued the cycle, but such a cycle need not, in itself, have closed off the marriage option for the next generation. Besides, youth was not always the best stage in life for a woman to get married: '*Pósadh go hóg mé mar gheall ar na puntaí . . . is níor shásaigh sé riamh m'intinn*' (I was married too young because of money . . . and my wishes were never satisfied), complains the young woman in a ballad.[13] The 'staid and mature' bride deplored by Connell[14] may have been a woman who knew what she wanted.

Moreover, by focusing on male reluctance or inability to marry, we are, as O Gráda wittily points out, ignoring the other side of the equation:

> A further drawback of both Guinnane's and Connell's interpretations of post-Famine marriage patterns is their undue focus on male strategies, as if there existed a limitless supply of women willing to marry the men if required.[15]

Historians used to believe that male reluctance to marry was something that made women's lives hard in these years. David Fitzpatrick comments:

> All too often the life of the unmarried Irishwoman, cut off from male companionship as well as independent employment, was one of humiliation and despair.[16]

It has not occurred to Fitzpatrick that women were the reluctant ones. Certainly, when women in twentieth-century Ireland had an alternative to the hard life of the farmer's wife, they often took it.[17] Could this be true of the nineteenth century? George Birmingham famously complained that convent schools gave farmers' daughters ideas unsuitable to their station in life, prompting them to flee the land.[18] Farmers' daughters and the provincial mercantile middle class – Catholic and Protestant – were the first to avail themselves of educational opportunities in the 1880s, and probably the first to postpone marriage thereafter. Alternatives to marriage in the form of work, the religious life, philanthropy on a private income or simply a genteel, single life in the home of origin evidently appealed to some girls.

All of this indicates that people had a choice about marriage, and, again, we cannot have it both ways. If parental authority about choice of spouse was so strong, why did they not force their offspring to marry? The defiance of the girl in the song quoted at the head of the chapter might have been true of many women – and men. Was there a conscious rejection (by both men and women) of the arranged marriage? The mercenary match was condemned in Kickham's hugely popular *Knocknagow* (1875). Connell quotes in evidence of clerical disapproval of love an exchange between the two priests in Sheehan's *My New Curate* (1899), where they lament the passing of the old-style marriage arranged by parents, but in this passage Sheehan (never an opponent of romantic love) is gently mocking the innocence of these two unworldly celibates.[19] People laughed in gleeful recognition at the story of McBreen's daughters and their indecisive suitor:

> Now there's no denying Kitty was the girl that was pretty
> But you can't say the same for Jane.
> And still there's the differ of the price of a heifer
> Between the pretty and the plain.[20]

Irish people were well aware of their reputation as dilatory courters and marriers. Evidence of that awareness should not be taken as further evidence of their caution.

The decline of cousin-marriage

The decline of marriages between blood relations could be an additional reason for falling marriage rates in these years. The practice of first or second cousins marrying each other was common in the seventeenth, eighteenth and early nineteenth centuries; in 1835, seven religious dispensations (or permissions) for such marriages were sought in one Catholic parish in Tyrone. By the end of the nineteenth century, applications for such dispensations were increasingly rare – the largest diocese in Ireland granted only 70 dispensations in the years 1879–89, and many dioceses had no applications at all.[21] In 1894, some doctors expressed their belief that consanguineous marriages had contributed to insanity in Tipperary, Clare, Kilkenny, Kerry, Waterford and Sligo; the marriages they were referring to had taken place 30–40 years earlier. Charles McGlinchey believed that 'sib marriages' in his part of Donegal had led to insanity in the past, but that they died out in the late nineteenth century.[22] The Catholic Church and prevailing scientific opinion were agreed on the undesirability of these alliances (whether they were right or not is beyond the scope of this book), and the rising social power of the Catholic Church cannot but have discouraged them. Cousin-marriage continued, if on a small scale. However, no canonical prohibition on cousin-marriage existed for Protestants, who were as slow about marrying as their Catholic neighbours, although Swanton refers quite often to the intermarriage of first and second-cousins among Wicklow Protestants in the late nineteenth and early twentieth centuries.[23] A comparative study is long overdue.

An over-parented family?

Guinnane argues convincingly that comfortably-off farmers postponed marriage because of the ready availability of what he calls 'marriage substitutes'. These he identifies as company (parents, other siblings, married or single), friends (encountered locally and regularly, quite often in the course of work and recreation), social status (due to ownership of the farm), housekeeping (in the form of an unmarried sister or surviving mother) and an attachment to the younger generation through the crop of nieces and nephews supplied by the only-marrying sibling.[24] This depiction of the single person as part of a lively, well-populated environment, not an isolated figure against a deserted landscape, rings true.

Developing this argument, I suggest that a pattern of *rare marriage* (only one or two of the offspring in every generation getting married) perpetuated itself; all it needed was one *founding* generation. In Ireland, this generation put down roots at various times (in prosperous farming, business and professional families) in the nineteenth and early twentieth centuries. From about 1870, children in many farming and business families grew up with several never-married aunts and uncles, and late-marrying or single elder siblings. Whether in Ireland or abroad as unmarried exiles sending home money, or as nuns or priests, or in the farthest reaches of the empire where spouses were not readily found, these relatives took an intense interest in the younger generation. Kate O'Brien recalls her two maternal aunts, nuns in Limerick's Presentation Convent, in the early years of the twentieth century:

> Aunt Mary wanted for every one of us the worldly success that she had eschewed . . . it was her intention that Katty's four daughters should marry well, marry young, and into Catholic bourgeois security.[25]

The presence of so many elders forged a strong family culture. Meanwhile, middle-class houses, urban and rural, were more capacious and comfortable than ever. Waters and Williams's exploration of the 1901 Census in a small Wexford village describes at least three businesses (public houses and merchants) with a high proportion of co-resident adult siblings. In one, the 81-year-old widowed shopkeeper was the head of the house, two single sons, aged 45 and 35, were shop assistants, and another son, 37, a magistrate. In another, a 67-year-old publican and his 52-year-old wife preside over a household where 4 of the 7 co-resident offspring, in their twenties, are described as 'shop assistants' (the eldest daughter had married in 1894 – would she be the only one to marry?).[26] Three daughters of a magistrate in Drumcollgher, Co. Limerick, entered the Mercy Convent in Limerick city for the period 1865–71; in 1901 their three sisters, in their forties, were still living in the family home, unmarried, with their brother, sister-in-law and nephew.[27] Examples could be multiplied; the writer Maeve Brennan (1917–93) had unmarried aunts, uncles, grand-aunts and grand-uncles on both her father's and mother's side of the family, in rural and urban Wexford, though some of them married, eventually, in their late thirties and early forties.[28] The child or children of the few who married grew up under the watchful eye of not one or two but several adult mentors. Released from this weight of supervision, and not beguiled by compensating domestic comforts, working- and labouring-class people, and small farmers, in the west were freer to follow their own destinies. When Cáit Ní Gaoithín, a fisherman's daughter, returned around 1920 from domestic service in Limerick to her home on the Blasket Islands and told her parents that she had no intention of ever going into service again, her disappointed father's only comment was '*Tá go maith, a nighean ó . . . beatha dhuine a thoil*' (All right, daughter . . . a person's life should be according to his own will).[29] It is impossible to imagine a large farmer, shopkeeper or landowner saying something similar to a teenage son or daughter.

Paid work and marriage

For girls and women from labouring backgrounds there was only domestic or farm service, and for many of their male counterparts the life of a servant boy continued long after boyhood – either that, or they moved around constantly, working first for one farmer or householder, then another. All this mobility made it difficult for men and women to get to know each other over a long period of time.

Counties with the highest concentration of agricultural labourers were also those where there were the most bachelors and spinsters. Granted that many of them were the labourers' employers, as discussed above, many were also labourers and servants. Delaney's retrieval of the 1901 Census in Co. Kilkenny shows plenty of labourers, as well as farmers, in sibling households or living with elderly parents. The Doran parents (father a labourer) in Aghamucky, with their 4 single offspring (3 sons, one daughter), aged 28–33, are probably an extreme example; more typical was the Bolger family in Aughatubrid, where 60-year-old Edward, a farm servant, lived with his two sisters Margaret, aged 55, and Honoria, 52.[30] These sisters probably did some daily work and agricultural labouring work in season. One grim reason for the decline in the number of agricultural labourers in Ireland between 1850 and 1911 is that economic forces were driving men and women at this level of society farther away from each other, robbing them of their chance to marry and have children. They are the forgotten demographic casualties of the post-Famine era.

A settled male artisan, on the other hand, had every opportunity to meet a wife. The farmer takes the brunt of historical criticism for crude patriarchal authority, but the artisan – the freeman, the *saor* – could be very domineering. Unlike in farming, the artisan's wife had no small income of her own, and unless she was the book-keeper she was often ignorant of what her husband earned, and so was utterly dependent on him. Michael O'Beirne's mother in Dublin in the early years of the century called her carpenter husband 'Mister' and served him meals separately at his own table (in a two-roomed flat!).[31] Admittedly, this was extreme, but other accounts of Dublin family life identify tradesmen (rather than labourers) as those least likely to hand over control of the money to their wives.[32] A study of courtship and marriage among those archetypal males, the trades, would be very welcome.

People working in large shops and businesses had the most chance of meeting partners on a level with themselves. Old photographs of works outings and company picnics, with the men in straw boaters and the women in white blouses, give a clue about how courtships were nurtured. With factory workers and town labourers, courtship was more direct, even adversarial: girls and boys walked around in same-sex groups on summer evenings, calling insults and challenges to each other, stealing caps and running away, eventually pairing off:

I'll tell my Ma when I go home, the boys won't leave the girls alone.
They pulled my hair, and stole my comb, but that's all right till I go
home.
She is handsome, she is pretty, she is the belle of Belfast city . . .[33]

Parents thundered and threatened to no avail. Cramped accommodation made it sensible for lovers to marry young and move out into
small rented rooms, however temporary the initial space and
prosperity ('two can live as cheaply as one').

The upper-middle and upper classes

Courtship was most elaborate where marriage was most mercenary,
at the levels of society where men were destined for the learned
professions, politics or management of their landed estates, and
women were not expected to earn money either before or after
marriage. George Moore's cringe-making description of the Dublin
husband-hunting season is no great exaggeration, judging by the
Countess of Fingal's memoirs.[34] Mary Butler describes some of the
leftovers of the Dublin season:

> [L]evee and Drawing-room came and went year after year, and tea-
> party and dance and concert and dinner, were attended with tireless
> persistence by her five nieces, and still they remained the Misses Lynch.
> Everyone said 'the Lynch girls are so popular' but somehow it seemed
> to end there.[35]

A family over-supplied with daughters could not provide dowries
for all of them to find partners of equivalent social status, and some
of the daughters would remain single rather than marry 'beneath'
them. Anna Parnell criticized the landlord custom of 'giving all, or
nearly all, to the sons and little or nothing to the daughters',
describing (rather outrageously) females of the landed classes as 'little
less the victims of the landlords than the tenants themselves'.[36] There
were petty humiliations: the odd habit of dressing sisters identically
for drawing-rooms at Dublin Castle or other glittering social
occasions (a habit also common in Britain) suggests interchange-
ability.[37] But women from financially secure backgrounds, if they
had congenial and generous parents, could enjoy some freedom
in their choice of marriage partner. Kate Cullen, the daughter of a
high-ranking army officer from Sligo, married Michael Mitchell of
Parsonstown in 1860 when she was 28; he was her own free choice,

following several other courtships which did not work out.[38] The single daughter who remained at home looking after her parents could lead a happy life and attain a high social status, but she was also a soft target for parental ill-humour and petty tyranny. 'M.A. continues to ballyrag Flo', is a concise entry in 1893 in the diary of a Justice of the Peace in Wexford. 'M.A.' was his wife, Flo his adult daughter.[39]

Conclusion: *Is Fearr an Troid Ná an tUaigneas?* (Conflict is better than loneliness?)

> I had made up my mind that I couldn't get married during my mother's lifetime, and after her death in 1890 my whole energies were bent to the preparation for the examination for First Division of First Class ... (Edward O'Toole)

Once he passed the examination, the 36-year-old Edward fell 'in love at first sight' (his words) and married in 1896. He had held back because he could not envisage supporting both mother and wife to the desired standard on a National School teacher's salary, but once free to marry lost no time about it.[40] Those who married most and married young had lower expectations. Mayo and Kerry may have had the poorest quality of life in Ireland in 1841 and in 1861, as Jordan argues,[41] but both counties had more actual life than any other part of Ireland, right up to 1911. When George Moore wrote, in 1887, that 'in Ireland you seldom see a young man who is not married', he was only telling the truth as he saw it in his native Mayo.[42] In other parts of the country comfort, choice and elders' advice caused many to delay. Of the four daughters in Kate O'Brien's heavily aunted family mentioned above, only one married. Was it despite or because of their aunts' interference that the other three O'Brien daughters stayed single? Or were they simply following the example of their contented, unmarried aunts?

When marriage took place, the economics were important at all social levels. Strength and ability to work were highly prized among all working people, farmers included; it ensured survival, and cemented partnerships. Such pragmatism could, and can, co-exist with sexual attraction, friendship and joy in one another's company. Our view of country people is relayed to us by city people, through the lens of nineteenth-century urban sentimentality, and if Irish farmers were reputed to lack romance, so were rural people everywhere – French peasants in particular.[43] The Victorian urban middle-class courtship, hedged round with lockets and love-letters and mementos and poems, was just as money-conscious. And one need not demonise the 'made match' as such: arranged marriages, still the norm in many parts of the world, can be successful, provided both parties are reasonably good-tempered, not physically repelled by each other, and able to give and take, according to the *seanfhocal* (proverb), *Is fearr an grá a fhásann ná an grá a fhuarann* (The love that grows is better than the love that grows cold]. But fewer and fewer Irish people in the post-Famine period were prepared to take this chance. Perhaps their caution had its origins in emotion rather than economics. Instead of the over-practical and materialistic attitude to marriage portrayed for us in most of the secondary sources, cultural change, rising levels of comfort and an abundance of loved authority figures seem to have bred generations of comfortable, lazy or timid romantics, who turned firmly away from the proverb that heads this section. Besides, married or single, they would not be lonely.

Notes

1 There are many sources on Irish marriage and family life, but only the major and most important works are referred to here: O Gráda, *Ireland*, pp. 236–54; K. H. Connell, *Irish Peasant Society* (Oxford 1968), particularly pp. 113–61; Kennedy, *The Irish*; Art Cosgrove (ed.), *Marriage in Ireland* (Dublin 1985); D. Fitzpatrick, 'Divorce and separation in modern Irish history', *Past & Present*, No. 114 (1987), pp. 172–96; S. J. Connolly, 'Illegitimacy and pre-nuptial pregnancy in Ireland before 1864', *Irish Economic and Social History*, Vol. 6 (1979), pp. 5–23; Linda May Ballard, *Forgetting Frolic: marriage traditions in Ireland* (Belfast 1998); the most recent and most authoritative is Timothy Guinnane, *The Vanishing Irish: households, migration and the rural economy in Ireland 1850–1914* (Princeton, NJ 1997). On women in particular and their apparent loss of power, see Janet Nolan, *Ourselves Alone: women's emigration from Ireland 1885–1920* (Kentucky 1989) and, loth though I am to admit it, Clear, *Nuns in Nineteenth-Century Ireland*, pp. 1–35; Jenny Beale, *Women in Ireland: voices of change* (London 1986), pp. 1–39, gives a good summary of this view.
2 Fallon, *A County Roscommon Wedding, 1892*, pp. 20–1.
3 Miller, *Emigrants*, p. 408; Carbery, *The Farm by Lough Gur*, pp. 252–69. Similar books which appeared in the 1930s and early 1940s were Uttley, *Country Child*; George Orwell, *Coming Up for Air* (London

1939); Flora Thompson, *Lark Rise to Candleford* (London 1939–43); Laverty, *Never No More*; and Eric Cross, *The Tailor and Ansty* (London 1942). But even Guinnane cites Carbery unproblematically, *Vanishing Irish*, p. 236. Details about Mary Carbery are taken from Sandford (ed.), *Mary Carbery*, pp. 7–12.

4 Elizabeth Malcolm, 'House of strident shadows', p. 184.
5 Sidney Gifford Czira, *The Years Flew By*, ed. Alan Hayes (Galway 2000 [1974]), p. 38.
6 *Census of Ireland*, 1881, General report, table 83, showing the proportion of single, married and widowed persons of each sex to 100 men and 100 women of the age 20 and upwards; *Census of Ireland*, 1911, General report, table 67, showing the same for 1911. Married women rather than married men are singled out because of the reproductive implications of late marriage for women rather than for men.
7 George Grossmith (1847–1912), *Diary of a Nobody* (Oxford 1998 [1892]); Guy de Maupassant (1850–1893), *Contes et nouvelles* (Paris 1996); W. S. Gilbert and Arthur Sullivan, *HMS Pinafore*, premiéred 1876, where this theme is comically explored; see also Tommy Traddles's predicament in Charles Dickens, *David Copperfield* (London 1850).
8 Brian Griffin, 'The Irish police: love, sex and marriage in the nineteenth and early twentieth centuries', in Kelleher and Murphy (eds), *Gender Perspectives*, pp. 168–78.
9 Lee, *Modernisation*, pp. 1–25.
10 Connell, 'Catholicism and marriage'.
11 According to Lee, *Modernisation*, pp. 4–5, the old woman is definitely the villain of the piece.
12 See, e.g. the disgust for the extended family of Ezra Pound-quoting David Fitzpatrick in 'The modernisation of the Irish female', in Patrick O'Flanagan et al. (eds), *Rural Ireland 1600–1800: modernisation and change* (Cork 1987), pp. 162–80.
13 'Fuigfidh Mise an Baile Seo', in M. O hEidhin, *Cas Amhrán*, Vol. 1 (Inreabhán 1975), p. 31.
14 Connell, 'Catholicism and marriage', p. 117.
15 O Gráda, *Ireland*, p. 218.
16 Fitzpatrick 'Modernisation of the Irish female', p. 173.
17 Clear, *Women of the House*, pp. 171–215.
18 Bermingham quoted in Connell, 'Catholicism and marriage', p. 143.
19 Kickham, *Knocknagow*, pp. 30–1; Connell, 'Catholicism and marriage', pp. 159–60; P. A. Sheehan, *My New Curate* (Dublin 1928 [1893]), pp. 276–7.
20 *The Immortal Percy French Sung by Brendan O'Dowda*, Dublin 1958, re-released by Polygram 2000.

21 Jack Johnston, 'Society in the Clogher Valley c.1750–1900', in C. Dillon and H. Jefferies (eds), *Tyrone: history and society* (Dublin 2000), pp. 543–65; C. J. M. 'The intermarriage of relatives and its consequences', *Irish Ecclesiastical Record*, Vol. 11 (February 1890), pp. 97–100.

22 McGlinchey, *The Last of the Name*, p. 143.

23 Daisy Lawrenson Swanton, *Emerging from the Shadow: the lives of Sarah Anne Lawrenson and Lucy Olive Kingston 1883–1969* (Dublin 1994), pp. 1–26.

24 Guinnane, *Vanishing Irish*.

25 Kate O'Brien, *Presentation Parlour* (London 1963), pp. 111–13 and generally.

26 Des Waters and Tom Williams, 'Taghmon village: the 1901 Census', *Journal of the Taghmon Historical Society*, Vol. 4 (2001), pp. 150–94.

27 Clear, *Nuns in Nineteenth-Century Ireland*, p. 146.

28 See Angela Bourke, *Maeve Brennan: homesick at the New Yorker – an Irish writer in exile* (New York 2004).

29 Mieheal O Gaoithín, *Is Trua ná Fannan an Oige* (Baile Atha Cliath 1953), p. 66.

30 Tom Delaney (comp.), *Irish Genealogical Sources No. 19: Castlecomer, Co. Kilkenny Census 1901* (Baile Atha Cliath 2000).

31 Micheal O'Beirne, *Mister: a Dublin childhood* (Belfast 1979).

32 Kevin Kearns, *Dublin Tenement Life: an oral history* (Dublin 1994), p. 118 and generally; Alexander Humphreys, *New Dubliners: urbanisation and the Irish family* (London 1966), pp. 99, 203. Although Humphreys carried out his research in the 1940s, some of his comments relate to the generation of grandparents at that time, who would have married in the 1880s and 1890s.

33 Traditional, popularised by the Clancy Brothers in the 1960s, and revived on Van Morrison and the Chieftains, *Irish Heartbeat*, Dublin 1986.

34 George Moore, *A Drama in Muslin* (London 1886), and Elizabeth, Countess of Fingal, *Seventy Years Young* (Dublin 1992 [1937]).

35 Mary Butler, *The Ring of Day* (London 1906), p. 9; see Mairead Ní Chinnéide, *Maire de Buitléir: Bean Athbheochana* (Baile Atha Cliath 1993).

36 Margaret Ward, *Unmanageable Revolutionaries: women and Irish nationalism* (Dingle and London 1983), p. 7.

37 A detailed account of ladies' toilettes for the drawing-room at Dublin Castle is given in *Freeman's Journal*, 2 February 1865. 'Same as sister' is common. Also see Judith Flanders, *Victorian House* (London 2003), pp. 258–9. Of course, it was probably cheaper to get the dressmaker to make up one design and copy it than to commission two different designs.

38 Hilary Pyle (ed.), *The Sligo–Leitrim World of Kate Cullen (1832–1913)* (Dublin 1997).
39 Nicky Rossiter, 'The life of a Wexford gentleman 100 years ago: based on the diaries of Edward Solly-Flood J.P.', *Journal of the Wexford Historical Society*, Vol. 13 (1990–91), pp. 117–29.
40 O'Toole, *Whist for Your Life*, p. 103.
41 Thomas E. Jordan, *Ireland and the Quality of Life, 1841–1861* (New York and Lampeter, Wales 1997).
42 George Moore, *Parnell and His Island* (Dublin 2004 [1887]), p. 37.
43 Martine Segalen, *Love and Power in the Peasant Family* (London 1991).

6

Public health

On 27 February 1873, William Corcoran, a baker in Tuam, Co. Galway, summoned the doctor to look at his 22–year-old assistant William Burke. The doctor took one look, diagnosed smallpox and ordered young William to the local workhouse hospital. Instead, however, Corcoran brought him to the railway station and settled him on the train home to Athenry. By the time William Burke died, some days later, a full-scale public health alert was in place. Kineen's hotel in Athenry was closed by public health order; Loughrea workhouse infirmary van was burned maliciously to make sure it could not be used to transport patients. There was even talk of a detachment of militia from Galway to guard the twelve-bedded, temporary, iron hospital set up in Athenry. By July the epidemic, which saw over 200 cases in east Galway, had run its course. William Corcoran was fined £2 10 shillings, and on July 13 every house in Athenry was thoroughly disinfected with chloride of lime, carbolic acid and Condy's fluid.[1]

This smallpox outbreak was probably a lingering trace of the big epidemic which had killed over 4,000 people in Ireland in 1871–72; the disease would flare up again, in 1878–80, and in 1895–96, before almost dying out in the early twentieth century.[2] We will never know why the baker acted as he did. Was he simply sorry for a young man who begged to go home to his own place instead of being among strangers? In June, when the epidemic was starting to wind down, Dr Digby French came across a family, three of whom had smallpox, but had not reported it for fear of being sent to the workhouse.[3] Or was Corcoran afraid of word getting out, in Tuam, that one of his assistants was in the workhouse hospital with smallpox? The refusal of Athenry's hotel to close its doors, the objections of the locals to the temporary hospital and the reluctance of many to report disease shows how fear of infection was inextricably mixed with fear of *reputedly* being infected. The story of poor William Burke illustrates how developments in commerce and transport aided the spread of disease even as modern public health authorities tried to curb it. Dr Charles Cameron told of a butcher's assistant who was cutting up carcasses 'with the [smallpox] pustules on him'.[4] Irish people's health in general improved over these seventy-odd years, but butchers, bakers, railway lines and commercial hotels gave diseases, old and new, several additional leases of life.

In 1850 health provisions in Ireland were patchy. Cities were well supplied with voluntary hospitals for the poor, and most county towns had public infirmaries and fever hospitals. Geary counts 171 hospitals in Ireland by 1845, and 664 charitable dispensaries (outpatient clinics). These varied widely in capacity and quality, and were unevenly distributed – there was one hospital for every 141,885 people in Connacht in 1846, compared with one for every 48,901 in Munster.[5] Successive reforms between 1850 and 1922 saw steps taken towards the piecemeal establishment of free health care. The collection of health statistics, urban sanitary reforms and other health legislation led to an improvement in what is known as public health, but did the people's health improve in equal measure?

Dispensaries, diseases and drains: 1851–75

A person suffering from a contagious disease is, with respect to the rest of the community, very much in the same condition as a lunatic – both are dangerous to health and life. They are, however, usually treated in a very different manner. The lunatic, if he exhibit the slightest tendency to do violence to anyone, is, on the production of a medical certificate, summarily deprived of his liberty . . . On the other hand, the smallpox or scarlatina patient is not interfered with. He may, when barely convalescent, mix, without let or hindrance, in crowds, travel in tram-cars, railways, carriages and cabs, go to places of worship and amusement and in a word, scatter the seed of disease broadcast amongst the population.[6]

This quarter of a century is bounded at one end by the setting up of the dispensaries in 1851 and at the other by the Public Health Act of 1874. The first step addressed the individual, the second the environment. Over these two and a half decades the main killers were what doctors called the 'zymotic' diseases – 'fever' (typhus), scarlatina, smallpox, measles, whooping-cough and diarrhoea or enteric fever.

The Medical Charities Act of 1851 set up dispensaries, or clinics, linked to the Poor Law Unions throughout the country. People unable to pay for medical care could obtain a ticket from the dispensary committee, see the doctor and obtain medicine. Each Poor Law Union was divided into several dispensary districts – 40 Poor Law Unions in Leinster, for example, had 208 districts, with sometimes more than one doctor for every district. At its inception, the scheme employed 776 doctors and 29 apothecaries (chemists). Geary argues that the scheme as it developed was wide open to corruption in both appointments and in provisions: 'lack of definition led to widespread abuse of the system by individuals who could afford to pay for medical treatment'.[7] This is said of many free medical systems in any era, and when one considers the paucity of medical resources in some parts of Ireland prior to this, it is arguably a 'good complaint'. The 1851 Act established the principle that everyone, regardless of income, had the right to see a doctor and obtain medicine. There was now a free doctor within a day's walk, everywhere in the country; doctors also made house calls. They could have private practices on the side, but many, Farmar suggests, were kept so busy by their dispensary patients that they would not have had the time.[8] Dispensary doctors had a reputation for drunkenness and disreputability, but this may be due partly to the snobbery of urban hospital doctors. With its risk of disease and its exposure to all kinds of weather and terrain, the dispensary post was no sinecure, at £50 a year in the 1850s. There was also some accountability, as shown by a public investigation in Lusk, Co. Dublin, in 1855, of a dispensary doctor, Dr Barry. He did not visit a child with scarlatina from a Wednesday until the following Monday; he did not remove the bonnet of a child with a sore head so as to examine it; he addressed one of his patients as 'you fool of a woman', asked another patient why she was 'making a beggar of herself' and, most seriously of all, called one patient a pauper.[9] These charges were taken very seriously, the doctor either denying them or insisting that his words and actions had been misinterpreted.

The next important step was the opening, in 1861, of the workhouse infirmaries to non-workhouse residents who could not afford to pay for hospital care. Catholic nuns managed, after a landmark initiative in Limerick Poor Law Union in 1861, to get jobs as nurses in workhouse infirmaries. By 1900 nuns were nursing in half of all workhouse hospitals, and were avidly sought after, because of their economy and efficiency, by Poor Law boards in parts of the country where Catholics were in a majority.[10]

Systematic annual collection of statistics on births, marriages and deaths began in 1864. The registrars' annual reports included discussion of the health of the people over the course of the year. In the 1860s scarlatina, 'fever' (usually typhus but sometimes typhoid, according to Crawford) and smallpox were the major causes of concern. Asiatic cholera, ranging over Europe throughout 1865, reached Ireland in 1866, affecting Dublin, Wexford, Down, Wicklow, Queen's County, Donegal and Roscommon.[11] There was some panic: in Rathdrum, Co. Wicklow, O Cathaoir tells us, staff fled the workhouse hospital, people blocked the road to the fever hospital and the hospital van was stoned.[12]

Doctors worried about the cleanliness of water and, because they did not know that typhus was lice-borne, they worried about the cleanliness of the air, and complained about the dirt and overcrowding in many of the dwellings of the poor.[13] There was certainly a connection between dirt, poverty and disease, if not quite one that the doctors understood, but their trenchant observations drew attention to the inadequate living conditions of many small farmers, labourers and slum-dwellers. Three doctors in the Dublin area alone lost their lives through 'fever' in the autumn and winter of 1864–65.[14] Health in general, however, was good in the 1860s and 1870s. Deaths in Ireland in 1873 from the principal 'zymotic' diseases were 212.4 per 100,000 of the population, compared to 291.4 per 100,000 in England and Wales. The death-rate in Ireland as a whole, from all causes, was 18.3 per 1,000 compared to 21.2 in England and Wales and 22.4 in Scotland. Smallpox in Ireland in 1871–72 killed far fewer people than in England and Wales, due to the almost universal take-up of vaccination in Ireland from 1858, as Brunton shows.[15] Death-rates from all the major killers, including 'fever', diarrhoea, and scarlatina, fell significantly between 1861 and 1871.[16] Rural areas were the healthiest. Ireland's death-rate was inflated by its cities: Dublin and Belfast stood at 26.1 per 1,000 population, Cork at 27.3, exceeded only by Liverpool, Manchester, Salford, Oldham, Leeds, Sheffield, Newcastle-on-Tyne and Glasgow.[17] In Ireland as a whole, the rate of sickness in 1861 was higher in Leinster at 16 per 1,000 and in Munster at 14 than it was in Ulster and Connacht, both at 11.

(The figure for Ireland as a whole was 13: table A7, Appendix). Water in rural areas was cleaner; Cameron worried about the run-off from animal waste but families often may have been immune to their own livestock's germs – particularly if they lived right beside them. Overcrowding in the tiny cabins was a problem, but much time was spent out of doors. Food was simple and nutritious: oatmeal, yellow meal, potatoes and buttermilk had not yet been challenged by tea, white bread and American bacon.[18]

The Public Health Act of 1874 divided the country into sanitary districts – 38 of them urban and 163 rural. Medical officers of dispensary districts were to be supplemented by sanitary officers, and they were to report to the Poor Law Guardians – now the Local Government Board – in rural and small-town areas, and in cities to the Corporation. These authorities were responsible for providing clean water, preventing pollution of air and water, dealing with overcrowding, cleansing streets and roads, disinfecting clothes and bedding, providing recreation grounds, maintaining cemeteries and burying the very poor. They could also, if funds were available, construct dwellings for artisans. The Act also prohibited the keeping of animals in dwellings, though that was difficult to enforce. The ideal medical officer should, according to Cameron, as well as treating the sick and dispensing medicine, investigate the causes of diseases, and 'make himself acquainted with the topography of his district, the nature of its rock formation and soils, the position of its drains and sewers . . . [and] the social condition and habits of the humbler classes'.[19] It was an ambitious agenda, which made great demands on the medical and sanitary officers; it was also an optimistic one.

Prior to the Public Health Act, one kind of disease was singled out for special treatment because it was seen as physically, morally and socially infectious. The notorious, though short-lived, Contagious Diseases Acts of 1864, 1866 and 1869 applied only in the catchment areas of the three largest garrisons/ports – the Curragh of Kildare, Queenstown and Cork city in Ireland – and similar areas in Great Britain (Aldershot and Portsmouth, for example). Here, police could arrest any woman they suspected of being a prostitute and compel her to undergo a doctor's examination. If diseased, she would then be detained in hospital until cured, and after release was obliged to return for regular check-ups. These measures were undertaken in response to the belief that the armed forces were being infected by a huge hidden army of syphilitic women, though the official belief that the infection operated only in one direction was vociferously challenged by a large public campaign in opposition to the Acts in Britain.[20] In Ireland, those operating Magdalen asylums often worked hand in hand with the sanitary authorities in implementing the legislation.[21] These laws were repealed by popular outcry in 1885, but they highlight the potential, and the limits, of coercive health legislation in the nineteenth century. Despite Cameron's heartfelt lament, quoted above, people were never arrested or forcibly detained for smallpox, scarlatina or enteric fever. And even Cameron and his contemporaries did not fully understand that one of the deadliest diseases of all, phthisis/consumption/tubercolosis, was not only highly contagious, but was gathering its forces for a ferocious attack in the closing years of the nineteenth century.

New problems and responsibilities: 1875–1922

[W]hile Andy Flaherty had once been the best runner and jumper in the county, he was now in the last stages of consumption and could barely hold himself erect. His poor ravaged face with its hollow temples, sunken flushed cheeks and drawn white lips was a fevered death mask that night. But it became happy and less feverish when Andy sat down with us and commenced to go back over the days when no athlete could beat him . . . As the days of his glory came vividly before him, Andy Flaherty was no longer there on our settle . . . losing his lungs cough by cough. He was in a summer field somewhere, flying from the starter's pistol like an arrow from a bow, the wind rushing to meet him . . .[22]

The years 1875–95 saw the steady retreat of scarlatina, typhus and smallpox. A scarlatina epidemic killed 2,424 people in 1886–88, and smallpox's last stand killed 218 in 1894–95.[23] In 1891, as in 1861, Connacht and Ulster tied for the lowest proportion of sick people to the total population, on the night the Census was taken. This was, fortuitously, in early April, a time of year when the last blast of winter weather often brings on illness – the notorious *riabhóg* days,[24] and it is therefore a good time to evaluate general vulnerability to bad health (see table A7, Appendix). The overall rate of sickness fell dramatically from 13 per 1,000 in 1861 for Ireland as a whole, to 7 in 1911. Proportionately, the fewest sick people in the country in precarious early April 1891 were in Londonderry (4.2), Down (4.4), Sligo (4.9) and Roscommon (5); the highest numbers were in Dublin city (13.2), Clare (11.8), Kildare (10.5) and Limerick (10.1). Twenty years later Dublin and Clare still contained black spots, while three different Connacht and Ulster counties and one Leinster – Mayo, Leitrim, Longford and Cavan – had the fewest sick people[25] (tables A8a and A8b, Appendix, give a breakdown of the districts within these counties which were most or least afflicted with illness for the years in question). Only 7.6 per cent of those who died in the scarlatina epidemic of 1886–88 were in Connacht, and the western province had dramatically lower rates of diarrhoea and enteric fever than the other provinces between 1886 and 1895, though it was hit very hard by whooping-cough in 1889 and influenza in 1890, 1892 and 1894.[26] It also had, throughout the period, the lowest death-rate from tubercolosis.

Some Poor Law Unions began to employ district nurses from the 1890s. The more high-profile but less numerous Jubilee and Lady Dudley District Nurses also began work in these decades; local voluntary initiatives had to pay for these.[27] Highly-valued, hard-working public health apostles and midwives, district nurses of whatever kind covered miles on their bicycles in their everyday work, and in contrast to many urban 'lady visitors' they seem to have been loved rather than resented by the people they treated and advised.[28]

In the second decade of the twentieth century deaths from scarlet fever/scarlatina, typhus, diarrhoea/enteritis continued to fall, while deaths from influenza, pneumonia and bronchitis rose. At that stage, doctors had something else to worry about: rates of tubercolosis, or consumption, began to rise in the late 1880s. An average of 12,135 people were lost to it every year between 1899 and 1908. Then the death-rate fell, although very slowly; in 1918 it killed 9,576. Even on the wane, tubercolosis was a bigger killer than the epidemics of cholera (1865–66) and smallpox (1871–72). Diet and accommodation were improving; people were more amenable than ever to health advice, and more aware of infection; local authorities were taking responsibility for cleansing public space; transport and communication were better than ever before. Yet this disease gathered strength. It was a heartbreaking affliction, as the extract from Laverty illustrates, striking down the young and the healthy, advancing and retreating, giving false hope of recovery and often in its last stages leaving its sufferers ethereally beautiful. More prevalent in the towns and cities than in the country, and in the east rather than the west (Connacht's tuberculosis death-rate was 1.13 per 1,000 in 1918, compared to Leinster's 2.01, Ulster's 1.74, and Munster's 1.68), it throve in dusty, enclosed environments. Tailors, dressmakers and stonemasons were particularly vulnerable, as were porters and labourers. Poor housing was not necessarily a trigger – rates of the disease were far higher in Belfast (which had quite good working-class housing) than in many British cities where the housing was far worse, and the disease rampaged thoughout Ireland in places where housing had improved since the 1870s. The improved transport and commercial life of the 1880s and 1890s – the introduction of light railways, for example, creating far more commercial traffic than ever before – played its part in disease transmission.[29] Was compulsory schooling, introduced in 1892, also partly to blame? Children were not the primary victims of the disease, but schools, by gathering and mixing large numbers of people in enclosed and often unhealthful buildings for hours at a time may have helped to spread the disease from family to family. Rapidly changing diet in some parts of the country may have played a part in lowering resistance, and rising levels of church attendance no doubt helped to spread infection. A vigorous campaign against consumption/tubercolosis began towards the end of the nineteenth century. Between 1899 and 1903 the National Association for the Prevention of Tubercolosis and Consumption was set up, with offices in Belfast, Dublin and Cork. The Women's National Health Association, founded in 1907 by Lady Aberdeen, had a roadshow to educate the public about the prevention both of tubercolosis and of other diseases.[30] Houses should be kept ventilated, dung-heaps should be moved some distance from the house, and advice was also given on nutrition and cleanliness.

The fall in the death-rate from tubercolosis after 1910 may have been due partly to education about contagion. Certainly, clinics were opened, sanatoria were built, the Tubercolosis Act of 1908 increased the powers of local authorities to deal with the disease, and public awareness had risen. Yet the death-rates fell all over Britain and Ireland before these vigorous initiatives had had time to take effect – the first sanatorium was built only in 1908. One explanation could be an exhaustion of the bacillus, as sometimes happens in the case of virulent diseases. Another could be the introduction of the Old-Age Pension, from 1 January 1909. While the elderly were not the primary victims of the disease, their new income lessened the strain on family resources, and that in turn could have improved nutrition and boosted resistance to disease in general. Again, however, these improvements would have needed time for their effects to be felt.

Improved nutrition did not protect people from the great influenza epidemic of 1918, which claimed between 17 and 22 million lives worldwide and over 10,000 in Ireland alone. The "flu' was at its worst in the towns and cities: people were afraid to board the Dublin trams and city streets were washed with disinfectant. There were alarming stories of the rapid decomposition of the bodies of those who died from this disease; this was no ordinary epidemic. The young and the strong were not spared: 28–year-old Michael Whelan, a tram conductor, left his house in Donnybrook, Dublin, collapsed from the influenza, fell in a pond near the tramway depot and drowned; his body was not discovered until some time later. Philip MacDonnell, the State Solicitor for Galway, came home from his honeymoon in a coffin. Glasnevin cemetery in Dublin had 240 funerals over 8 days – the norm would have been 12 or 13.[31]

A less talked-about public health problem, which was not resolved in this period, was sexually transmitted disease. The Contagious Diseases Acts were repealed in 1885, but this was only the beginning, rather than the end, of increased policing of prostitutes. The Criminal Law Amendment Act, brought in in the same year, clamped down on brothels and street-walkers, introducing stronger penalties. Although there were complaints about the 'boldness' of prostitutes on the main streets of the capital, oral evidence and popular memory suggests that by the early twentieth century many of them were virtual prisoners in the 'kip-houses' (brothels) of Montgomery Street ('Monto') and other areas.[32]

Infant mortality is the preventible death of an otherwise healthy baby aged 6 weeks to 2 years, usually from gastro-enteritis, but also from the various childhood diseases – measles, diphtheria (a terrible killer), scarlet fever/scarlatina and mumps, among others. More babies died in all social classes then than they do today – over half of Dr Charles Cameron's own children did not reach adulthood.[33] Infant mortality was always highest among the poorest people living in poor conditions, the urban casual labouring class, but more babies survived in poor, tenement-ridden Dublin than in better-housed Belfast, because Dublin mothers were able to breast-feed their babies longer than their mill-working northern counterparts. (In Britain, according to Smith, the presence of Irish people in any city invariably brought down the infant mortality rate, because of Irish women's almost universal breastfeeding.[34])The danger time was when babies were weaned from the breast on to cows' milk served in glass bottles with rubber teats, which impossible to keep clean. On farms, a baby weaned on to milk from the family herd was fairly safe, as the family and the family herd were usually immune to one another's germs. And if the milk was bought locally, it could be obtained fresh, daily, and was easier to keep clean and free of flies. Milk in cities was notoriously unreliable and in the days before refrigeration impossible for either the supplier or the consumer to keep fresh in summer. In the 1850s wet-nurses advertised occasionally, and were advertised for, in the *Freeman's Journal*: a 'strong, healthy respectable young woman, on her second child' sought a situation as a 'nurse (wet)' in 1876.[35] Babies' deaths declined in the second decade of the twentieth century, no doubt due to improved overall nutrition and accommodation, and probably (though this is a controversial point among historians worldwide) partly due to greater knowledge and awareness of cleanliness among mothers.[36] Ireland's infant mortality in 1922 was by no means the worst in Europe, which makes its persistence up to 1950 all the more shameful.[37]

Maternal mortality, like infant mortality, was worst among those whose resistance was low – the badly-fed. The major killers were toxaemia of pregnancy (associated with high blood pressure and poor nutrition), haemorrhage at or after childbirth and puerperal fever. The most reliable birth attendant, according to the international historian of death in childbirth, Irvine Loudon, was the trained midwife.[38] The experienced and sympathetic handywoman with only informal training might also have been good, although doctors sending in reports to the Registrar-General throughout the nineteenth century often complained of these women, who were, they alleged, the cause of 'flooding' (haemorrhage) and uterine damage. Given the poor standard of training in midwifery which many doctors had, the same could be said of them.[39] Puerperal fever, the most unpredictable cause of maternal death, could strike a healthy mother a few days after delivery of a healthy baby. Rates of this disease fluctuated from year to year; it was not confined to hospitals or infirmaries, and the most careful and cleanest doctors, midwives or handywomen could transmit it. Deaths in childbirth fell from 6.18 per 1,000 in 1900 to 4.87 in 1920.[40] There was no relationship between tubercolosis and maternal mortality, but good nutrition and a strong constitution certainly helped women to survive haemorrhage and other obstetric complications, including puerperal fever. The Old Age Pension and National Insurance Act (1908–11) may have boosted family nutrition and access to health care. Separation allowances for soldiers' wives, often the first regular income these women had ever enjoyed, may have played a part in their improved health; trade union successes and wages boards of 1914–18 could also have improved their standard of living. But the problem was by no means solved by 1922, and maternal deaths – individual tragedies, family catastrophes – continued, north and south.

Conclusion

Great ignorance of both sick-room cookery and sick-room nursing prevails in many homes where love and affection abound, and it is not through carelessness but through ignorance that many invalids are allowed to suffer unnecessarily. Knowledge is power; and the knowledge of the above subjects will give us the power of adding to the comfort of those we love.[41] (Kathleen Ferguson, 1903)

O Doctor O Doctor O dear Doctor John,
Your cod-liver oil is so pure and so strong,
I'm afraid of my life I'll go down in the soil
If my wife won't stop drinking your cod-liver oil. ('The cod-liver oil song', traditional[42])

Public health in the first three decades after the Famine was dominated by medical men, intrepid, hands-on practitioners who were as interested in drainage and soil composition as they were in lungs and bowels, holistic in their approach, treating the entire society as an organism. Like most social and medical reformers in all countries at the time, they thought of the poor as a particularly disorderly and troublesome organ of that body or sometimes even as waste matter; burial of the dead poor was on a par with drain clearance, and knowing the habits of the labouring class was like knowing about laws of nature and climate. That said, people in medicine and local government drew attention to the living conditions of the poor in a way that nobody had done before, and spurred government responsibility for housing. Provision of clean water and sewers benefited the poor first and foremost. Vigorous promotion of vaccination through the country-wide system of dispensaries reduced smallpox deaths dramatically, while the opening of workhouse infirmaries provided hospitals, however rudimentary, in every part of the country. There was no retreating from such responsibility.

Doctors and local government officials concerned themselves with the cleanliness of public space and the provision of facilities to the public, but a later generation of public health promoters, women and men, focused on the home. Worldwide, the era from 1890 to about 1940 was a time of *maternalism* in politics, where some women not only assumed a measure of public responsibility for the health of women and children, but used their maternal authority to advise working-class women.[43] In Ireland Poor Law Unions hired district nurses, two prominent women (Queen Victoria and Lady Dudley) served as patrons of voluntary district nursing bodies, and Lady Aberdeen was a patron of the highly visible Women's National Health Association and closely identified with the anti-tubercolosis campaign. Classes in housecraft and domestic health spawned penny booklets like Kathleen Ferguson's *Lessons in Cookery and Housewifery*, published in 1900, her *Sickroom Cookery* published three years later, and Josephine Redington's *Economic Cookery Book*, published in 1905, and used by instructors and schools as well as private individuals.[44] One of the founding aims of the United Irishwomen, founded in Wexford in 1911 (and later to become the Irish Countrywomen's Association) was the promotion of health, hygiene and good nutrition.[45] There is a refreshing absence of patronising 'meddling' in the writings and activities of health reformers in Ireland in this period: note the insistence, in the passage quoted from Ferguson at the head of this section, that it is not carelessness, but ignorance which is to blame, and the two-fold use of the word 'power'. And most of the improvements recommended were necessary – moving dungheaps some distance from the house, letting in air and light, washing clothes and bodies, boiling milk if uncertain of its origin, cleaning all vessels and utensils, and valuing commonplace, easily grown foodstuffs instead of expensive, adulterated ones.

The promotion of good, simple food may well have been the most important part of their message. That part of the country where the accommodation and diet remained the most primitive – the west or, more specifically, Connacht – was also the place which consistently had, despite some aberrations, the lowest death-rates from the most virulent diseases and the lowest proportion of sick people. Connacht's comparative health cannot be attributed to its remoteness. As many as 78,000 people a year left *and came back to*

Mayo, Galway, Roscommon and Sligo until the late 1870s, and thereafter as many as 19,000 a year, and possibly more, made this journey. While away, they lodged in damp, warm, overcrowded conditions ideal for the transmission of disease. Connacht's resistance to disease is all the more remarkable when one bears in mind the distress of the late 1870s, the droughts of the mid-1880s, and the visible hardship and extreme poverty which prompted the government to pump hundreds of thousands of pounds into the region by way of the Congested Districts Board in 1891. (This money certainly improved life in Connacht by providing employment, but the – comparative – good health predated it.)

Sickness rates in Connacht, however, while they were lower than elsewhere in Ireland, did not improve in the last decade of the nineteenth century. Uniquely in western Europe, typhus survived there until the 1940s, and when influenza and typhus hit – as the latter did the Iniskea Islands, off Mayo, in 1897 – they spread quickly and were quite severe.[46] On Iniskea, the dwellings worst hit by the infection were solid, whitewashed houses with stone chimneys, proper beds with good bedding, furniture crafted from driftwood and clean, bright interiors, according to one doctor.[47] Parts of Ulster were also consistently and puzzlingly 'healthy'. If good land and tillage-farming were sources of health and strength in Londonderry and Down in 1891, why did the small pasture farms of Sligo and Roscommon yield a similar result, as did those of Leitrim and Cavan 20 years later? If the cottage industry and factory work common in Derry and urban Down were a reason for this good health, why were Antrim and Armagh not equally healthy? Looking more closely at the Superintendent Registrars' districts, the lowest incidence of sick people in the entire country on Census night in 1911 was in Stranorlar (2.2), followed by Limavady (2.4), Ballymahon (2.5), Swinford and Killala (2.8), Inishowen (2.9), Kilkeel and Castlederg (3.3) and Ballina (3.4). All, except the Longford town of Ballymahon, are in the north and west, and all are characterized by hard work (agriculture or textiles and garments) and a large, young population. Cork city, probably because it was low-lying and liable to flooding, had very poor water quality, and it also had a very high proportion of sick people in Ireland in 1891 and 1911. However, it is difficult to explain why certain districts in both east and west Clare were blackspots in both years[48] (see tables A8a and A8b, Appendix). More research is necessary.

Rates of death and sickness certainly fell over this period, and medical resources became more effective and more evenly distributed throughout the country. The environment also became more healthful, with improved drainage, better water and more awareness of cleanliness in people's homes. However, there were new threats to health. Shops, billboards and newspapers encouraged people to purchase useless and often harmful pre-packaged and marketed 'remedies'.[49] More trains and better roads meant that doctors and medicines travelled more quickly, but so did germs. More people than ever before were going into shops, around the streets, working in offices, hospitals, schools, institutions, going to weekly and even daily church services. The bicycle played its part; new organizations for leisure and for political and cultural activities brought people to mix, often for long periods, in stuffy and badly ventilated settings, and then sent them out in the damp and cold. Respiratory and pulmonary diseases took over from scarlatina, smallpox and typhus, and these diseases (with the exception of fast-acting influenza) were held at bay for long periods or, as in the case of bronchitis, became chronic conditions. The problem of tubercolosis had not been solved by the end of this period; neither had maternal and infant mortality. They were, however, recognized as problems, even if it would be another thirty years before they were all tackled.

All we can know about people's health and sickness is what they chose to tell the doctors, nurses and workhouse attendants, who then recorded it, though they did not always explain it. One unexplained phenomenon is the extraordinary incidence of blindness in Munster. (The Census assigned to blind asylum inmates their counties of origin, so it was not simply that Munster had more institutions.) In 1861, 1891 and 1911 there were substantially more blind people in Munster than in any of the other three provinces[50] (see tables A9a and A9b, Appendix). If home-based needlework in poor light were the cause of sight loss, one would imagine Ulster to have been the most afflicted area; if smoke-induced ophthalmia from chimneyless cabins were to blame, Connacht; if too much reading in poorly lit dwellings, Leinster would surely have equalled Munster. Looking more closely at the distribution of blindness throughout the Munster counties, there is no clear connection between urbanisation or rurality and this disabling condition. Measles and smallpox are notorious for causing blindness in many who survive them. Rates of these diseases throughout the period were no higher in Munster than elsewhere, but as always, our source for this information is *reported* illness and infection. Perhaps many people in Munster recovered from smallpox and measles, but lost their sight, without ever consulting a doctor or becoming a public health statistic. While the records can tell us something of *public* health, certain aspects of the *people's* health will remain hidden.

Notes

1 *Correspondence with regard to epidemic of smallpox at Athenry 1875* (422), Vol. 60.
2 Deborah Brunton, 'The problems of implementation: the failures and success of public vaccination against smallpox in Ireland 1840–1873', in Malcolm and Jones (eds), *Medicine, Disease and the State in Ireland*, pp. 138–57; Cameron, *Manual of Hygiene*, generally, but especially pp. 146–7.
3 *Correspondence with regard to epidemic of smallpox at Athenry 1875*, letter dated 25 June 1875.
4 Cameron, *Manual of Hygiene*, p. 178.
5 Laurence M. Geary, *Medicine and Charity in Ireland 1718–1851* (Dublin 2004), pp. 1–92.
6 Cameron, *Manual of Hygiene*, pp. 177–8.
7 Geary, *Medicine and Charity in Ireland*, p. 214.
8 Tony Farmar, *Patients, Potions and Physicians: a social history of medicine in Ireland* (Dublin 2004), pp. 85–7.
9 *Freeman's Journal*, 3 March 1855.
10 Sr Patricia Kelly, 'From workhouse to hospital: the role of the Irish workhouse in medical relief to 1921' (MA thesis, University College Galway 1972); Clear, *Nuns in Nineteenth-Century Ireland*; see also M. Luddy, 'Nuns as workhouse nurses 1861–1898', in Malcolm and Jones (eds), *Medicine, Disease and the State in Ireland*, pp. 102–13.
11 Joseph Robins, *The Miasma: epidemic and panic in nineteenth-century Ireland* (Dublin 1995), p. 205; *Report of Registrar-General* for 1865 (1870) [c. 4], Vol. 15 and for 1866 (1870) [c. 130], Vol. 16.
12 Eva O Cathaoir, 'The Poor Law in Co. Wicklow', in Ken Hannigan and W. Nolan (eds), *Wicklow: history and society* (Dublin 1994), pp. 503–80.
13 Robins, *The Miasma*; also *Reports of the Registrar-General for Ireland 1864–*, passim, but especially *Registrar-General of Births, Marriages and Deaths (Ireland) 1865* (1870) [c.4], Vol. 15, and ditto for 1866 (1870) [c.130], Vol. 16, introductory reports. On typhus see E. Margaret Crawford, 'Typhus in nineteenth-century Ireland', in Malcolm and Jones

(eds), *Medicine, Disease and the State in Ireland*, pp. 121–37; on Asiatic cholera see Cameron, *Manual of Hygiene*, generally.

14 *Freeman's Journal*, Editorial, 24 February 1865; they were Doctors Speedy, Anderson and Healy.

15 Brunton, 'Problems of implementation'.

16 Cameron, *Manual of Hygiene*, p. 43; Crawford, 'Typhus in nineteenth-century Ireland'.

17 Cameron, *Manual of Hygiene*, pp. 34–44 and generally.

18 See chapter 9, on living standards.

19 Cameron, *Manual of Hygiene*, p. 10.

20 Elizabeth Malcolm, 'Troops of largely diseased women: VD, the Contagious Diseases Acts and moral policing in late nineteenth-century Ireland', *Irish Economic and Social History*, Vol. 26 (1999), pp. 1–14. On the English campaign, see Judith Walkowitz, *Prostitution and Victorian Society: women, class and the State* (Cambridge 1980).

21 Frances Finnegan, *Do Penance or Perish: a study of Magdalen asylums in Ireland* (Oxford 2004), pp. 157–96.

22 Laverty, *Never No More*, pp. 208–9.

23 *Twenty-Third Annual Report of the Registrar-General 1886–7* [c. 5153], Vol. 23, table 10, p. 14, showing the number of deaths from the febrile or zymotic diseases 1876–85; and *Thirty-Second Annual Report of the Registrar-General 1895–6*, 1896 [c. 8236], Vol. 23, table 10, ditto for 1886–95.

24 The *riabhóg* was the speckled cow, and the first days of April were, in the folklore, the days particularly dangerous to that animal, and to human beings too.

25 *Census of Ireland*, 1851–1911, General reports, tables on sickness in Poor Law Union registrars' districts; 1891, pp. 30–5; 1911, table 77.

26 See note 24 and also *Thirty-Seventh Annual Report of the Registrar-General 1900*, table 12 (deaths from influenza), table 13 (deaths from tubercolosis and phthisis), pp. 12–16 (1901) [cd. 697], Vol. 15.

27 I am indebted to Mary Clancy for this important distinction and clarification about the difference between Poor Law Union nurses and Dudley Nurses.

28 Caroline Hynes, 'District nursing in Ireland 1880–1939', M.Phil thesis, NUI, Galway, 1999; Ann Wickham, '"She must be content to be their servant as well as their teacher": the early years of district nursing in Ireland', in Gerard M. Fealy (ed.), *Care to Remember: nursing and midwifery in Ireland* (Cork 2005), pp. 102–37.

29 Greta Jones, *Captain of All These Men of Death: the history of tubercolosis in nineteenth- and twentieth-century Ireland* (Amsterdam 2001).

30 Joanna Bourke, '"The health caravan": domestic education and female labour in rural Ireland 1890–1914', *Eire–Ireland*, Vol. 24, No. 4 (1989), pp. 21–38.

31 *Freeman's Journal,* 26 and 28 October 1918, oral evidence from Eithne MacCormack (born 1920).

32 Malcolm, 'Troops', pp. 13–14; Finnegan, *Do Penance or Perish,* pp. 157–96; Kearns, *Dublin Tenement Life,* generally, but particularly pp. 69–70, 218–19; B. Murnane, 'The recreation of the urban historical landscape: Mountjoy Ward, Dublin, c.1901', in W. Smyth, K. Whelan and T. Jones Hughes (eds), *Common Ground: essays on the historical geography of Ireland* (Dublin 1988), pp. 189–207.

33 M. Daly, M. Hearn, P. Pearson, *Dublin's Victorian Houses* (Dublin 1998), p. 10.

34 F. B. Smith, *The People's Health 1830–1910* (Canberra 1979, London 1990), pp. 90–1.

35 *Freeman's Journal,* 26 January 1876, Situations Wanted.

36 The controversy rages, the principal contributors being Gisela Bock and Pat Thane (eds), *Maternity and Gender Policies: women and the rise of European welfare states* (London 1991); Jane Lewis, *The Politics of Motherhood: child and maternal welfare in England 1900–1939* (London 1980); and Deborah Dwork, *War Is Good for Babies and Young Children: a history of the infant and child welfare movement in England 1891–1918* (London 1987).

37 Ibid.: *Detailed Annual Report of the Registrar-General for Saorstát Eireann 1923* (1924), T.3, table 9, showing, by certain causes, the mortality among infants under 12 months per 1,000 births, 1913–23.

38 Irvine Loudon, *Death in Childbirth: an international study of maternal care and maternal mortality 1800–1950* (Oxford 1992), remains the definitive source on maternal mortality in all countries at this time, including Ireland; H. Marland and A. M. Rafferty (eds), *Midwives, Society and Childbirth* (London 1997), is also very useful. For Ireland, see Clear, *Women of the House,* pp. 96–125; and Tony Farmar, *Holles Street, 1894–1994: the National Maternity Hospital – a centenary history* (Dublin 1994); Alan Browne (ed.), *Masters, Midwives and Ladies in Waiting: the Rotunda Hospital, Dublin 1745–1995* (Dublin 1995).

39 See *First Report of the Registrar-General, 1865*; Loudon, *Death in Childbirth*; and for an account of a well-trained handywoman, see Leslie Matson, *Méiní: the Blasket nurse* (Cork 1996).

40 Figures taken from Jones, *Captain of All These Men of Death,* p. 90.

41 Kathleen Ferguson, Preface to *Sickroom Cookery with Notes on Sick Nursing* (Athlone 1903).

42 I heard this song from my mother (born Limerick city, 1926), who got it from her mother (born King's County, 1892).

43 See note 39.

44 Kathleen Ferguson, *Lessons in Cookery and Housewifery: Leabhairíní na Seamróige* (Dublin 1900), and *Sickroom Cookery*; Josephine Redington, *An Economic Cookery Book* (Dublin 1905).

45 Pat Bolger (ed.), *And See Her Beauty Shining There: the story of the Irish countrywomen* (Dublin 1986); Sarah McNamara, *Those Intrepid United Irishwomen: pioneers of the Irish Countrywomen's Association* (Parteen 1995).
46 Robins, *The Miasma*, p. 204.
47 *Freeman's Journal*, 12 July 1897.
48 See note 26; on water, see Cameron, *Manual of Hygiene*, pp. 78–94.
49 Tony Farmar, *Patients, Potions and Physicians*, pp. 124–7.
50 *Census of Ireland*, 1851–1911: 1861, general report; 1891, table 100, showing by counties and provinces the number of blind at their own homes and in workhouses; and 1911, table 82.

7

Institutions

Nineteenth-century institutions lasted a long time in Ireland. Reformatories and industrial schools still operated in the 1970s. Psychiatric hospitals began to experiment with 'care in the community' in the 1960s and 1970s, but many of the features of the old lunatic asylum remained until much later. Magdalen asylums lasted until the 1980s. The hated workhouses were more or less abolished after independence, though the more benign county homes which replaced them continued to house some homeless people until long after that.[1] And in Ireland, as elsewhere, the founding principles of the nineteenth-century prison still inform judicial punishment in the early twenty-first century.

The lunatic asylum

Although there were some asylums in the eighteenth century, most people who were seen to need restraint due to insanity were detained either in 'houses of industry' (eighteenth-century workhouses of a sort, few in number) or in prison. The 'harmless' insane either lived at home or wandered around begging, 'at large' as the worried authorities put it. Between 1817 and 1854, twenty-two lunatic asylums were built, equipped and staffed, out of government funds. It is not entirely clear why the government decided to make such a large financial outlay on a relatively small section of the needy. Perhaps because there was no poor law of any kind in Ireland at the time, the government, with civic disorder forever bubbling to the surface, wanted to be seen to do something for the poor. The medical profession had a high reforming profile in the early nineteenth century, and although the terms 'psychiatrist' and 'psychiatry' were still in the future, 'mad-doctors' and 'alienists' were becoming more respectable. The new asylums sought to replace chains, cells and physical punishment with beds and timetables. The reforms of the Monroe family in London and Philippe Pinel in the Salpetriere in Paris were followed avidly in Cork by William Saunders Hallaran, whose *Practical Observations on the Causes and Cures of Insanity*, published in 1810, recommended kindness, fresh air and the 'talking cure'.[2]

Once built, the asylums filled up. This was true of every country where there were state-provided asylums, and there is much debate about why this was so. Did the asylums fill an urgent need to have many insane people who had hitherto been 'at large' locked up? Did the definition of insanity broaden, so that more people were seen as insane? Was the social and economic dislocation brought on by industrialization and modernization quite literally driving people mad at a greater rate than before? This argument still rages, but certainly, judging by the Irish experience, industrialization and urbanization were not preconditions for asylums to be filled to capacity.[3]

In the early nineteenth-century asylums used 'moral treatment': madness was seen as a temporary aberration brought on by shock or some other outside cause. Asylum inmates were kept clean and their behaviour was regulated; they had to work, but they had copious quantities of fresh air and exercise in the well-kept grounds, and plenty of bed rest. People came voluntarily into the asylum, as well as being placed there. However, under the Dangerous Lunatics Act of 1838, a person deemed to be a dangerous lunatic – not having committed any crime, but dangerous to himself or herself and others – could be certified by a relative, a doctor or a justice of the peace, and compulsorily committed to an asylum. According to Finnane and Robins, this piece of legislation was used more often in Ireland than in England, Wales and Scotland: in 1875, for example, 50 per cent of all admissions to Irish asylums were of 'dangerous lunatics', and two years later 66 per cent. It was as high as 90 per cent in some asylums in 1891. In 1887 the comparable figure for Scotland was 0.4 per cent.[4]

It is difficult to believe that Irish people were really that much more dangerously insane than the Scots. The 'dangerous lunatic' was kept in the asylum free of charge, so many who entered voluntarily might have arranged to be committed, to save money. Many, however, must have been sent in against their will. Malcolm argues that the asylum was a 'friend of the family', used as a place to keep (temporarily or permanently) unruly members; certainly that is the image of the asylum in Irish lore and oral history.[5] Police and people used the Dangerous Lunatics Act to lock up wandering homeless individuals. In 1873, of those committed as dangerous lunatics 62 per cent were 'dangerous persons at large, vagrants and insane persons wandering without control'.[6]

By the late nineteenth century asylums were bursting at the seams, and doctors and administrators were anxious to 'cure' people and move them on. Women in Ballinasloe asylum, according to Walsh, had a higher recovery rate because they were kept occupied at sewing and embroidery in a light, airy room;[7] women in general were more likely to recover and less likely to be committed (rather than to enter voluntarily), probably because they were often needed at home, and in any case were more easily subdued if violent. In Ireland, mental illness does not seem to have been the 'female malady' that it became in the upper-middle-class Anglophone world.[8] More men than women were committed as 'dangerous lunatics', probably because of drink and domestic violence, though the number of females committed in this way rose in the last quarter of the century.[9]

The asylum was a major employer: an institution could provide up to 200 permanent jobs; many keepers or attendants (later called nurses) male and female, were part-time small farmers. Tradesmen – painter-decorators, tailors, plumbers, plasterers, gas-fitters and chemists – also did work for asylums, and while they had their own home farms and bakeries, local grocers, drapers and hardware merchants got plenty of business from them.

The prison

Like the asylum, the prison was reinvented in the late eighteenth and early nineteenth centuries on both sides of the Atlantic.[10] The pre-reform prison had been mainly a holding centre for criminals awaiting trial and punishment – transportation, death, a fine, flogging. The new prison conceived of imprisonment itself as punishment, of the mind rather than the body. Uniformity, supervision and separation were the key elements of the new imprisonment. Prisoners, theoretically at least, were clothed, fed and treated the same; their day was strictly time-tabled, and, apart from supervised interludes, they were separated from each other and from the outside world. The late eighteenth century saw the construction of jails throughout the country, under the control of the local authority (the Corporation or the Grand Jury). By 1850 there were 41 such prisons in Ireland, mainly for those serving sentences of up to 2 years. Mountjoy Prison opened in 1850 for convicts (more serious offenders) serving longer sentences. Transportation to Australia ceased in 1853, so there was a problem of what to do with those convicted of serious crime but who did not merit the death penalty. After a few false starts, the system developed by Walter Crofton was employed. This was gradated imprisonment, becoming less severe as the sentence was served and culminating in an 'open prison' at Lusk, in Co. Dublin. Prisoners could earn 'marks' for good conduct, and in the final stages wear their own clothes and earn money. This 'Crofton system', which Carey considers to have been moderately successful in reforming criminals, was inexplicably abandoned in 1880.[11]

Local prisons were harsher, because the sentences were short and intended to deter rather than reform. Authorities struggled to impose the 'separate system' whereby prisoners had only minimal contact with each other during the day, but were constantly defeated by the fact that there were often 4–5 to a cell. Those serving sentences of less than a month received no meat, and survived on stirabout, bread and milk; those on longer sentences had meat soup twice a week.[12] Work was both punishment and 'training': the women in Antrim County Prison (in Belfast) in 1854–55 were 'employed at knitting, needle-work, prison duties, spinning and carding, veining, washing and in school, and 'a contract has lately been obtained for washing for the military'. In the 1870s this prison also became a laundry for private families. Men in prison worked at everything from mat-making to timber-cutting, but in Clonmel in 1886 they were mainly pumping water, rope-picking and 'labouring'. Turnkeys were often tailors, weavers and schoolmasters, teaching as well as keeping discipline.[13] The same individuals were detained again and again for minor offences. More females were imprisoned in Ireland for petty offences than elsewhere, according to Carey, and Conley tells us that Irish women's propensity for violent assault brought them constantly before the courts. Maryborough Prison in 1862 had a stream of 'constantly recurring prostitutes' and insubordinate paupers from the workhouse.[14] In Galway, Curtin shows, these women were predominately middle-aged, illiterate and unskilled, and their crimes largely alcohol-related.[15]

In 1878 the General Prisons Board amalgamated responsibility for local prisons and convict prisons, and standardized prison routines throughout the country, prescribing strict summer and winter time-tables. Prison reports in the 1880s and 1890s are far less detailed and personal than those of the three earlier decades, when every prison was visited, diet described (and tasted), prisoners interviewed, their work detailed, and all the prison workers named individually. The dwindling prison population led to the closing of several local prisons and an attempt at what we would call 'centralization'. By 1895 there were only twenty-six local prisons, with convict prisons in Mountjoy, Maryborough and Philipstown. The comparatively open prisons of Lusk and Spike Island had been closed. By 1914, Maryborough was the main convict prison, Mountjoy had become Dublin's local prison, and there were only 14 others throughout the country; 'bridewells', holding centres for remand prisoners, had also dwindled in number to 5.[16]

The workhouse

To end up in an institution in nineteenth-century Ireland or Britain one did not have to be insane or a criminal – destitution would suffice. In Ireland the Poor Law of 1838, modelled on the British Poor Law of 1834, was welcomed by some as the first country-wide system of government-funded poor relief. But it was conceived as a harsh, punitive, degrading system, designed as such so as to deter the 'undeserving' – the lazy and the idle – from seeking poor relief.[17]

The Poor Law established workhouses all over the country, organized in local areas known as Poor Law Unions. Rate-paying property-owners in these areas paid for the workhouse and its officers; there was to be no relief outside the workhouse. Rate-payers also elected the Poor Law Guardians who administered the Unions. Guardians were local people, usually those whose way of life enabled them to give up a day a week to attend meetings on matters relating to workhouse administration – 'gentlemen' and, after 1896, 'ladies' – people of the upper-middle class. The workhouse master and matron were employees who worked under their authority and were answerable to them.[18]

When a man, woman or child entered the workhouse he or she gave up all rights to freedom of movement and even to family. Although children, the old, the sick and nursing mothers received better food than the able-bodied, incarceration was the same for all inmates. By 1850 widows with small children could apply for relief in their own homes, outside of the workhouse; this was 'outdoor relief', considered to be against the spirit of the Poor Law, though Guardians, in times of crisis, often voted for outdoor relief to be given to all applicants, as in Dublin city in the severe winter of 1854–55.[19]

The workhouse split up families: husbands were separated from wives and parents from children, though mothers kept the babies they were nursing. This was partly so as to make workhouse life unpleasant, thus acting as a deterrent, but there were also practical reasons. The workhouse could not provide separate apartments for families and it did not want people reproducing while they were living at the ratepayers' expense. Besides, the entire workhouse system was an attack on the only sphere of authority poor people had – their families.

The 'work' was nondescript. There was always basic domestic work, cleaning and cooking, for the women, and a few enterprising workhouses had small cottage industries, using women's skills.[20] There were schools, but their quality varied widely. Some believed that the workhouse could be an experiment in social engineering, taking children from their idle, feckless parents and training them to be model citizens. It was even claimed that girls reared in the workhouse were cleaner and neater than those sent to board with private families, where standards were lower.[21] By 1876, however, workhouse children boarded out with foster parents were allowed to stay with them until they were 15.[22] The original idea, when boarding-out began in 1862, was that children would be taken back to the workhouse when they were 5 years old. It would be hard to find anyone by the end of the century who believed that the workhouse was a good place for a child to grow up.[23]

But if human beings endured the system, human beings ran it, too. Women on the move, McLoughlin shows, used it as a place to leave children until they could afford to take them out, and though this was strictly against workhouse rules the harshest official would not turn out a small child to starve.[24] The workhouse established a standard subsistence diet. The food, if monotonous, was at least nourishing and adequate, with milk for children who might never have tasted it otherwise, plenty of carbohydrates and even some protein. And the Guardians were not made of stone. In 'perpetual conflict' with the Poor Law Commissioners (the central authority in Dublin Castle) because of their liberal interpretation of the workhouse rules, were the Guardians in Lismore, Co. Waterford. Good beef for Christmas dinner, eggs for Easter, snuff and tobacco for the elderly, freedom to leave the workhouse on certain days, food for inmates leaving, oranges and currant buns, were just some of their indulgences.[25] In Rathdrum from 1868 tobacco and alcohol were issued to the elderly for medicinal purposes, and at Christmas and Easter meat, toys, snuff and tobacco were available.[26]

Insubordination was such a real problem that pauper inmates had to be led rather than driven – boys cleaning cesspools in Carlow Union in 1853 were given whiskey and tobacco to 'compel' them to carry out this task.[27] Loughlinstown workhouse allowed out fathers of families on 'passes' to look for work, a pragmatic practice probably connived at in several Poor Law Unions. What began as a system of intentional deterrence evolved into a more 'user-friendly' place by the end of the nineteenth century. The rule that mothers could keep with them only the children they were actually breast-feeding, resulted in children being 'nursed' for 3–4 years, if Clones Union in 1860 is anything to go by.[28] In the second half of the 1860s the Poor Law Commissioners recommended that able-bodied inmates be provided with an evening meal and when some miserly Boards of Guardians refused to change lengthy correspondence ensued.[29] Robins cites several instances of treats and excursions for children, usually provided by local ladies, from the 1860s on.[30] When Ginnett's Circus played Wexford in 1895 it informed the Board of Guardians that workhouse inmates would be admitted to an afternoon show free of charge.[31] By the 1860s overnight beds were being provided to people on the move, or 'night-lodgers'. The work-house was used by some women to tide them over the temporary destitution occasioned by childbirth, judging by the number of children born there who were subsequently 'discharged', i.e. neither boarded out nor kept in the workhouse.[32]

All that said, no matter how the workhouse developed or how humane (and indeed accountable) its officers and Guardians some-times were, it remained a place for punishing the destitute. Child mortality was high. Of the 18 infants (under 12 months) who were sent out to foster parents in Belfast Union in 1872–74, 11 (61 per cent) died; in Dublin city (north and south), the rate was almost identical at 60 per cent (52 out of 86). Urban life was notoriously unhealthful and babies boarded out in rural areas had a much better chance of survival in those years – for example, 5 out of 6 children boarded out in Newcastle West Union, Co. Limerick, remained 'healthy'– but the fact that such a high mortality-rate was tolerated in Belfast and Dublin speaks volumes about the value of baby paupers.[33] And though there was an improvement in the last quarter of the nineteenth century, it was not a dramatic one. In the three years ending 30 June 1904, there were 402 deaths out of 'probably less than 1000 children' under 2 years of age in the 2 nurseries of the North Dublin Union – a mortality-rate of over 40 per cent (and note that chilling 'probably').[34]

Industrial schools and reformatories

They played marches and dance music with great spirit and precision, but an operatic *fantasia* was not so perfectly rendered. (Inspectors' report on Glencree Reformatory, 1866)[35]

At first glance this comment makes the reader smile: no one expects rough, teenage lads to play operatic works as they should be played. Yet the inspectors were probably in earnest, such was the faith of Victorian reformers in the potential of educational reform. To understand the widespread support for reformatories and industrial schools in the nineteenth and early twentieth centuries, one must first understand the opposition. Opponents of the system claimed that these institutions pampered the criminal and destitute poor, and that some parents deliberately abandoned children so that they could be fed, clothed and taught a trade. It was not fair on the respectable poor, they argued, that the disreputable poor got better chances than they did.[36] Reformers pointed out that the alternatives were the adult prison (where juveniles were still occasionally kept), the workhouse, the (perhaps) neglectful home and the street. The reformatory, established in 1858, was for criminals aged 12–16, the industrial school, licensed in 1868, for criminals under 12 and for those under 16 without proper homes.[37] By 1894 there were 7 reformatories and 68 industrial schools in Ireland 12 of these institutions – 2 reformatories and 10 industrial schools – were for Protestants, the remainder for Catholics. The number of reformatories in general had fallen since 1858, while the number of industrial schools had risen.[38]

Initially, the industrial school seems to have operated like the orphanage it often replaced: 84.9 per cent of the children committed to industrial schools in 1873–74 had only one parent or both had died; only 3.9 per cent were illegitimate, and only 3 per cent had been sent for criminal offences. By 1883, however, a big change is evident: only 37.9 per cent of children sent to industrial schools were orphaned or had but one living parent, while 39.7 per cent were committed for a criminal offence or being destitute, although in that year an even smaller proportion – 3.39 per cent – were illegitimate.[39] The definition of 'criminality' and 'destitution' had broadened considerably in the intervening ten years, and subsequent legislation, in 1886 and thereafter, would further extend the definition of neglect and cruelty to children.

Sir John Lentaigne's inspectors' reports between 1869 and 1886 are valuable because his visits to the schools were unannounced.[40] Much preoccupied with health, living conditions, diet and training, he was also alive to less tangible factors, though we cannot know today what precisely he meant by 'happy' and 'cheerful'. In 1873 the girls at Balmoral Industrial School in Belfast 'appear bright and happy', and the girls in St Joseph's Good Shepherd Reformatory in Limerick were described as 'contented and happy'; and 'the cheery happy appearance of the girls' was noted in St Bridget's Industrial School in Loughrea. He questioned the usefulness of the girls in Sunday's Well Industrial School in Cork, run by the Good Shepherd order, making hair-nets for the shops, a skill which he doubted would be useful to them in later life. The children in the Carmelite Industrial School in Sandymount, Dublin, should not be drinking out of tin mugs. The girls in Middletown Industrial School run by the Sisters of Mercy, in Armagh, in 1883 were 'well-cared [sic.] and the picture of health'; the Protestant girls in Cork Street Industrial School, Dublin, were 'industrious, cheery and happy'; while those in the care of the deaconesses in Glanmire, Cork, were 'one happy family'.[41]

In most of the schools boys were taught agricultural work, with tailoring, shoemaking and carpentry; in the girls' schools, housework, cookery, needlework and laundry. Though useful training was certainly given, all these skills were needed in any case for the upkeep and maintenance of the school and its inmates, and these institutions were practically self-sufficient as a result. There were specialisms: the training ship *Gibraltar* in Belfast trained Protestant boys to be sailors; the St Nicholas Industrial School for Protestant boys in Cork taught bell-chiming; the Merrion Industrial School for girls in Dublin, run by the Sisters of Mercy, had a lithographic studio with photographic equipment to train the girls; and the boys in the 700-strong Artane

Industrial School made 15,000 shirts, 3969 pairs of socks, 12,655 teapots and sundry other items in the year prior to the 1883 inspection. The care of fine linen and china, and hairdressing are stressed in some girls' schools, where inmates were being trained for the upper reaches of domestic service, as parlour maids and ladies' maids. A South Kensington-trained cookery teacher was employed at a number of schools in 1883, to train girls as cooks, the skill summit of the below-stairs' world. By the 1880s swimming-baths were being encouraged, 'so necessary', as Lentaigne commented in one of his reports.[42]

The belief that industrial-school children were being pampered died hard, as the following exchange from a meeting of the Wexford Board of Guardians in 1902 shows:

> Mr John Lambert said – 'He was opposed to sending the [workhouse] children to the convent [industrial school], and anyone who had any experience of the children trained there would not be in favour of the proposition. He asked Mr Ennis if he had had any servant from the Convent of Mercy? If you get one, do not let her see the moon, or she will want to get it.' (laughter)

> Lady M.Fitzgerald – 'I had often girls from the Convent of Mercy and I found them most satisfactory.'

> Mr John Lambert said – 'He was satisfied to send the children outside to board with private people, but he objected to sending them to the Sisters. The Convent of Mercy was the means of taking work out of the hands of many honest labouring families in Wexford. Why should these workhouse children be trained up for fine situations? There should be someone to do the rough work, and why should they not do it?'[43]

By 'fine situations' Lambert meant good domestic service. Wexford was a tillage county where there was still great demand for part-time agricultural labourers; former workhouse girls and women, the cheapest of cheap labour with poor bargaining power, were ideal for this. The nuns were giving them ideas above their station in life.

Most industrial schools were run by and for Catholics, and thus by religious orders. In contrast to Protestant schools, they did not have boards of management and therefore developed an autonomy which was not, Barnes suggests, receptive to change. Inspectors occasionally criticised the schools, but they seemed to be running well, weren't overspending and had few discipline problems. There were three times as many industrial schools for girls as for boys, and twice as many reformatories. To claim that this is because girls were seen as more vulnerable than boys is to miss the point. Industrial schools and reformatories were set up, not by government, but by voluntary organizations which then looked for government licensing and funding. There were about fifty times more women than men working voluntarily with poor children in Ireland, therefore more female juvenile institutions were in operation. Thus there were even more female reformatories than male, despite the fact that there were more male than female criminals at every age. The Children's Act of 1908 did not bring about any real change in the schools as they operated, except that they allowed workhouse children to be admitted to them. (This was already happening in Wexford – see above – and probably in other Unions also.)

Undoubtedly some children were rescued from starvation and neglect, trained and given the only home they ever knew. But it was a home they had to leave, and Barnes points out that only half of those who left between 1869 and 1908 went directly to work (domestic service or apprenticeships), the army or the navy. A quarter of these teenagers returned to the families who had been considered (rightly or wrongly) unfit to rear them.[44] The management of the *Gibraltar* training ship lamented 'the continued indisposition of the owners of vessels and other employers of labour' to give their boys a chance when they left the ship.[45] Perhaps it was not so much fear of the boys themselves as of their families that gave employers pause. The Sisters of Mercy Industrial School for girls in Strabane told the inspector in 1883 that 'ladies who reside in England and know girls trained in this school who are living in their neighbourhoods, frequently apply to the manager for servants'.[46] Tyrone and Donegal 'ladies' were not applying. A 'good situation abroad' was the ideal, and industrial-school and reformatory children, like convicts,[47] were often encouraged to emigrate, though 'encouragement' might be somewhat euphemistic in the case of this incident recorded of the St Louis Reformatory in Monaghan in 1865:

> About eight months ago two girls, cousins, were to be released by expiration of sentence on a certain day. Their relatives, a gang of wandering tinkers, had been prowling around the reformatory and were driven off by the constabulary. Mrs Beale was determined to rescue the girls if possible. A steamer was to sail from Londonderry three days before the expected day of discharge. She telegraphed me to obtain a pardon from the Chief Secretary, which he kindly granted,

and three days before the day of discharge the two girls were sailing for New York, where careful friends and safe employment was secured for them.[48]

We have no way of knowing what the girls themselves thought of this plan, as the narrator does not see fit to tell us. What is striking, however, is that their families – described here as little better than wolves ('prowling', 'driven off') – knew exactly, to the date, when the girls were due to be released. A lot less shadowy and passive than the official reports imply, families are the hidden half of the history of nineteenth-century children's institutions. 'What the poor are to the poor is little known, except to themselves and to GOD', as Dickens remarked.[49]

Asylums for the disabled

In 1891 there were 13 asylums for the disabled, mainly those afflicted with loss of sight, hearing and speech, in Ireland; 12 of them were concentrated in Dublin, Belfast, Cork and Limerick, and there was also one in Armagh. Numbers of inmates ranged from 12, in Limerick Blind Asylum, to 300 in St Mary's Catholic Asylum for the Blind in Merrion, Dublin. The inmates of these asylums were often trained to play musical instruments and in crafts like basket-weaving. They made up only a tiny proportion of the blind, deaf and dumb in the country as a whole, however, and were most likely those who for some reason were unable to live with their relatives. The vast majority of people whose sight, hearing and speech were affected lived in their local communities or in the workhouse.

Penitent/Magdalen asylums

There were Protestant Magdalen asylums (James Joyce mentions one, the Dublin By Lamplight Laundry), but the majority of Magdalen asylums were Catholic.[50] These institutions did not receive any government funding, and before 1850 were often run by lay boards of management, sometimes partly by the 'penitents' – inmates – themselves, it seems; but after 1850 all Catholic Magdalen asylums were run by nuns. While they were certainly used by tired prostitutes, they became places of incarceration for women who had had a baby outside of marriage and, even more commonly, for girls and women seen to be in 'bad company' and in danger of 'falling'.

This mixing together of various degrees of sexual transgression is all the more surprising when we see that even the workhouses tried to separate unmarried mothers from prostitutes.[51] Magdalen asylums continued to admit, discharge and re-admit the prostitutes who used the facilities as respite care,[52] even as they permanently incarcerated the 'first-fallen' women and young girls 'in moral danger'. So, while they reformed the occasional prostitute, prolonged her life and, in their own terms and her's, saved her soul for all eternity, these institutions also contained non-prostitutes who could spend, on Finnegan's account, up to forty years there. The 'first-fallen' and the women in 'moral danger' were brought in by relatives who rarely took them back once the 'danger' had passed.[53] A case history from one of the asylums tells the story of 'Ellen'. The oldest girl in a motherless farming family, she had reared her younger brothers and sisters, and was sent to the Magdalen asylum by her father because she was keeping bad company. He promised to take her out after a few years, but in the meantime he remarried and the woman did not want Ellen: 'Her spirits never recovered this blow' and Ellen died soon afterwards in the asylum.[54]

Long-term incarceration in a Magdalen asylum, unlike a lunatic asylum, had no basis in law. People may have been confused on this point because nuns also ran reformatories and industrial schools, to both of which children were committed by the courts. Occasionally courts recommended that women be sent to Magdalen asylums but these women made up only a tiny minority of all inmates. The fact that these asylums were able to virtually imprison women testifies to the huge power and authority not only of the nuns and the Catholic Church, but of the families who placed the women there and refused to 'take them out'. M. J. F. McCarthy, in 1902, commented:

> I visited one of those penitentiaries, and saw the poor Magdalenes in chapel, and a more distressing sight I never saw. They were dressed as outcasts, and *they looked outcasts*.[55]

His view was exceptional. During the Dublin Lock Out in 1913, a strike supporter, Mary Ellen Murphy, was sent to High Park Reformatory by the courts, for a minor offence. The strikers objected vociferously because the reformatory was on the same site as the Magdalen Asylum. In the chapel, it was alleged, Mary Ellen had been 'brought into full view of the fallen women in the chapel of the institution'. The 'Magdalens' were so low that catching a glimpse of them could mark somebody for life.[56]

Conclusion

Whether an institution ended up as a welcome refuge or as a grim prison depended not on the function or the founding ideals, but on the power enjoyed by those running the institution, and the level of interest and intervention from outside.

The workhouse was deliberately designed as a joyless place where the destitute would not linger. The elected Boards of Guardians met weekly and discussed every detail of workhouse administration: diet, health, admissions, discharges, punishments. They moved people through the system as quickly as possible. No one on the outside wanted to keep people in the workhouse – certainly not the rate-payers. The only permanent jobs tied up in them were those of the master and matron. (The workhouse hospital certainly provided jobs, but these did not depend on the permanent incarceration of large numbers of people.) Families could not send in unwanted members and refuse to take them out; those running the institution were accountable. Workhouses never cast off their punitive character but they became less grim over time.[57]

The founders of the modern lunatic asylum, on the other hand, intended it as a benign institution providing a sort of kindness to the insane poor, but it developed into a prison by the early twentieth century. The relatively easy committal procedures and the sheer number of people dependent on the asylum for a livelihood ensured that these institutions would always be full, even as doctors and administrators tried to move people through the system and out the other side. Overcrowding was one of the chief causes of the outbreak of beri-beri in the Richmond Asylum in Dublin between 1894 and 1897.[58]

The biggest apparent change in the prisons was the rise and fall of optimism – the adoption and abandonment of Crofton's reforms. Because convicts made up only a small proportion of prisoners as a whole, however, an arguably more important change was the gradual closing down of local prisons and bridewells after 1878. Up to that time, the prison experience, though never pleasant, had some familiar elements: relatives could come and visit, or shout up at cells or through the gratings of bridewells; turnkeys and warders were often local,[59] which might have imposed some check on their treatment of prisoners who would not be serving sentences longer than two years. After amalgamation, there were more rules and time-tables. Visiting, never easy, became more difficult for many; and prison reports became a lot less personal, informative and detailed towards the end of the nineteenth century. This new reticence mirrors the retreat of execution by hanging behind prison walls, from 1868. The punishment was brutal and final, but it was less visible.

Historians' judgement of industrial schools in the nineteenth and early twentieth centuries (as opposed to the later twentieth century) varies. Boys' industrial schools, Barnes tells us, were more regimented, and less relaxed than girls'; Robins argues that boys' schools were more exuberant and active, and girls' schools depressing and regimented. This contrasting reading of the same evidence reminds us that judgements on the past treatment of children are of their very nature subjective. The nineteenth- and early twentieth-century industrial school, when staffed by responsible and kindly people, gave youngsters a chance to be trained, and provided food and shelter to many who would otherwise have gone without. But by the end of the nineteenth century most industrial schools and reformatories were run by religious orders operating under strict rules and living a regulated, collective life for which they had taken vows to devote themselves to the work in hand. Institutions were running institutions, and this made them effective, impervious to criticism and long-lasting.

Industrial schools and reformatories had some links with the world of the courts, detention orders and the police. Children could be taken out on appeal, and were discharged on their sixteenth birthday. There were no such checks on Magdalen asylums, which combined all the worst features of the other institutions. Like the industrial schools, they were run by permanent, dedicated, institutionalized and effective staff increasingly beyond criticism; like the workhouse, they provided a comfortless and punitive atmosphere; like the lunatic asylum, they gave families a chance to dump unwanted members; like the prison, they locked up the inmates, shaved their heads, made them wear special clothes and discouraged relationships among them – though, unlike the prison, there was no release date.

The inmates of institutions about whom we know least are people with a mental handicap. Robins believes that these people were probably better off 'at large', even if they became homeless targets of ridicule, than in the prison-like accommodation of workhouses or lunatic asylums. Specialized asylums were few in number by 1922,[60] and most of those afflicted were still looked after at home, though poverty and old age could make this impossible.

Can anything good be said about institutions in Ireland over this period? First of all, lives were undoubtedly saved by them. The workhouse in particular established the standard of a basic diet. Second, if the asylum was abused by those wanting to get rid of 'inconvenient' relatives, it was also used for its proper purpose – by wives wanting respite from violent or alcoholic husbands, by families terrorised by the unpredictable rages of one member, by people tormented with mental illness needing a sanctuary.[61] Many long-stay patients in nineteenth-century Ballinasloe asylum, according to Walsh, had relatives who were deeply concerned about them, visiting and writing regularly.[62] Third, the workhouse splitting up of families and the incarceration of children in correctional institutions could have been, for victims of domestic cruelty, neglect or starvation, the first respite they had had for years.

Notes

1 See Simon Community of Ireland, *Closing Down the County Homes* (Dublin 1980); when county homes stopped housing the homeless in the late 1970s, the results were catastrophic.

2 The three main works on lunatic asylums in Ireland are Mark Finnane, *Insanity and the Insane in Post-Famine Ireland* (London 1982); Joseph Robins, *Fools and Mad: a history of the insane in Ireland* (Dublin 1986); and Joseph Reynolds, *Grangegorman: psychiatric care in Dublin since 1815* (Dublin 1992).

3 See e.g. the debate by the contributors to Joseph Melling and Bill Forsythe (eds), *Insanity, Institutions and Society 1800–1914: a social history of madness in comparative perspective* (London 1999).

4 Robins, *Fools and Mad*, p. 146; Finnane, *Insanity and the Insane*, pp. 230–1.

5 Malcolm, 'Strident shadows'.

6 *Judicial Statistics (Ireland) 1873* (1874) [c. 1034], Vol. 71, p. 51.

7 Oonagh Walsh, 'The designs of providence: race, religion and Irish insanity', in Melling and Forsythe (eds), *Insanity, Institutions and Society*, pp. 323–41.

8 Elaine Showalter, *The Female Malady: women and madness in English culture 1830–1980* (London 1987).

9 Finnane, *Insanity and the Insane*, pp. 230–1 and generally.

10 Michael Ignatieff, *A Just Measure of Pain: the penitentiary in the industrial revolution* (London 1978); Michel Foucault, *Discipline and Punish* (London 1977); V. A. C. Gatrell, *The Hanging Tree: execution and the English People 1770–1868* (London 1994); Brian Henry, *Dublin Hanged* (Dublin 1994); Tim Carey, *Mountjoy: the story of a prison* (Cork 2000); and Geraldine Curtin, *The Women of Galway Jail: female criminality in nineteenth-century Ireland* (Galway 2001).

11 Carey, *Mountjoy*.

12 Curtin, *Women of Galway Jail*, pp. 61–2, 56–7.

13 *Thirty-Third Report of Inspectors-General of Prisons in Ireland 1854–55* (1956), Vol. 26, pp. 42–3 and generally; *Fifty-Third Report of Inspectors-General of Prisons in Ireland 1874–1875* (1876) [c.173], Vol. 37, pp. 82–3 and generally; *Eighth Report of General Prisons Board of Ireland 1885–1886* (1886) [c. 4817], Vol. 65, p. 109 and generally.

14 Carey, *Mountjoy*, pp. 95–102: Carolyn Conley, 'No pedestals: women and violence in late nineteenth-century Ireland', *Journal of Social History*, Vol. 28, No. 4 (summer 1995), pp. 801–18, and *Melancholy Accidents: the meaning of violence in post-Famine Ireland* (Lanham 1999).

15 *Forty-First Report of Inspectors-General of Prisons in Ireland 1862* (1863) [3214] Vol. 23, p. 363; Curtin, *Women of Galway Jail*.

16 Carey, *Mountjoy*, p. 124; *Seventeenth Annual Report of General Prisons Board 1894–5* (1895) [c.7806], Vol. 65, p. 967.

17 On the Poor Laws in Britain before 1834, and after, K. Snell, *Annals of the Labouring Poor* (Cambridge 1985) is about the best.

18 On workhouses in Ireland, see Helen Burke, *The People and the Poor Law in Nineteenth-Century Ireland* (Dublin 1987); Gerard O'Brien, 'The new Poor Law in pre-Famine Ireland: a case history', *Irish Economic and Social History*, Vol. 12 (1985), pp. 33–49; and Virginia Crossman, *Local Government in Nineteenth-Century Ireland* (Belfast 1994).

19 *Freeman's Journal*, 22 February 1855.

20 McLoughlin, 'Superfluous and unwanted deadweight: the emigration of Irish pauper women'.

21 See e.g. some of the comments in minutes of evidence in the *Report of the Select Committee to Inquire into the Relief of the Poor in Ireland* (1861) [408, 408.1], Vol. 11, p. 647.

22 Joseph Robins, *The Lost Children: a study of charity children in Ireland 1700–1900* (Dublin 1987 [1980]), pp. 271–91.

23 Burke, *The People and the Poor Law*.

24 Dympna McLoughlin, 'Workhouses and Irish female paupers 1840–1870', in M. Luddy and C. Murphy (eds), *Women Surviving* (Dublin 1990), pp. 117–47.

25 Christine Kinealy, 'The workhouse system in Co. Waterford 1838–1923', in W. Nolan and T. Power (eds), *Waterford: history and society* (Dublin 1992), pp. 541–78.

26 O Cathaoir, 'Wicklow'.

27 P. Foley, 'The Carlow Workhouse', *Carloviana: Journal of the Old Carlow Society*, Vol. 47 (December 1999), pp. 7–13.

28 O Cathaoir, 'Wicklow', p. 523; Michelle McGoff-McCann, *Melancholy Madness: a coroner's casebook* (Cork 2003), pp. 25–6.

29 *Return of names of Unions in which a third meal is not allowed daily to healthy inmates ... (1867–68)* [322], Vol. 61, Reports and correspondence.

30 Robins, *Lost Children*, pp. 287–9.

31 Rossiter, 'The life of a Wexford gentleman 100 Years Ago'.

32 *Return of infants born in Irish workhouses and attempted to be reared there 1872–4 (1878–79)* [245], Vol. 61, p. 173.

33 Rossiter, 'The life of a Wexford gentleman 100 years ago'.

34 *Freeman's Journal*, 23 February 1906.

35 *Fifth Report of Inspector of Reformatory Schools of Ireland June 1866* (1866) [3691], Vol. 38, Appendix 1, p. 22.

36 See M. J. F. McCarthy, *Priests and People in Ireland* (London 1902), pp. 455–6, and his objections to 'little vagrant children being maintained at the public expense', made throughout. Mrs Bosanquet, *Rich and Poor* (London 1896), pp. 170–4, believed that some parents deliberately abandoned their children so as to get them into industrial schools and reformatories. See also Jane Barnes, *Irish Industrial Schools 1868–1908* (Dublin 1989); and Robins, *Lost Children*.

37 The main source for industrial schools is Barnes, *Irish Industrial Schools*; Robins, *Lost Children*, is also very informative.

38 Clear, *Nuns in Nineteenth-Century Ireland*; Luddy, *Women and Philanthropy*.

39 *Thirteenth Report of Inspector of Reformatory and Industrial Schools in Ireland 1874* (1875) [c.1222], Vol. 36, pp. 14–16; *Twenty-Second Report of the Inspector Appointed to Visit Reformatory and Industrial Schools, Ireland 1883* (1884) [c.4163], Vol. 44, pp. 9–12.

40 *Annual Reports of the Inspectors of Reformatory and Industrial Schools of Ireland 1869–1886*; for 'unannounced' visits, see Barnes, Irish Industrial Schools, pp. 51–4.

41 *Thirteenth Report*, pp. 32–60.

42 *Twenty-Second Report*, pp. 32–95.

43 McCarthy, *Priests and People in Ireland*, pp. 455–6.

44 Barnes, *Irish Industrial Schools*, pp. 79–80.

45 *Twenty-Second Report*, pp. 41–2.

46 Ibid., p. 89.

47 Carey, *Mountjoy*, pp. 77–9.

48 Quoted from an inspector's report in 1865 in Sr Mary Pauline, *God Wills It: the centenary story of the Sisters of St Louis* (Dublin 1959), pp. 168–9.

49 Charles Dickens, *Bleak House* (London 1862), p. 192 (Everyman edn).

50 Luddy, *Women and Philanthropy*, pp. 97–148. Clear, *Nuns in Nineteenth-Century Ireland*, pp. 100–34; and the classic by Finnegan, *Do Penance or Perish*; 'Clay' is in James Joyce's *Dubliners* (London 1914).

51 Burke, *The People and the Poor Law.*

52 Luddy, *Women and Philanthropy*, pp. 97–148

53 Finnegan, *Do Penance or Perish.*

54 Sara Atkinson, *Mary Aikenhead, Her Life, Her Work, Her Friends* (Dublin 1878), pp. 468–9.

55 McCarthy, *Priests and People*, p. 421 (emphasis in original).

56 Peter Murray, 'A militant among the Magdalens?, *Saothar*, Vol. 20 (1995), pp. 41–54.

57 See annual reports of prisons, cited in notes 15–16 above.

58 *Freeman's Journal*, 14 July 1897.

59 They were not supposed to be; like policemen, people from outside the area were preferred. But looking at the local prison staff so obligingly identified in the reports up to the 1880s, there are often surnames associated with that locality, and also several of the same names over the years; see notes 14–18 above.

60 Joseph Robins, *From Reflection to Integration: a centenary of service by the Daughters of Charity to persons with a mental handicap* (Dublin 1992), pp. 27–8.

61 Diana Gittins, *Madness in its Place: narratives of Severalls Hospital 1913–1997* (London 1998); some elderly long-stay patients refer in this oral history to an institution similar to those in Ireland which they found a safe haven.

62 Oonagh Walsh, '"Tales from the big house": the Connacht District Lunatic Asylum in the late nineteenth century', *History Ireland*, Vol. 13, No. 6 (2005), pp. 21–6.

8

Extreme poverty: vagrants and prostitutes

Vagrants and prostitutes were among those who would have been described as 'poor' by everyone, including labourers and casual workers. As targets of repression and recipients of relief, they were in regular contact with government and voluntary agencies of the time. Vagrancy or wandering homelessness in Ireland and in Britain was seen as such an ongoing social problem that it prompted a special government commission in 1906; social panic about prostitution happened a little earlier, in the 1860s and 1870s, flaring and fading at intervals for the remainder of the period.

Vagrancy and homelessness

For being drunk and wandering about in suspicious circumstances and being a stranger in Macroom.[1]

Although, over time, many other offences were grafted onto it, vagrancy was essentially the crime of 'wandering abroad without visible means of support'; the crime was having no place of lodging and no money. Masterless men on the move have always been targeted by police. The huge and rapid rise of population all over Europe at the end of the eighteenth century and the newfound mobility of the very poor due to economic change sparked everywhere a new concern about vagrancy.[2] During the Famine, the Poor Law Amendment Act of 1847 made it a vagrancy offence to go from one Union to another seeking relief.[3]

The Poor Law Commissioners noted in 1856 'an almost total disappearance of deaths by the roadside through want of the necessities of life'. At this stage the authorities were still trying to distinguish between the respectable and the disreputable homeless poor. One observer writing from the north-east distinguished four distinct kinds of vagrants – professional beggars exposing deformities (real or faked); young, able-bodied beggars extorting money from a terrified populace; single homeless people rendered destitute by the Famine who preferred wandering to 'the restraints of the workhouse'; and mothers with children 'abandoned' by the head of the family. (Women begging with their children while their husbands were away on seasonal work or, indeed, begging on their own account were a common phenomenon in eighteenth-century Europe.[4]) Another observer, from Leinster, noted the decline of wandering homeless people and attributed this to the workhouse, 'because it is now generally felt and known that everyone who can work and is willing to work can live by the hire of their labour'. All noted a decline in the number of what they called 'professional beggars'.[5] It is hard to know what to make of these classifications, or of the belief – supported by the folklore – that there was a distinct group of disabled homeless people who lived off alms and their wits, had a strong, self-confident identity and were known as *bacaigh* (literally, lame people). Certainly the disabled always had a sense of entitlement about receiving alms as they were, in all societies down through the centuries, the archetypal 'deserving poor', on a par with 'the widow and the orphan',[6] but whether they were as confident or, indeed, as organized as this (some accounts claim that *bacaigh* held their AGM in Ballyvourney, Co.Cork, every year) is open to question. All accounts from the 1850s describe the mobile poor – petty dealers, pedlars, disabled and mentally afflicted people, and tradespeople. The perennial migrant worker was also a recognisable figure. One observer in 1861, who speculated (using the degeneracy theories which were coming into vogue at the time) that *bacaigh* were probably 'the slime or dregs of society', insisted on the need to differentiate between kinds of mobility so that the honest, destitute wayfarer looking for work would not be penalized.[7] But it is not at all clear that the homeless or vagrant could be so easily divided into the pathetic and the parasitical.

The early 1850s was a time of huge social upheaval and public order concern, when vagrants made up between a quarter and a half of those imprisoned in Clonmel and Galway. These were mostly teenage boys and men under 25, but occasionally older men and mothers with small children. Boys were hauled in in groups, like the 6 young men sent to Clonmel jail on July 3 1852, aged 24, 16 (2), 15 (2) and 14. Three months was the maximum sentence for vagrancy offences. By the end of the 1850s the proportion of vagrants committed to jail dwindled sharply.[8] The judicial statistics for 1866 noted a 'very satisfactory' decrease in the quantity of tramps and vagrants 'as the numbers of this class had been increasing for several years'.[9] The emphasis in the 1860s was on getting homeless people within walls of some sort. The category 'night-lodger' in workhouses was introduced in the early 1860s to cater in particular for people on the move. Nearly a third (30 per cent) of those admitted to the Thurles workhouse from 28 November to 11 December 1866 were put down as chargeable to the 'Union at large' meaning that they did not have an address in the Union. Most stayed only one night.[10] The Dublin Metropolitan Police instruction book published in 1865 advised officers to refrain from arresting those they suspected of vagrancy, directing them to the nearest workhouse instead.[11]

The Reformatories Act of 1858 played its part in reducing the numbers of homeless youths sent to jail. In Galway prison in 1861, a good half of the vagrants committed were 50 years of age and over, and the youngest was 25.[12] In the 1860s the old, the blind and the disabled often ended up in prison, like the 85-year-old blind man sent to Athy jail in 1862.[13] In the 1870s renewed concern about people on the move would lead to a rise in prosecutions of the young and able-bodied but in the 1860s the police (obviously supported and encouraged by the general public) directed their attention to the older cultural phenomenon of the disabled beggar.

It is unlikely that the antecedents of the people we now know as 'Travellers' were those steadily persecuted as vagrants. In the figures which police kept in the 1860s on 'known tramps and vagrants', children under 12 make up less than a quarter of the total number – had families been counted, children would have made up a greater proportion of the total. Travellers, moreover, went about in family groups, so the father of the family was clearly not leaving his wife and children to become a burden to others, which was always one of the primary objections to homeless men. Also, Travellers carried the tools of a trade (usually that of tinker or tinsmith) or goods to sell, so that even if they combined those trades with a little begging, as most did, they were not 'wandering abroad without visible means of support'. Travellers usually had strong identification with one part of the country or another;[14] crucially, they were *known*, and it was the unknown homeless person who was feared. The Industrial Schools Act of 1868 and later amendments to it empowered police to take children away from 'unsuitable' guardians – thieves, prostitutes and vagrants – but this was not generally applied to Traveller children. Individual Travellers ended up in jail on vagrancy charges, and individual Traveller children in industrial schools. There is a reference to two 'tinker' girls in the St Louis Reformatory for Girls in the 1860s.[15] But Travellers *per se* were not targeted. Indeed, until compulsory schooling (introduced only in 1892) had had a generation to take root, the cultural differences between Travellers and non-Travellers of a similar income level would not have been marked. Customs for which Travellers came (rightly or wrongly) to be notable in twentieth-century Ireland – early marriage, children trained in the family trade without formal schooling, strong family loyalty, strong local identity, occasional recreational violence[16] – were common in the general population until the late nineteenth century. By the early twentieth century, some Travellers were using the workhouse as a temporary stopover in bad weather or for childbirth. Was this a new development? Did travelling people survive as a distinct group because they used the workhouse or because they avoided it? There are also non-Roma (Gypsy) travelling people in Britain (not only transplanted Irish ones), which suggests that the Poor Law (similar in both countries) was instrumental in creating or maintaining these quasi-nomadic people.[17] It would be indeed ironic if an institution designed to curb proud and independent poverty ended up fostering it! Irish Travellers also have the same kinds of surnames and, often, trades as non-Travellers, so it is impossible to track them in the records.[18]

In the Vagrancy Act of 1871, the definition of *vagrancy* was broadened from begging, wandering abroad, being an incorrigible rogue and lodging in the open air to include loitering near warehouses, possessing picklocks and other instruments of burglary, telling fortunes and gaming. Not just people without money but those who seemed to be about to gain money by illegal means were targeted by the legislation. Nineteenth-century fears that a 'criminal class' would infect the rest of society, morally and physically, were reflected in this legislation. Vagrants, because of their mobility and idleness, seemed to be the vanguard of this 'criminal class'.

Poor Law records, workhouse admissions and judicial statistics all suggest a rise in wandering homelessness after 1875 (tables A9a, A9b and A10, Appendix). Numbers of night-lodgers might have risen because there was room in any given workhouse, due to a fall in the numbers of local people using it on a long-stay basis – rising numbers could indicate increased sympathy rather than increased incidence. But, by the same token, a rise in vagrancy prosectuions could indicate increased vigilance on the part of the police. It seems that both sympathy and persecution intensified at the same time, and that vagrants were seen as both pitiful and dangerous. After all, two government commissions of the early twentieth century, the Commission on Vagrancy (1906) and the Royal Commission on the Care and Control of the Feeble-minded (1908), linked vagrancy, or wandering homelessness, to 'feeble-mindedness' and 'degeneracy', so-called hereditary traits that were greatly feared.[19] Vagrancy prosecutions and convictions were always highest in the cities, particularly in Dublin. There were never as many in Belfast, probably because it was an urban economy which did not attract casual workers and would-be workers. Outside of this fairly predictable fact, prosecutions of vagrants were consistently highest in the prosperous regions of Leinster and Munster, and parts of Ulster. Kilkenny, Kildare, Tipperary South, Cork East and Kerry, and, less markedly, Meath, Clare, Tyrone, Down, Limerick and Westmeath, showed consistently high proportions (relative to the total petty crime) of prosecutions of people for begging, sleeping out and wandering abroad without visible means of support. Examination of the distribution of police shows no inevitable connection between police density and the prosecution of vagrants. Nor was it that police used the extended powers of the new Act of 1871 to prosecute agrarian offences: Connacht, the heart of the land agitation, did not see a rise in vagrancy prosecutions in the 1880s and 1890s. In 1884 there was only one vagrant committed to Castlebar Prison, a 41-year-old native New Yorker. Few mobile homeless people went to Connacht, and vagrants imprisoned in other parts of the country were only very rarely from the western province.[20] Seasonal migration from Connacht to fertile parts of Ireland and to Britain may have meant that Connacht people on the move were treated with less suspicion than those from other parts of the country whence no such systematic mobility emanated.

One Poor Law Inspector in 1887 attributed the rise in night-lodgers in workhouses to the depression in trade; certainly, an increasing number of artisans feature in both workhouses, as night-lodgers, and prisons, as vagrants, from 1875.[21] Of workhouse inmates *in toto* (not just night-lodgers) 5.5 per cent were artisans on

April 5 1891, and by 30 March 1901 their proportion of the total of workhouse inmates had risen to 8 per cent.[22] Trades were hard-hit by factory mass production and commercial distribution all over the Western world. The 30-year-old sawyer, born in Wicklow, who got one month in Clonmel in 1885 for 'wandering abroad', may have been finding it hard to get work, but the 76-year-old shoemaker from Bandon, locked up in Cork jail in 1882 for begging, was in a more pathetic position, as his age would have prevented him from getting a labouring job. Some travelled long distances to find work or to avoid acquaintances due to shame or cunning: a 26-year-old tailor from Thomastown, Co. Kilkenny, got fourteen days in Castlebar Prison in 1894 for 'begging on the streets of Newport', as did a cork-cutter from Newry of around the same age. Labourers however, made up the majority of homeless people who passed within the portals of workhouse and prison – of 17 people imprisoned for vagrancy in Carrick-on-Shannon prison in 1877, only 4 were artisans; the rest were labourers. A 25-year-old labourer, originally of Waterford, but of no fixed place of residence, arrested in Kanturk in 1882, and sent to Cork County Prison, is typical.[23]

Other people likely to be arrested as vagrants or relieved in workhouses were pedlars, ex-soldiers and sailors, and the mentally and physically handicapped. Sometimes the latter were treated with sympathy by the general public, sometimes not. It would be a mistake to see police prosecuting unfortunate homeless people, Poor Law officials grudgingly giving them relief, and people sheltering and loving them. The police, after all, acted on complaints from the public. The folklore records often recall the homeless with affection and insist that hospitality was an everyday social obligation, but there are some notes of wariness. One Mayoman noted that women on their own (a common feature of Mayo life when the men were away on seasonal work) were often very nervous of homeless men of erratic disposition – as well they might be.[24] Old pedlars, old women selling holy pictures and individual, eccentric, 'harmless' men are remembered with affection. Groups of young able-bodied men do not feature in nostalgic reminiscence. Many of those who ended up in Cork Prison were arrested in Kanturk, a big hiring town where the first labourers' trade union was formed in 1874. Farmers, shopkeepers and property-owners, when they felt threatened, were more likely to complain about men 'wandering abroad'. The rise in vagrancy prosecutions from 1875 is no doubt associated with the cultural changes of these years, when the standard of living rose and people (of all classes) became more vigilant about their property. But it could also indicate a fear and resentment of more confident and outspoken labourers, who had the temerity to reject farmers' offers of employment.

The homeless person was also increasingly likely to be a 'stranger' in the place he or she was arrested. In Clonmel, Cork and Galway prisons, in the 1850s and 1860s, nearly all vagrants were from the immediate locality, but as time went on more long-distance wanderers appeared: 15 of the 22 vagrants committed to Clonmel Prison in 1905 were from Tipperary and the surrounding counties of Waterford, Cork and Kilkenny, but the other 7 came from Roscommon, Wicklow, Donegal, Kildare, and Birmingham. There were also the occasional exotics, like the 27-year-old 'Mahometan' locked up in Cork in 1877, and two Italian men, aged 30 and 39, who got a month for begging in Cork in 1874.[25]

There were also female vagrants (apart from prostitutes), usually women who travelled within a limited circuit and ended up in the same prison maybe 3–4 times a year. Typical of the earlier period was Eliza Wilson, aged 21, and unusually a Protestant, who was sent to Athy Prison in January 1858 for vagrancy and breach of the peace, and again, in March of the same year, for vagrancy and 'exposing her person on the public street indecently'.[26] A woman of 49 who got 14 days for vagrancy in Cork county jail in November 1877 had been in jail 5 times before for the same offence; a 50-year-old Ballina woman who was sent to Castlebar Prison 4 times in 1888 and 4 times in 1889, cropped up again, times without number, in the 1890s.

Most of those arrested as vagrants were men, however, especially as time went on. It was not that women faced destitution and extreme poverty less often than men, but that state and voluntary institutions were more inclined to help females than males. A young, healthy male was by definition employable, and if he happened to be mobile and destitute the burden of proof of his 'innocence' and good intentions was placed squarely on him. Girls and women were helped because of the fear that they would become pregnant (thus adding to the numbers of dependent poor) or take to prostitution. Women with children, particularly widows, were always objects of sympathy, and a Poor Law official could get into serious trouble for turning away an exhausted woman and her hungry children. The Poor Law itself was amended in the 1850s to allow outdoor relief to widows with young children, which cut down on their mobility.[27] There were also far more voluntary and charitable organizations catering to females than to males, charity schools, hostels for working girls, even Magdalen asylums. The philanthropic activity of upper-middle-class women (nuns and lay-women of all religions) was at its height, and poor females were the focus of their concern. This kind of relief, and low-paid service employment available to girls and women, kept them in one place rather than moving them around. The kind of employment available to males moved them from place to place, as freelance agricultural and construction workers, and the only kind of poor relief they could get was as night-lodgers going in search of work. T. Jones Hughes mentions clusters of poor female-headed households, particularly in Waterford and Wexford, who lived in small, tumbledown settlements on main arterial roads, their menfolk evidently on the road in search of work or subsistence.[28]

There was little difference between the workhouse night-lodger who was considered deserving of a bed for a night or two, and the vagrant, imprisoned for anything from a week to three months. Had the prosecuted vagrant used abusive or aggressive language, that would have been mentioned in the charge; threatening behaviour, breach of the peace and using foul language were occasionally mentioned alongside the charge of vagrancy, but in the main they were not. A labourer or a tradesman of whatever age and level of ability or disability could end up in either workhouse or prison, according to the disposition of the countryside or town at the time and the mood of the arresting or relieving officer. People on the move had to be extra careful, too, not to be charged with 'going from one Union to another seeking relief', as were the 4 men and 2 women, all in their thirties, sent to Castlebar Prison on the same day in October 1892. All were from different parts of the country – Tralee, Co. Wicklow, Dublin city, Cavan, Limerick city and Waterford. The sheer unlikelihood of their finding work in Mayo at that time is probably why they were charged rather than relieved in the workhouse as 'honest wayfarers'.

The numbers using the workhouse as 'night-lodgers' rose significantly in the first decade of the twentieth century (see table 11, Appendix): 92 'tramps' visited Dunshaughlin workhouse in one week in February 1905, and as many as 100 during a week in April.[29] Cullen tells us that William Bulfin met a tramp in 1907 who complained that there was not the same feeling in the people for a beggarman any more. What Cullen does not tell us is that Bulfin was at one with the people on this subject:

> He was the only beggarman I met during the whole of the month. When I was a lad the country was infested with them. I was glad to note the change that had taken place in this respect.

The man, whom he met in Knockshigowna, Co. Tipperary, lacked even a decent hard-luck story with which to amuse Bulfin.[30] The Montreal-born travelling clown and musician who had served time in the East Lancashire Regiment and was sent to Castlebar Prison in 1901 might have had a more colourful tale, but most destitute people on the move went round and round a shrinking circle of deprivation as monotonous as it was debilitating.

A well-known woman of bad character – the prostitute

Prostitution was a vagrancy offence, and women could be arrested for 'prostitution' just as men (and women) were arrested for vagrancy. The prostitute, like the vagrant, was charged with a state-of-life rather than an act, with being rather than doing. ('Soliciting' was a separate crime.[31]) Most towns and cities had their *own* prostitutes, women who were well-known to the police and the people; garrison and port towns were particularly notorious. Yet it is very difficult to track the incidence of prostitution through the judicial records. In 1866, for example, 3,848 women appeared in court for prostitution in Dublin city, 28 in Cork city, 8 in Waterford, 82 in Kildare (the biggest garrison in the country) but only 8 in Belfast, and none in Derry. Can it be true that prostitution was almost unknown in the cities of the north, or was limited to the smaller towns of Tyrone (where 30 women were prosecuted) and Down (50)? If so, what happened in the succeeding half-century or so to push the numbers in Belfast up to 453, and to shrink the Dublin numbers to 787? A more likely explanation is that police, acting on complaints from the general public and directives from above, clamped down on these women in some years and left them alone in others. Rising population and economic uncertainty in Belfast could have inflated the numbers of visible and actual prostitutes in the intervening years, but it is highly unlikely that they were as few in number in 1866 as the prosecutions would suggest.

It seems (we cannot be certain) that far more women worked as prostitutes in Ireland in the 1850s and 1860s than at the end of the century. The police count was 13,076 'known prostitutes' in 1866. One historian argues that prostitutes as such did not exist, and that observers tended to ascribe the label 'prostitute' to women behaving in a disorderly manner in public places.[32] But women themselves, brought before the courts, often gave their occupation as prostitute. O Murchadha suggests that prostitution was so much a part of urban life that it went all-but unremarked, unless prostitutes were involved in fights or other crimes.[33] Another body of historical opinion argues that the numbers of prostitutes in the records are a vast under-statement, that hundreds of thousands more women were involved in this way of life than we can ever know;[34] many contemporaries shared this belief, in a familiar blend of moral panic and sexual fantasy. However, it is almost impossible to get accurate numbers of prostitutes in the past. The police in Ireland believed that the numbers of 'known prostitutes' had shrunk to 7,999 by 1873, and certainly the number of prosecutions showed a matching decline in that decade and thereafter, though they rose again in the first decade of the twentieth century. At this stage, Dublin was believed to be the pros-titution capital of Europe, with one side of Sackville Street/O'Connell Street allegedly given over to women plying this trade.[35]

Were prostitutes getting more desperate for business or just bolder, venturing into public thoroughfares? The large increase in the number of women in the urban workplace – in offices, shops and businesses – made prostitutes touting for business unacceptable in a way that they had not been before. Women of all social classes were going unchaperoned and unaccompanied in the city streets; a woman did not want to brush up against prostitutes or, worse, be mistaken for one. Such a mistake would have been difficult to make in the 1850s and 1860s: one account describes Cork prostitutes in these years as 'bare-headed and bare-breasted, in coloured dresses, dis-porting themselves at the quay end of [North] Street'.[36] ('Bare-breasted' means without a kerchief or other covering for the upper part of the chest.) Perhaps prostitutes began to dress more discreetly by the end of the nineteenth century. Prosecution of prostitutes was stepped up in the first decade of the twentieth century – in 1900 no woman in Cork city was brought before the courts for this crime, but 10 years later 128 women were, and the numbers in Dublin and Belfast also increased.[37] Popular tolerance was falling. Kevin Kearns's oral history of Dublin in the 1910s and early 1920s recalls the 'unfortunate girls' (as locals called them) of Dublin's prostitution district as virtual prisoners in the 'kip-houses', throwing down money to the children to buy them cigarettes and other articles in the shops.[38]

Most research on Irish prostitutes focuses on the institutions which tried to change them.[39] We know little about their backgrounds, except the bare, unadorned facts we can glean from prison records. Many were illiterate, like the 34-year-old woman from Cashel who spent 14 days in Clonmel Prison in February 1885.[40] Research in France and Germany shows that most prostitutes came from casual labouring backgrounds, the class most vulnerable to economic change (*les filles du peuple*); but some came from broken-down artisan backgrounds, with a tradition of independence and an aversion to working for anyone else.[41] They began their working lives around the age of 16, and many had lost one or both parents at an early age. However, as some contemporaries pointed out, if a prostitute took care of herself and went for regular check-ups – syphilis and gonorrhea were curable in the nineteenth century – she could save some money from her earnings and move on.[42] This way of life was neither necessarily permanent nor a death-sentence.

Prostitutes were always plentiful in towns where there were large numbers of single men passing through, with money in their pockets, and a shortage of regular female employment. The regular job, however poorly paid, was the strongest insurance against prostitution, which is why there were more prostitutes in Limerick than in Derry, in Dublin than in Belfast. Finnegan quotes one source for the late nineteenth century according to which most prostitutes were 'feeble-minded', but it was a common belief at that time that only 'defective' women could thus 'pervert' what was seen to be women's 'true nature'. Indeed, it was also believed that male (and female) vagrants were defective and feeble-minded.[43] However, unprotected women with learning disabilities fell easily into this way of life; whether they would have been more contented or better treated as 'idiots' in workhouse, lunatic or Magdalen asylum, we will never know.

Judges and magistrates were often more sympathetic to prostitutes than were doctors, policemen, social reformers and the general public; Conley tells us that Irish judges in the nineteenth century dealt seriously with the crime of raping a prostitute, often handing down severe prison sentences to the perpetrators.[44]

Conclusion

The male vagrant provoked contempt not only because he was a 'masterless man' but because he was not master even of his own house. Seen to be running out on responsibilities (real or imagined), he was also – by being reduced to begging and pleading – a pathetic, unsexed creature. There were fewer female vagrants because statutory and voluntary relief agencies were more sympathetic to women in general, though there *were* women on the move, often with their menfolk. Prostitutes' movements as they plied their trade were of the utmost importance, and that is why most countries at the end of the nineteenth century brought in laws limiting them to certain parts of towns. Such laws did not exist in Britain or Ireland, but the invasion of 'respectable' urban space by prostitutes was resisted strongly, and Dublin had developed a *de facto* red-light district by 1900. Vagrants were seen as spreading disease (they were suspected of introducing smallpox to Galway in the 1880s, for example[45]) but also of infecting the working class with the germ of idleness. Prostitutes were feared as sources of sexually-transmitted disease and immorality. These way-of-life 'criminals' had a social impact out of all proportion to their numbers. Vagrants were often considered potentially violent and were often scapegoated for crimes – rural arson for example; prostitutes, on the other hand, had more opportunity than most for 'stealing from the person' as they consorted, by definition, with men with money in their pockets. Yet those vagrants who were caught do not seem to have been particularly calculating or malevolent. Even after the amended legislation of 1871, nearly all those prosecuted as vagrants were charged with the traditional offences of begging or wandering abroad. The numbers charged with the new offences of loitering, possessing picklocks, or other directly criminal activities were infinitesimal, statistically invisible.[46]

Prostitutes were subjected to quite energetic persecution by working-class and artisan townspeople in eighteenth-century Ireland, while wandering beggars in pre-Famine Ireland were often hunted and persecuted.[47] Life on the margins was always difficult, uncomfortable and disease-prone; there was never a 'golden age' when women offering their bodies for hire and men and women on the move were accepted and tolerated. By the early twentieth century, however, there was no longer any attempt to distinguish between *deserving* and *undeserving* people on the move – they were all undeserving.

Notes

1 Given as the grounds for vagrancy imprisonment, in Clonmel, 1883, of a 30-year-old Waterford-born dealer in rags and feathers, of 'no fixed place of residence': National Archives, Dublin, Clonmel Prison register 1883.

2 General works on vagrancy include D. J. V. Jones, *Crime, Protest, Community and Police in Nineteenth-Century Britain* (London 1982); Lionel Rose, *Rogues and Vagabonds: the vagrancy underworld in England 1815–1945* (London 1988).

3 Burke, *The People and the Poor Law*.

4 Hufton, *Eighteenth-century France*, pp. 318–53.

5 See *Reports and Communications on Vagrancy 1847–8* (987), Vol. 53; *Irish Poor Law Commissioners' Annual Report 1856*, pp. 14, 50–9.

6 IFC, Vol. 686, pp. 525–6, 578: Seán O Cróinín, *Seanchas Amhlaoibh Uí Luínse* (Baile Atha Cliath 1980), p. 134; G. Murphy, 'Bacaigh Baile Mhúirne', *Eigse*, Vol. 3 (1941), pp. 101–2.

7 W. Hackett, 'The Irish *bacach*, or professional beggar, viewed archeologically', *Ulster Journal of Archeology*, Vol. 9 (1861–62), pp. 255–71.

8 Galway and Clonmel prison registers.

9 *Judicial Statistics (Ireland), 1866* (1867) [3930], Vol. 66, pp. 9–10.

10 Indoor Register, Thurles Poor Law Union, consulted at Tipperary County Library, Thurles.

11 Inspector John Ward, *Instruction Book for the Dublin Metropolitan Police* (Dublin 1865), p. 148.

12 Galway Prison register – see chapter on institutions for information about reformatories.

13 Athy Prison register.

14 Any Traveller will tell you that there are those of their number who *belong* to specific parts of the country; Nan Joyce, *Traveller: an autobiography*, ed. Anna Farmar (Dublin 1987), pp. 1–5, discusses this.

15 See chapter 7, section on industrial schools.

16 Conley, *Melancholy Accidents*, pp. 17–50.

17 Judith Okely, *Traveller–Gypsies* (Cambridge 1983).

18 The following are some of the relevant sources: P. MacGréine, 'Irish "tinkers" or travellers', *Béaloideas*, Vol. 3 (1931–32), pp. 170–86; S. MacEinrí, 'Ceant agus saol na dtincéirí', ibid., Vol. 9 (1939), pp. 219–39; IFC, Vol. 1436, pp. 3–39, and Vol. 688, p. 141; J. Gow, 'The Irish tinkers', *Ulster Folklife*, Vol. 17 (1971); S. O Catháin, *Irish Life and Lore* (Cork 1982), pp. 76–89; Seán Maher, *The Road to God Knows Where* (Dublin 1972); Sharon Gmelch, *Nan: the life of an Irish Travelling woman* (New York 1986); A. Court et al., *Puck of the Droms: the lives and literature of the Irish Tinkers* (Berkeley, CA 1985); Joyce, *Traveller*; Mary O'Malley Madec, 'The Irish travelling woman: mother

and mermaid', in Ailbhe Smyth (ed.), *Irish Women's Studies Reader* (Dublin 1993); Jane Helleiner, *Irish Travellers: racism and the politics of culture* (Toronto 2000); University of Limerick, *Historical Resources for Research into the Social, Economic and Cultural History of the Irish Travelling Community* (Limerick 2005). The most recent and authoritative work is Aoife Bhreatnach, *Becoming Conspicuous: Irish travellers, society and the State* (Dublin 2006).

19 *Report of the Special Commission on Vagrancy 1906* (cd.2852, 2891), Vol. 103 (Appendix 14 refers to Ireland). *The Royal Commission on the Care and Control of the Feebleminded*, Vols 1–7 (Cd. 4215–21) (London 1908). On the rise in vagrancy prosecutions, see *Judicial Statistics (Ireland)*, 1866–1914, Returns of persons proceeded against for offences determined summarily, variously tables 9, 7, 16; and on the rise in night-lodger admissions to workhouses, see *Annual Reports of the Local Government Board Ireland*, 1870–1914. For the present study, numbers of prostitutes have been taken out of the vagrancy prosecutions and are looked at separately, below.

20 Prison registers, Clonmel, Athy, Castlebar, Cork, Galway,

21 Letter from Thomas Mooney to Local Government Board, 2 June 1887, cited in *Special Commission on Vagrancy*, Appendix 14, p. 88.

22 *Census of Ireland*, 1891, General report, table 131, pp. 443–5; *Census of Ireland*, 1901, General report, table 136, pp. 487–8.

23 Prison registers for Cork County Prison, Clonmel, Castlebar, Carrick-on-Shannon.

24 IFC, Vol. 688, pp. 137–44

25 Prison registers.

26 Athy Prison register

27 On charitable institutions for women, see Clear, *Nuns in Nineteenth-Century Ireland*; Luddy, *Women and Philanthropy*; and McLoughlin, 'Irish female paupers'.

28 T. Jones Hughes, 'Landholding and settlement in Co. Tipperary in the nineteenth century', in W. Nolan and T. McGrath (eds), *Tipperary: history and society* (Dublin 1985), pp. 339– 46; and 'Continuity and change in rural Wexford', in K. Whelan (ed.), *Wexford: history and society* (Dublin 1987), pp. 342–72.

29 Gilligan, 'Murrays of Dunshaughlin'.

30 Louis Cullen, *Life in Ireland* (Dublin 1968), pp. 155–6; Bulfin, *Rambles in Eirinn*, pp. 13–15.

31 Prostitution was a vagrancy offence – the numbers which follow here are taken from the *Judicial Statistics (Ireland)*, Tables of persons proceeded against summarily, 1866–1910; see notes 7 and 17.

32 Linda Mahood, *The Magdalenes: prostitution in the nineteenth century* (London 1990).

33 Ciaran O Murchadha, 'Paphian nymphs and worshippers of the Idalian goddess: prostitution in Ennis in the mid-nineteenth century', *The Other Clare*, Vol. 27 (2000), pp. 32–6.

34 E.g. Ronald Pearsall, *The Worm in the Bud: the world of Victorian sexuality* (London 1971).

35 Joseph V. O'Brien, *Dear, Dirty Dublin: a city in distress 1899–1914* (Berkeley, CA 1982); Murnane, 'Mountjoy Ward'; John Finegan, *The Story of Monto: an account of Dublin's notorious red-light district* (Cork 1978).

36 McCarthy, *Priests and People*, pp. 287–8.

37 *Judicial Statistics (Ireland)*, Tables of persons proceeded against summarily, 1866–1910.

38 Kearns, *Dublin Tenement Life*, pp. 69–70, 218–19 and generally.

39 Maria Luddy, 'Prostitution and rescue work in nineteenth-century Ireland', in Luddy and Murphy (eds), *Women Surviving*, pp. 51–84; Malcolm, 'Troops'; Finegan, *Do Penance or Perish*.

40 Clonmel Prison register; Curtin, *Women of Galway Jail*.

41 Alain Corbin, *Women for Hire: prostitution and sexuality in France after 1850* (Cambridge, MA 1990); R. J. Evans, 'Prostitution, state and society in imperial Germany', *Past and Present*, Vol. 70 (1976), pp. 106–29.

42 Walkowitz, *Prostitution and Victorian Society*.

43 Finnegan, *Do Penance or Perish*; see also *Royal Commission on Vagrancy*; *Royal Commission on Care and Control of the Feeble-Minded*; and Mark Jackson, *The Borderland of Imbecility: medicine, society and the fabrication of the feeble mind in late Victorian and Edwardian England* (Manchester 2000).

44 Conley, 'No pedestals'.

45 J. P. Murray, *Galway: a medico-social history* (Galway 1993), p. 107.

46 *Judicial Statistics (Ireland)*, Persons proceeded against for offences determined summarily, 1871–1920.

47 David Fleming, 'Public attitudes to prostitution in eighteenth-century Ireland', *Irish Economic and Social History*, Vol. 32 (2005), pp. 1–18; Laurence Geary, 'The whole country was in motion: mendicancy and vagrancy in pre-Famine Ireland', in Jacqueline Hill and Colm Lennon (eds), *Luxury and Austerity: historical studies 21* (Dublin 1999), pp. 121–36.

9

Houses, food, clothes

Houses

*Bhí áthas orainn go léir a bheith ag aistriú as an seana-pholl gránda
... Bhíomar múchta 'nár mbeathaidh istigh ann agus dá fheabhas a
dheineadh mo mháthair a dícheall chun é a choimeád slachtmhar do
theipeadh uirthe.*

(We were all glad to be moving out of the ugly old hole ... We were
smothered alive inside in it and however hard my mother tried to keep
it tidy, she couldn't manage it.)[1]

A combination of legislation, town planning and cultural change led
to the gradual disappearance of houses like those noted by Henry
Coulter in Scariff, Co. Clare, in 1861 – 'wretched-looking hovels
with fermented manure heaps outside' – and complained about by
health authorities in several parts of the country in 1873 as a 'fertile
source of zymotic disease'.[2] But the thatched house (with walls
sometimes of mud but, from the 1850s, more often of stone) could
be roomy, comfortable and snug, its cleanliness or otherwise
depending on the household's level of income and means of disposing
of waste. Thatch was reputedly warm in winter, cool in summer,
mud or stone walls were clean and strong under several layers of
whitewash or plaster, and clay floors were stamped down until they
were level and fairly clean. Various incentives to landlords and local
government from 1870 onwards made money available to build
labourers' houses. By the early 1890s, 94 out of 161 rural Poor Law
Unions had begun housing schemes, mostly in Munster and Leinster
where labourers' organizations were strong and clamorous. In
Connacht and Ulster, the Congested Districts Board in the 1890s
began to build solid 3- or 4-room slated houses, only recently
replaced by new bungalows, and provided money to improve existing

houses.[3] According to Bradley, nearly every house built since 1883 by local government or philanthropic organizations was still occupied in 1945, and Fraser tells us that two-thirds of the rural housing stock still occupied in the early 1960s had been built before 1914. In Enda McKay's memorable phrase, the early twentieth century was the period when the rural labourer was 'at last coming in from the cold'.[4]

Wealthy farmers built large houses with Georgian-type windows and fanlights, or invested in the more modest but solid two-storey slated houses still to be seen in the midlands and Munster. Farmers who could not afford this made themselves comfortable in the long, low, three-roomed, thatched or slated whitewashed houses, with out-buildings for animals on either side. In the 1870s and 1880s the poorest people began to banish the larger beasts from the living space, though cats, dogs and hens continued to come in and out until well into the twentieth century. The farmhouses which survived long enough to be 'preserved' and faithfully rebuilt were in parts of the country where a certain level of modest comfort prevailed among medium-sized dairy and tillage farmers – Wexford, Down, Tyrone, the Golden Vale, south Galway, Wicklow.[5] O Danachair, Gailey and Aalen classify these houses into various types, but all had large fireplaces and most had more than one room.[6] Kinmonth's meticulous study of the furniture of these dwellings reveals a multi-functional domestic interior, with as strong an aesthetic sense as was compatible with practicality.[7] Dressers with delph, mantelpiece ornaments and painted tables and chairs were starting to feature even in the poorest dwellings by the 1890s. While there were still people sleeping on straw in front of the fire, covered by clothes and shawls, the wooden box–bed had become popular enough in labourers' dwellings to be condemned by public health officials in 1872.[8] Localized traditions of carpentry and cabinet-making survived in parts of the country until well into the twentieth century.[9]

Some labourers' dwellings were built by companies and, less commonly, by landlords. Guinnesses in Dublin famously built many of the houses and flats in Dublin 7 and Dublin 8, and the Great Southern Railway was responsible for the rows of red-brick houses in Inchicore. Most towns with a railway station had between 4 and 8 'railway cottages'; prison workers and asylum attendants, too, often had tied houses.[10] The company houses built by Malcolmson, in Portlaw, Co. Waterford, are still occupied, as are those built in

Bushmills, Co. Antrim, and other company villages in the north. Fishery houses in Baltimore, Co. Cork, built in 1893, were a vast improvement on what had preceded them.[11]

Villa-style housing for upper-middle-class people was built in these years, and most of these large, three-storey houses still survive. Much more numerous, particularly in Dublin, Belfast, Limerick and Cork, were terraced, red-brick, three-bedroomed houses, catering for clerical workers, teachers and better-off artisans. These had three bedrooms, usually, a long kitchen, separate dining room and parlour, and sometimes an indoor bathroom and lavatory.[12] These were built in their thousands in the 1880s and 1890s near bus, tram and train routes. Kate O'Brien, with her usual snobbery, describes one of them, in Limerick, as 'a mean little brick villa . . .', but such houses have lasted just as long as their larger neighbours.[13]

Working-class housing was mixed in quality. Belfast had the best of all, with most of its working-class population in two-up, two-down (two rooms upstairs, two rooms downstairs) housing in 1911. There was also good housing in Dublin, though not enough of it, and it was relatively expensive; artisans as well as labourers often lived in the tenements. In 1900 over a third of Dublin's population lived in these one-room dwellings in Georgian houses, with about 5 or 6 families to a house. All water had to be carried up, all slops to be carried down. Bad as the tenements were – hot in summer, cold in winter, often infested with vermin – they were more healthful than the lanes and courts because the latter were right beside effluent and dirt. Most towns and cities had their lanes and courts; like the tenement-dwellers, those living there could pay up to a third of their income in rent. Proximity to docklands, the city centre and other sources of casual work was a priority in the days before public transport systems.

Drinking water came from a well or spring, and in towns, from a pump or tap. Cameron complained in the early 1870s about the uncertain quality of much town water. Rain-water, for washing, was gathered in a barrel in country dwellings. Buckets, chamber-pots and other receptacles did duty as toilets; in cities and towns these were emptied into the wet or dry latrine. (On one half-street in Tipperary town in 1901, according to Marnane, a single earth-closet served 36 families.[14]) The new villas and terraced houses usually had piped water and, sometimes, flush toilets; they were worlds away from rural life. There, a sheltered spot in the open air often sufficed, as the

Dublin cousin who asked for the toilet in a Kildare farmhouse around 1915, discovered:

> M'Cabe took him to the back door . . . 'There you are now *avic*', said he hospitably. 'The whole Bog of Allen is wide open to you.'[15]

Chamber-pots, used indoors, were usually emptied at some distance from the house. Throwing 'slops' out the front door seems to have been common among some people up to the 1870s, a habit of the very poor in Britain as well as in Ireland.[16] The better-off, with more household help and higher standards, or those who simply were naturally cleaner, had dungheaps some distance from the house, which after a year or so could be moved and used as manure. New houses built in the late nineteenth century always had a back door to facilitate the disposal of waste (not just the contents of chamber-pots, but dirty water, dregs of tea, cooking water and other liquids). The two-storey artisan's dwelling owned by Kilkenny Corporation, in which Mary Healy grew up, had a back and a front door at either end of the hall, a house-type also common in parts of Belfast. This arrangement was considered good for ventilation and the disposal of waste from the dry lavatory out the back, but it created a fierce draught.[17]

Food

> *Cuardóifidh mé bean agus spré duit*
> [. . .]
> *Is déanfaidh sí stampy is té duit.*
> (I'll find you a wife and a dowry
> [. . .]
> And she'll make stampy and tea for you.) (Traditional 'coaxing' sung to a child)

George Russell (AE) and the other food reformers of the early twentieth century would have approved of the stampy – described by Sexton as 'a deluxe version of boxty bread, made with cream, sweetened with sugar and spiced with caraway seeds'[18] – but not of the tea. Indeed, a moral panic about tea in Ireland in the 1890s and early 1900s blamed it for everything from lethargy to insanity.[19] There was also fear that oatmeal, buttermilk and potatoes would be edged out of the diet completely. These remained as mainstays of the rural diet for another fifty years at least, but tea, popular in cities,

towns and in the east since the early nineteenth century, and brought
to the more remote areas of the west by charming tea salesmen in the
1870s,[20] had come to stay.

The unavailability of food reduced the Irish population by over
2million between 1845 and 1851. Another crisis like the Famine of
the 1840s was never allowed to develop, and when famine threatened, in parts of western Mayo, Galway and Donegal in 1879–80,
in the late 1880s and again in the 1890s, resources were rushed to
the 'distressed' areas. Pockets of population were still almost totally
dependent upon the potato, but variety had been introduced into
most people's diets since 1850. Indian meal, or yellow meal,
introduced as famine-relief food, was used quite a lot in the second
half of the nineteenth century, but faded in popularity in the early
twentieth century. It was sometimes eaten as hot porridge or was left
cold and cut up and fried for tastiness. Oatmeal porridge was tastier,
more filling and certainly more traditional; easy to grow and to
harvest in the Irish climate, it long pre-dated the potato.[21] Oatcake
needed only hot water and salt, and was baked on a stand before the
fire; coarse oatmeal was fried with onions and bacon in parts of Ulster
as 'crushy'. Wheaten soda bread became popular as soon as people
were able to buy bicarbonate of soda in shops, and it had become the
most common kind of bread in the country by 1900. Until this
relatively inexpensive and handy raising agent appeared, leavening
was laborious and space-consuming. The buttermilk needed for soda
bread was plentiful for most of the year; when it was scarce, a buttermilk substitute, made with a combination of flour and raw and
mashed potatoes, was used. Indian meal was often used to
supplement white flour, and, according to one Ulster source, it
'lightened' soda bread – certainly it gives a distinctive flavour – and
was used also to make 'ashcakes' and other sweet buns of various
kinds. Oatmeal and potato were also mixed with wheaten flour to
make certain breads and cakes – farls, potato bread, boxty, potato
apple cake, reusel (a mixture of oatmeal and potatoes) and fadge.[22]
Bread was baked on the fire in a closed pan known in some parts of
the country as a 'bastable', or 'pot oven', but the popularity of 'drop'
scones and 'griddle' cakes – cooked on a hot pan over the fire –
illustrates the scarcity of cooking vessels in some households.
Florence Irwin, a cookery instructor for the Department of
Agriculture and Technical Instruction in Ulster between 1905 and
1913, describes this scarcity – and the ingenuity used to overcome it:

When I arrived in the kitchen there was no mixing bowl – only the basin
the 'wee fellas' washed their faces in – it also did duty for the dirty
dishes, no rolling pin, no bake board, no scales. She suggested that if I
return in twenty minutes all would be ready for me. In the meantime
the china flower-pot disappeared from the geranium in my window
. . . there it was on the well-scrubbed table to serve as my mixing bowl.
A length newly sawed off the window pole was my rolling pin . . .

Later, she learned to get a supply of the cheapest household utensils
she could find from the 'Penny Bazaar' in Belfast to bring with her to
rural areas, where they sold like the hot cakes they would be used
to make.[23]

Rural diet may have been monotonous, but it was healthful.
O Gráda's research suggests that nineteenth-century Irish men were
the tallest in Europe next to the Norwegians.[24] Height is not always
an indicator of health, but the Irish navvy, from the early nineteenth
until well into the twentieth century, was prized for his ability to
work hard, his strength and staying power, and Irish countrywomen
were also considered to be strong, able to carry loads (seaweed and
fish) on their heads, and to walk to market with eggs, butter and
sometimes live hens on their backs to sell. Potatoes, oatmeal, soda
bread and buttermilk were the staples, with a bit of bacon once
or twice a week, cabbage usually the only vegetable, and eggs at
particular times of the year. Onions were considered medicinal and
were seen as flavouring, rather than as a vegetable in themselves,
though they were used. There was a prejudice against turnips, which
were seen as animal feed, but people ate them too, though they might
have kept quiet about it. There was plenty of regional variation in the
diet. Coast-dwellers always ate fish, shellfish and even seaweed.[25]
Blasket Islanders ate puffin and cormorant,[26] midlanders feasted on
'salt ling' (fish) and river eel, northerners ate boxty (pancakes made
of raw, grated potato, mashed potato and flour), and ways of making
soda bread varied from one region to another – in some parts of the
country, caraway seed was used. Potatoes were eaten in a variety
of ways: in *Knocknagow*[27] Mat the Thresher's Tipperary family sit
down to a meal of potatoes and leeks, and a single herring for
flavouring, with roast potatoes as a delicious second course.

'Baker's bread', or yeast bread, became more popular towards the
end of the nineteenth century, because available in shops, and mass-
production techniques meant that it became cheaper (and less
nutritious). But for country people it was thought of more as an

occasional treat, spread with jam, 'like cake nowadays', according to oral evidence from the 1930s.[28] Vegetable variety was fairly poor, however. In rural Kildare, Maura Laverty, born in 1907, tells us (half-jokingly), only Protestants grew carrots, parsnips, beans and peas.[29] The Allen family in east Cork, of Quaker origin, are famous for their tradition of simple, home-grown, Irish food.[30] Prosperity over several generations instilled a self-confidence which did not shy away from using despised vegetables, herbs and offal; did Protestant big farmers have more of this confidence than their Catholic neighbours? In the country as a whole, middle-class rural Protestant women were in the vanguard of food preservation and reform, notably in the United Irishwomen, founded in 1912. They encouraged the growing of a variety of fruit trees and diversification in vegetables. This was most feasible on the large farms in Leinster, Ulster and parts of Munster, where some of the work of dairying had been taken away from the women and located in creameries, freeing time for this kind of cultivation, which had previously been possible only in big houses and large suburban gardens.[31]

Urban diet, in contrast, was at best precarious and at worst downright dangerous. Cameron tells several stories of rancid butter and bad meat causing severe food-poisoning, sometimes death, among artisan families in Dublin – the kind of people who could afford to eat meat daily, but not to guarantee its quality.[32] In towns and cities imaginative and ingenious ways of cooking and serving cheaper cuts of meat and offal, emerged – the Ulster fry, drisheens and crubeens in Cork, sausages, rashers and blood puddings in Limerick, skirts and kidneys, liver, tripe, brawn, hazlett, spiced beef at Christmas, kippers on fast days. It was here rather than in the country that 'one-pot' cooking was most common, because of the smallness of the fireplace, the scarcity of pots and the slowness of the fire – Dublin coddle (layered rashers, onions and potatoes) is one example, and Kearns's former tenement-dwellers recall cooking oxtail stews.[33] Town-dwellers, though they had access to a greater variety of food if they could pay for it, had one huge disadvantage compared to even the poorest rural people: they could not grow or rear their own food, and they had no ready or guaranteed access to clean milk. Many city children missed out on milk entirely in their formative years, and had no nutritional substitute for it. The quantity of urban food improved, especially for casual labouring people, between 1850 and 1922, with the overall rise in wages. However, as the accommodation of the poorest townspeople worsened over these years, the preparation and preservation of food suffered.

Clothing and appearance

There's no dress nowadays looks half so well on a man as the dress they used to wear in those days. They would wear knee-breeches of corduroy, a 'bawneen', a pair of low shoes and sheep grey stockings. It was the biggest pity you ever saw to do away with them. (The Tailor Buckley, Iveleary, Co. Cork to Eric Cross, c.1940)[34]

The Tailor Buckley's description recalls the 'knee-britches and coat of emerald green' of popular ballads,[35] the descriptions of Carleton, Lover, Lever, Boucicault and other writers revelling in the colourful and feckless stratum of Ireland's poorest, and the *Erin Go Bragh* postcards of the late nineteenth century. As late as the 1860s and 1870s, however, such clothing was still worn; although Edward O'Toole's artisan father, in Rathvilly, Co. Carlow, wore a coat of black cloth with a vest (waistcoat) and trousers of the same material for Sundays, and brown frieze and white corduroy on weekdays, without a waistcoat, old men still wore swallow-tailed coats, knee-breeches and home-knit grey stockings.[36] Charles McGlinchey, born in Inishowen, Co. Donegal, in 1861, gave detailed descriptions of such apparel as worn 'in my father's time'; Irish-speaking Donegal was probably more up-to-date than rural Leinster, given its proximity to Derry and links with the cities of Scotland.[37]

Change in many parts of the country was slow. A group photograph of the first old-age pensioners in Clonown, Co. Roscommon (in 1909), shows all the women in checked shawls, with white aprons in front, some with white linen caps. All the men were bearded, in suits, some with bowler hats, some with cloth caps. They probably dressed up for the occasion, but their 'good' clothes made no concessions whatsoever to the high fashion of the day.[38] Edward O'Toole's mother and her neighbours in 1870s' Carlow wore voluminous cloaks of black cloth with quilted silk linings, and the white, linen-bordered, gophered caps also discerned in Clonown thirty years later.[39]

What happened in Ireland over these 70 years happened in most Western countries over this time – the gradual, but never total, replacement of local, regional styles of dress by approximation to or adaptation of metropolitan styles or 'fashion'. The last decade of this period saw a permanent shortening of women's skirts and a simplification and elongation of the 'line'. Dunlevy's classic work gives a vivid and pictorial idea of how people's clothing changed over this period. The northernmost province of Ireland gave its name to the caped, woollen, travelling coat worn by men, particularly those who had to be out in all weathers, like cabbies (drivers of horse-drawn cabs) and carters; with the oils left in, it was not only warm but waterproof. In the West of Ireland, particularly in Galway, *báinín* (woollen cloth) protected people from the ever-present rain.[40]

It is relatively easy for us to find out what the fashionable upper and upper-middle classes were wearing at any given time – any history of fashion will tell us. There was certainly popular interest in fashion, or the *Freeman's Journal* would not have regularly devoted a close-printed half-page to the *toilettes* worn by ladies presented at viceregal 'drawing rooms' as it did in 1865:

> Miss Daly, Castle Daly – Train and corsage of fine white gros D'Oran, lined with white Florence silk, trimmed with ruches of white Indian gauze; corsage of drapery, of tulle illusion and blonde lace, petticoat of white glace with tunic of illusion and boiullionnes of same. Headdress – plume of ostrich feathers, tulle lappets, and coquette of Veodard, ornaments, torquoise and pearls.[41]

The detail of the description indicates that the women themselves (or their mothers) handed in these descriptions as 'press releases'; they were probably pored over by many a dressmaker or woman with a special occasion to plan. People adapted high fashion to their own needs. The advent of the sewing-machine in the 1870s was a boon: not only did it give women a chance to earn money at home, but it enabled them to make clothes for themselves, their daughters and younger sons. Clothes for older males had to be tailored and were far more expensive – it always cost more to dress a man than a woman. Clothes were expected to last, even at a time of changing fashion. The Tailor Buckley of west Cork knew a man who, through his entire life, had owned only two linen shirts; Charles McGlinchey of Donegal knew a man who had been married in the second pair of shoes he had ever owned.[42] That these facts were subject to comment shows that such thrift was unusual even at the time when they were noticed – the late nineteenth–early twentieth century. Still, only the very rich could afford to have and to maintain many items of clothing: Mary Dugan and her sisters in late nineteenth-century

Antrim (daughters of a farmer–businessman) were brought to the dressmaker yearly to be fitted for their 'annual dress, which remained Sunday-best for a year and then descended to secular use', which implies that they had (depending on how quickly they grew) at most three dresses at any given time.[43] Cotton, linen, wool and frieze were practically indestructible, and even cheap, ready-made clothes could last a long time. Clothes were 'made over' several times in different styles and cut down to smaller sizes; good material was not thrown away. Garments were heavy and dark in colour so as not to show the dirt. According to Sidney Czira,

> heavy materials, sombre colours and tight-fitting garments were the fashion, everyone had the appearance of being upholstered, rather than being clothed ... when my sisters and I took part in a Nationalist demonstration outside the City Hall in 1911, dressed in light-coloured linen dresses, we were described in a daily newspaper as looking as though we had come out of a musical comedy.[44]

The voluminous garments worn by most women at that time meant that the making of baby clothes was often the first visible sign of pregnancy – 'Did you think it would come dressed and all?' was the caustic remark to a woman in early twentieth-century Kilkenny who had made no such preparation. Boys were usually kept in skirts until they were about the age of 4, when they were 'breeched' (put into britches, or pants).[45] This is usually said to have been a deterrent to the 'little people', or fairies (who will not steal girls), but the fact that it was common in towns and cities and among classes where belief in the fairies was non-existent indicates that there were practical reasons for it too. Putting pants which are difficult to unbutton (no zips then!) on small boys not yet fully toilet-trained was asking for more trouble than mothers or nannies needed. People wore layers of clothing, even in summer, having to be out in all weathers. Antrim girls walking to National School wore 'several petticoats, long woollen dresses, frilled linen pinafores, black knitted stockings and buttoned boots'.[46] Though the aprons might not always have been frilled, they were nearly universal for school-going girls, as photographs from around the country show.

The Dugans' mother had all her clothes made up by a travelling sewing-woman who came and stayed in the house for a fortnight; ready-made clothes, McDowell tells us, were unheard of. A short distance away at the Giant's Causeway they were very much in evidence, though, according to the disdainful Madame de Bovet, quoted by Horgan: 'a maiden aunt showing off a belt of sky-blue on a grey skirt, in the latest fashion of Ballybrophy or Carrickmacross . . .'[47] being the mildest of her comments. Labourers in Roscommon in the 1850s were wearing ready-made clothes, and even in areas where there was a traditional expertise in needlework and weaving, bought items could sometimes surface, probably due to fashion. All the women's shawls in Inishowen in the 1860s and 1870s were bought either in Derry or at fairs.[48] Dedicated followers of fashion were noticed by Henry Coulter as he travelled around Clare in the 1860s, and while he questioned the practicality of small farmers' daughters wearing the hoops and crinolines fashionable at the time, he welcomed the cleanliness and freshness.[49]

The emergence of a uniform for certain kinds of work also raised the standard of clothing and popularised the full-length coat. Railway employees got good, heavy, all-weather coats; policemen, prison wardens (turnkeys) and lunatic-asylum attendants wore uniforms of various kinds; shop assistants often had to wear livery; domestic servants of large houses wore uniforms, as also, of course, did soldiers and sailors. The army greatcoat was prized for its warmth, and was often used as a quilt by soldiers' families. Employees often had to buy their uniforms themselves (or at least contribute to the cost), but they were good quality and long-lasting.

Then, as now, people dressed up for special occasions. Only brides from very wealthy families wore once-off white dresses; blue and even brown were popular colours. Linda Ballard tells us that men's wedding-coats had to last them for years;[50] among Mary Healy's artisan neighbours and relatives in early twentieth-century Kilkenny, brides wore a 'costume' – a coat and skirt.[51] More out-of-house entertainment meant more dressing up to go out:

> She had her Sunday finery on. Her blue serge skirt was held at the waist by a belt of black leather. The great silver buckle of her belt seemed to depress the centre of her body, catching the light stuff of her white blouse like a clip. She wore a short black jacket with mother of pearl buttons, and a ragged black boa. The ends of her tulle collarette had been carefully disordered and a big bunch of red flowers was pinned in her bosom stems upwards.[52]

This is Joyce's description of an early twentieth-century Dublin servant on her night out. George Russell would have winced at the girl's clothes, but even Irish language and culture enthusiasts would not be caught dead in the kind of free-flowing tweeds Russell recommended, unless they were featuring in a *tableau vivant*. The jacket, straw hat and narrow skirt giving just enough room to cycle (elastic stirrups sewn into the skirt to keep it from blowing up)[53] were the familiar uniform of the early twentieth-century young woman out and about at work, politics and play. A gulf yawned between her and the countrywoman coming into market, and the older, married, working-class woman, who continued to wear the shawl for every day. This large garment covered a multitude, hiding the hair, the bodice and the upper part of the skirt, and it could be fixed in such a way that a baby or small child could be carried, leaving the hands free. There was a less dramatic difference between the clothes of men at different social levels – the full-length trousers, jacket, or 'frock' as it was called in some parts of the country, and sometimes waistcoat had become universal by the early twentieth century. Some trades continued to wear distinctive attire, the flat cap being associated with the working man, the hat with the white-collar worker. However, many tradesmen started wearing a collar and tie, and waistcoat and watch-chain, by the end of the nineteenth century.

Beards were very common in the nineteenth century and were still popular among older men in the early twentieth. Younger men at this stage shaved their chins and sported moustaches, sometimes waxed and twirled, more often neatly clipped. All of this took maintenance, and Ireland's 605 male barbers in 1861 had become 2,261 in 1911. Most men, however, shaved themselves at home every morning with razor and soap. In small dwellings they were competing for mirror-space with womenfolk putting up their hair. There were only 57 female hairdressers in Ireland in 1911.[54] Ladies of fashion had their hair done by their maids, but women of lesser means did their own or had it done for them by sisters or mothers. Before the 1920s, short hair on women was a catastrophe, a shame or a sacrifice, seen only in fever, incarceration or when taking religious vows. Long hair, almost universal among women, would be 'put up' at around the age of 16 or 17:

> The long heavy plait of hair which hung down my back was transformed into a sort of coiffure . . . the hat slipped its moorings a little and so I made my entrance into young womanhood . . .

Thus did Mary Colum recall her coming of age in the 1890s. Training locks deftly, with pins and grips, into a neat and non-straggly 'bun' was a time-consuming daily ritual; curly or frizzy hair was very difficult to manage. No wonder the harried mothers running to work in the mill in Antrim in the 1890s and 1900s often had their hair 'in greasy and sometimes grey plaits rather in the manner of aged schoolgirls, or even in unkempt locks without benefit of braiding . . .'. The young, unmarried mill-workers, however, took great trouble with their appearance, using oatmeal bags to whiten their chapped hands and washing their hair in rain water.[55]

Conclusion: 'do not send her looking shabby'

Accommodation, clothing and diet all changed significantly over the seventy-year period considered in this study. Housing improved overall; the Irish interiors painted by the naturalistic Helmick, Brenan, O'Kelly, Magrath, Sheil and others in the last four decades of the nineteenth century have tables, dressers, clocks, ornaments and mirrors.[56] The various new housing initiatives from the 1860s, though they did not benefit everyone all over the country, helped to raise the minimum standard of accommodation. In dwellings new or old, rural or urban, there remained problems of ventilation when the fire had to be kept going morning and night, summer and winter, for cooking, for boiling water and for drying clothes. The half-door was a necessity rather than a picturesque detail – it kept the bigger animals outside and maintained a flow of fresh air. Economic necessity often worsened conditions, and lack of space never stopped anyone keeping lodgers – women living in one-room tenements often had paying guests, as well as their often large families.[57] An extreme example, noted by Marnane, was a thatched, one-room dwelling in Tipperary town, in 1901, with no front windows and no outoffices, which a husband and wife, their adult daughter and grandchild shared with ten boarders.[58]

Clarkson and Crawford point out that even though Irish people's diet in general became less healthful over these years – with the advent of tea, which was often consumed stewed and over-strong, white bread of questionable value and sugar – it probably became more varied and more palatable, thus representing an improvement in the quality of life.[59] Changing diet, however, could have lowered protection against some diseases: rates of tuberculosis were consistently lowest in Connacht, where diet had changed the least by the end of the nineteenth century. The cookery reformers of the early twentieth century did their best to make tasty meals out of cheap, nutritious ingredients, and they often succeeded.[60] Josephine Redington's insistence, in 1905, that skim milk was not only fit for calves, and her many imaginative ways with Indian meal, probably fell on deaf ears, but the books and demonstrations which she, Kathleen Ferguson and others gave had some impact on Irish cookery and Irish life. In Dromore, Co. Donegal, in 1905, after one such demonstration, 'the audience sat down [to eat] and straightaway wanted that kind of cooking in their own homes'. Admittedly, our source for this is George Russell, the apostle of reform, but he could also be blackly pessimistic about rural life, and he did not praise easily.[61]

Changes in education, work and leisure meant that people of all ages were going out in public more, and so needed presentable clothes. Improved communications and a thriving retail sector disseminated fashion – and local adaptations of it – into the smallest towns. The number of drapers increased dramatically. Emigrants' parcels and letters, and indeed, the demands of emigration itself, played their part: 'Do not send her looking shabby',[62] an Antrim woman in New York exhorted her sister, whose daughter was emigrating, a remark which probably infuriated the woman in Ireland and confirmed for her that 'Yanks' had high notions of themselves. But Irish people too were starting to have 'notions'. Bridget Cleary was looked on with suspicion by her neighbours in Co. Tipperary in the 1890s because she, a working-class, married woman, wore a hat and jacket rather than a shawl.[63]

Notes

1 Micheal O Gaoithín on the new houses built by the Congested Districts Board on the Blasket Islands in the early twentieth century: *Is Trua ná Fannan an Oige* (Baile Atha Cliath 1953), p. 8.
2 Henry Coulter, quoted in Brian O Dalaigh (ed.), *The Stranger's Gaze*, p. 258 and *Reports from Poor Law Inspectors in Ireland in pursuance of instructions dated 9th May 1872 . . . obtaining information on the subject of labourers' dwellings in that country 1873* (1873) [c.764], Vol. 22, Report of Dr King for Cork, Limerick and Waterford, p. 72.
3 Breathnach, *The Congested Districts Board of Ireland*.
4 The information on housing is taken, unless otherwise stated, from two main sources, Murray Fraser, *John Bull's Other Homes: state housing and British policy in Ireland 1883–1922* (Liverpool 1996); and Enda McKay, 'The housing of the rural labourer 1883–1916',

Saothar, Vol. 17 (1992), pp. 27–39; see also Bradley, *Farm Labourers*, pp. 20–3.

5 I refer to the excellent loving reconstructions in the Ulster Folk and Transport Museum in Cultra, Co. Down, and Bunratty Folk Park in Co. Clare.

6 Alan Gailey, 'Changes in Irish rural housing 1600–1900', in O'Flanagan et al. (eds), *Rural Ireland 1600–1900*, pp. 86–103; and A. Gailey, *Rural Houses of the North of Ireland* (Edinburgh 1984).

7 Claudia Kinmonth, *Irish Country Furniture 1700–1950* (Yale, CT 1993).

8 *Reports from Poor Law Inspectors 1873*, Report of Denis W. Pack, Beresford, Co. Carlow, p. 55.

9 Kinmonth, *Irish Country Furniture*.

10 E.g. St Dympna's Terrace, Mulgrave Street, Limerick, is a row of late nineteenth-century houses built originally for attendants in the adjoining lunatic asylum and still inhabited at the time of writing.

11 Seamus Fitzgerald, *Mackerel and the Making of Baltimore, Co. Cork, 1879–1913* (Maynooth 1999).

12 Daly, Pearson and Hearn, *Dublin's Victorian Houses*, pp. 17–23.

13 O'Brien, *Presentation Parlour*, pp. 103–4.

14 Marnane, 'Tipperary town'.

15 Laverty, *Never No More*, p. 158

16 Smith, *The People's Health*, pp. 195–248.

17 Healy, *For the Poor and for the Gentry*, p. 3; Ulster Folk and Transport Museum, Caltra, Co. Down: Sandy Row houses.

18 Sexton, *Little History of Irish food*, p. 82.

19 See, for example *Special Report on Alleged Increasing Prevalence of Lunacy in Ireland 1894, in Parliamentary Papers* (1894) [c.7331], Vol. 63.

20 O Gráda, *Ireland*, pp. 236–54; Mary Kelly, 'Down memory lane: the tea travellers', *Cathair na Mart: Journal of the Westport Historical Society*, Vol. 15 (1995), pp. 66–9.

21 Clarkson and Crawford, *Feast and Famine*, pp. 88–110.

22 A vivid description of the diet of small farmers/labourers in Antrim is given in Florence Mary McDowell, *Other Days Around Me* (Belfast 1966), pp. 31–6.

23 Irwin, *Cookin' Woman*, pp. 2–3.

24 O Gráda, *Ireland*, pp. 243–6.

25 Danaher, *In Ireland Long Ago*, pp. 26–44.

26 Máire Ní Ghuithín, *Bean an Oileáin* (Baile Atha Cliath 1985).

27 Kickham, *Knocknagow*, pp. 143–5.

28 Oral evidence, see Clear, *Women of the House*, chapter 8.

29 Maura Laverty, *Kind Cooking* (Tralee 1946), p. 29

30 Myrtle Allen, *The Ballymaloe Cookbook* (Dublin 1984).
31 Bolger (ed.), *And See Her Beauty Shining There*; and McNamara, *Those Intrepid United Irishwomen.*
32 Cameron, *Manual of Hygiene.*
33 Kearns, *Dublin Tenement Life.*
34 Cross, *The Tailor and Antsy*, p. 27.
35 E.g. the early twentieth-century song 'The golden wedding': 'Put on your old knee-britches/ and your coat of emerald green./ Take off that hat, me darlin Pat/ put on your oul caubeen/ Today's our golden wedding/ And I want them all to know/ How we looked when we were wed/ Fifty years ago'.
36 O'Toole, *Whist for Your Life*, pp. 22–3.
37 McGlinchey, *The Last of the Name*, pp. 16–17.
38 Clonown Community Centre, *Clonown: the history*, p. 61.
39 McGlinchey, *The Last of the Name*, pp. 16–17.
40 Mairéad Dunlevy, *Dress in Ireland* (Cork 1999); Elizabeth McCrum, *Fabric and Form: Irish fashion since 1950* (Belfast 1996).
41 *Freeman's Journal*, 2 February 1865.
42 Cross, *Tailor and Antsy*, p. 28; McGlinchey, *The Last of the Name*, pp. 16–17.
43 McDowell, *Other Days*, p. 15.
44 Czira, *The Years Flew By*, p. 3.
45 Healy, *For the Poor and for the Gentry*, p. 51.
46 McDowell, *Other Days*, p. 15.
47 Quoted in Donal Horgan, *The Victorian Visitor to Ireland: Irish Tourism 1840–1910* (Dublin 2002), p. 113.
48 McGlinchey, *The Last of the Name*, p. 17.
49 Coulter in O Dálaigh (ed.), *The Stranger's Gaze*, p. 256.
50 Ballard, *Forgetting Frolic*, pp. 77–104.
51 Healy, *For the Poor and for the Gentry*, p. 30
52 James Joyce, 'Two gallants', in *Dubliners* (London 1914).
53 Czira, *The Years Flew By*, p. 3.
54 *Census of Ireland*, 1911, General report, occupational tables.
55 Colum, *Life and the Dream*, p. 86; McDowell, *Other Days*, p. 86.
56 William Magrath (1838–1918), 'Paddy's honeymoon', c. 1879; Edward Sheil (1834–69), 'Home after work', 1863 (Gorry Gallery Dublin); Aloysius O'Kelly (1853–1941), 'Mass in a Connemara cabin', 1883 (National Gallery Ireland, on loan from St Patrick's Parish, Edinburgh); Howard Helmick (1845–1907), 'Bringing home the bride', 1883 (Gorry Gallery Dublin); James Brenan (1837–1907), 'Words of counsel', 1876, and 'Patchwork', 1892 (Crawford Gallery Cork). For discussion of these works as historical sources, see Julian Campbell, 'The representation of everyday life in Irish painting of the nineteenth century: the European

158 *Ireland, 1850–1922*

context', in P. Murray (ed.), *Whipping the Herring: survival and celebration in nineteenth-century Irish art* (Cork 2006), pp. 24–33; and P. Murray, 'Realism versus romanticism in framing national identity', in ibid., pp. 10–23.

57 Mary E. Daly, 'Late nineteenth and early twentieth century Dublin', in Harkness and O'Dowd (eds), *The Town in Ireland*, pp. 221–52.

58 Marnane, 'Tipperary town'.

59 Clarkson and Crawford, *Feast and Famine*, pp. 108–10.

60 Josephine Redington, *Economic Cookery Book* (Dublin 1905); Kathleen Ferguson, *Lessons in Cookery and Housewifery: leabhairíní na seamróige* (Dublin 1900).

61 *Irish Homestead*, 7 October 1905; this is also Joanna Bourke's central thesis in *Husbandry to Housewifery: women, housework and economic change 1890–1914* (Oxford 1993).

62 Brigid McGay, 'Emigrant's letter 19th March 1999'.

63 Angela Bourke, *The Burning of Bridget Cleary: a true story* (London 1999), p. 43.

Conclusion

When William Bulfin travelled in Tipperary in the early twentieth century, he was struck by the importance of Charles Kickham's *Knocknagow* in the lives of the farmers and labourers:

> His works are as familiar to them as the fields amidst which they were reared. They are always quoting him ... from its pages they take standards of conduct and criterions [*sic*] of life. You will hear them give the names of Kickham's characters to people of their acquaintance.[1]

In 1910–14 an American film company, in Ireland to make a film about the Colleen Bawn,[2] went to Dingle to make a documentary on emigration. There they staged a mock farewell scene at Dingle railway station, observed by an interested crowd.[3]

To people who grew up and came of age between the Famine and Independence/Partition, the past was always present. Later marriage, where it happened, meant generational stretching – 'my father's time' and 'my time' could encompass a century. And seventy-two years is a very short time: someone born in the 1850s could be entering the grandparent generation when the Treaty was signed. Changing patterns of work, migration and emigration, new ways of dressing, eating, working, furnishing houses, all happened within the comfortable memory-span of an adult. It was this apparently rapid pace of social change, as well as nationalism, which fostered self-consciousness. If the past was unusually present, maybe the present (as in Dingle, above) sometimes seemed like the past. In the 1860s disabled beggars were being written of with affection and wonder even as they were being hounded from workhouse to prison.

A smaller population, more cash in circulation (some of it from emigrants), better communications and transport and higher literacy led to a short-lived boom in the 1880s and 1890s. More things could be bought for the house and for the self. Heightened awareness of healthful diet in the early twentieth century did battle with fashionable notions of what constituted good food. In 1897 *Freeman's Journal* readers were invited to be shocked at the Belmullet diet of oatmeal, Indian meal, buttermilk, fish, potatoes, soda bread and tea,[4] which – except for the absence of green vegetables – was a far more healthful diet than anything enjoyed by the town or the inland rural poor. All eyes were drawn to the obvious and distinctive poverty of the west, but there was poverty and hardship everywhere.

Traditional objects of historical pity, women on farms, were not necessarily miserable, put-upon drudges, slaves to their menfolk. Indeed, as time went on, later marriage and more opportunity to get involved in poultry-rearing, fruit-growing and other diversifications meant that farm women everywhere were likelier than non-farming women to be independent, authoritative and, indeed, comfortable. Segalen suggests that women on nineteenth-century Breton and Norman farms were actually quite powerful and that the grumbling proverbs about women's wickedness and the need to keep them under control came from men's resentment of women's authority.[5] The same could be true of Ireland. Women' subordination was not necessarily worse on the farm than elsewhere. The women – and men – most deserving of our sympathy are those who eked out an existence on tiny smallholdings, bent double under turf and hay, those who said goodbye to their loved ones for half of every year just to stay alive, the 'town poor' who felt lucky if farmers on outlying hinterlands gave them a day's work, harried mothers in woollen and linen mills doing the family wash after a twelve-hour working day, exhausted servants in cold suburban sculleries, women in shawls queuing outside pawnshops, men at the dockside waiting to be picked for a day's work, parents who watched one child after another die.

There were some success stories. Luck, skill or both enabled some people to make the vital step from chronic hardship to some kind of security; parental and elder-sibling struggle and sacrifice produced clerks, shop-workers, secretaries, administrators, teachers and uniformed workers of various kinds, in police barracks, hospitals, asylums, prisons and railways. These anxious employees have not been paid much attention by historians. But even those who have been subjected to intensive and extensive historical scrutiny – the big farmers – remain in permanent shadow. Everything we 'know' of their values, motivations, beliefs or tastes is speculation; they were not targeted by the folklore collectors of the twentieth century and produced few memoirs.[6]

Thanks to the meticulous record-keeping of the era, the people in the past about whom we now know most are those who were hidden away in institutions at the time. But how *hidden* were they, really? Asylum inmates' relatives often kept in touch with them, many industrial-school and reformatory graduates returned to their families, the Magdalen asylum was often used as a temporary rest-cure by tired prostitutes and the workhouse was used, more and more as time went on, by people on the move. Irish institutions were not as cut off from the outside world as they were to become in the mid-twentieth century. However, the Victorian habit of classification, incarceration and supervision put down roots which long outlasted that era. Nineteenth-century Ireland, like all Western countries, saw the rise of the official busybody. Increased entitlements – to medical attention, poor relief, schooling, housing, emigration – gave rise to increased scrutiny; the conditions of entitlement had to be fulfilled, and the age of questions and form-filling had begun. Those whose job it was to make judgements on others multiplied – policemen, prison officers, asylum attendants, relieving officers, registrars of births, teachers, nurses, doctors (in hospitals and dispensaries), district nurses, clerks, secretaries and, from the 1890s, Congested Districts Board officials, inspectors from the Department of Agriculture and Technical Instruction and 'middle managers' in industry, commerce and government. The shopkeeper had to decide who was credit-worthy and who was not. The property-owner had to decide if that group of lads joking at the street-corner who were not from the locality were potential thieves. The householder had to decide if the beggar at the door was genuine or not, and, even if genuine, whether he or she would be better off in some institution than going the roads. The policeman, magistrate and doctor had to decide which institution. Yet one group of people seem to have slipped the net of supervision and institutionalisation – the antecedents of modern-day Travellers. Understanding how Travellers survived or how they evolved into a distinct group over this period could be the key to understanding the extent, and the limits, of the social discipline instilled in this era.[7]

The survival – or emergence – of Travellers is not the only un-expected aspect of Irish social change in these years. Another is that the *fin-de-siècle* Ireland described by Russell, Plunkett and Filson Young[8] (among others) as gloomy, moribund and lethargic was in fact alive with organizations of various kinds – political, labour, cultural, religious and sporting: in early twentieth-century Dublin, if one of the six Gifford sisters ever stayed at home of an evening, their father would ask sarcastically if she were ill.[9] But even outside of Dublin social life was jumping. In Wexford town alone in 1885, according to Nolan, there were clubs for cycling, cricket, boating, hunting and athletics; there were well-supported libraries, frequent theatrical events, debating societies, art clubs and miscellaneous organizations, including St Vincent de Paul, the Temperance and Altar Society, Peter's Pence, the Wexford United Agricultural Society, the Society for Prevention of Cruelty to Animals and the Ladies Land League. (And this was before the explosion in popularity of Gaelic games![10]) There was a suffrage society in the small village of Annaghdown, Co. Galway; there were labourers' and shop assistants' organizations in the smallest Connacht towns by 1905.[11] More people had free time to attend meetings, concerts and other events. Bicycles opened up rural Ireland, even labourers and servants able to afford them on the hire purchase from local shopkeepers.[12]

We only have to move one step away from the doom-sayers – to contemporary newspapers, memoirs, autobiographies and local histories – to glimpse a population which was sociable, able to embrace change, enthusiastic. Some of what the pessimists said was right: enthusiasm carried many people out of the country for good, chronic under-employment and industrial under-development left little room for complacency, and the gloomy and depopulated Ireland foretold by Russell and Plunkett came to pass about fifty years later.[13] But people live in the day-to-day present, not in some feared future, and the world of late nineteenth- and early twentieth-century Ireland, with its short-term boost in retailing, administration and transport, must have seemed full of promise. We might be tempted to see all this activity as shiny and feverish; tuberculosis stalked houses where delph shone on the dresser, the bicycle and the meeting spread disease as never before, and the puffing steam train of progress did not offer the same comfortable accommodation to everybody. By the turn of the century 40 per cent of Achill Islanders were spending half the year on migratory labour in tough conditions in Scotland, a population movement that had begun only in the late 1860s in response to the need for cash.[14] The higher standards propagated by public health apostles saved lives, but knowledge without power often led to frustration and despair. No matter how 'spotless'[15] the tenement mother kept her room and her children, her weekly income did not stretch to clean milk. No wonder the Iniskea Islanders wept to see their new beds and bedding destroyed by public health order during the typhus epidemic of 1897.[16]

At the end, we have to try to answer the basic question of whether life got better or worse for most Irish people over the years 1850–1922. If quality of life is measured by things like emergency food supplies, health-care facilities, sound housing, warm clothing and basic education, then it undoubtedly got better – though not at the same rate for everybody. The biggest change happened between 1860 and 1900. At the latter date most people believed (or affected to believe) that they should send children to school for a few years, at least, remove large animals and human waste from the dwelling-place, wash clothes and themselves regularly, and consult a doctor or nurse in case of persistent illness. Their diet was more varied, though not necessarily more healthful, and in towns and cities the familiar institutional landscape of convents, lunatic asylums, reformatories, industrial schools, prisons, hospitals, Magdalen asylums, and National Schools was firmly in place. Though many houses, in town and country, were still thatched, and most rural houses still without piped water (not to mention electricity) in 1922, the internal furnishings and decoration had become more elaborate. Young people of both sexes and of all classes, in town and country, had more freedom than ever before. In the 1860s there were no bicycles, no trams and few trains for a quick getaway, but few places to go anyway. Associations for working-class or lower middle-class men (mostly trade union- and/or Fenian-related) were few and far between, and there were few for women. Taking the air for pleasure was developed by people penned-in all day by factory, office, school or institution, and the fact that sporting and other outdoor organizations grew and throve from the late 1890s is as much an indication of changes in waged work as in anything else. The acceleration must have seemed dizzying to those who lived through it; not just recreation, but every kind of work, even pasture-farming, became more demanding (though probably physically less hard) because of intensified competition, higher standards, more inspections and more regulations.

The rise in the numbers convicted (and relieved) for homelessness and prostitution was part of this speeded-up way of life. There was, after all, more moving around for everyone, and more buying and selling of all kinds of commodities. Policing was more vigorous, and long-stay institutions were getting greedier by the year. We see these people only through the eyes of those whose job it was to help or harass them (or both); their relationships with each other and, indeed, their opinions on the institutions which recorded them so meticulously, yet so inadequately for our purposes, remain the great untold story of a modernising Ireland.

Notes

1 Bulfin, *Rambles in Eirinn*, p. 348.
2 The story of the 'Colleen Bawn' (murder victim Eily Scanlan, 1819) inspired a play by Dion Boucicault, a novel by Gerald Griffin (*The Collegians*, 1841) and an operetta by Julius Benedict (*The Lily of Killarney*, 1868); W. MacLysaght and Sigerson Clifford, *The Tragic Story of the Colleen Bawn* (Tralee 1953).
3 David Rowlands and Walter McGrath, 'The Dingle train in the life and lore of Corkaguiney', *Journal of the Kerry Archeological and Historical Society*, No.11 (1978), pp. 85–133, p. 124.
4 *Freeman's Journal*, 12 July 1897.
5 Martine Segalen, *Love and Power in the Peasant Family* (London 1991).
6 See note 2 in chapter 5, on marriage, as to why Carbery, *The Farm by Lough Gur*, while brilliant on everyday life (food, clothes, routine, housing, schooling) is not entirely reliable on values, beliefs and feelings.
7 Travellers' distinct identity should not be seen as freedom: from the 1920s the Travellers were hunted and harassed (in different ways) by both jurisdictions: Breathnach, *Becoming Conspicuous*.
8 See Russell's various musings (accompanied, in fairness, by plenty of practical schemes for reform) in *The Irish Homestead*; also Horace Plunkett, *Ireland in the New Century* (London 1904); Filson Young, *Ireland at the Crossroads* (London 1903); McCarthy, *Priests and People*.
9 Czira, *The Years Flew By*, p. 30.
10 Fionnuala Nolan, 'Aspects of social life in County Wexford in 1885', *Journal of the Wexford Historical Society*, No. 9 (1983–84), pp. 55–65.
11 Mary Clancy, 'The western outpost: local government and women's suffrage in Co. Galway 1898–1918', in R. Gillespie and G. Moran (eds), *Galway: history and society* (Dublin 1996), pp. 557–88; Cunningham, *Labour in the West of Ireland*.
12 Gilligan, 'Murrays of Dunshaughlin'.
13 On Ireland after 1945 as strangled and depressed, see e.g. J. J. Lee, *Ireland 1912–1985: politics and society* (Cambridge 1989), pp. 271–327; for a slightly alternative view, Dermot Keogh et al. (eds), *Ireland in the 1950s: the lost decade* (Cork 2004).
14 Coughlan, *Achill Island*, pp. 16, 52.
15 Kearns, *Dublin Tenement Life*.
16 Robins, *The Miasma*, p. 204.

Appendix

Table A1 *Farms, 30 acres and less (30 <) and 50 acres and less (50 <) as %s of total holdings, 1901 and 1911*

	1901 30 <	1901 50 <	1911 30 <	1911 50 <
IRELAND	72	84	69	86
Leinster	70	81	66	79
Munster	58	74	55	71.9
Ulster	78	90	74.9	88.8
Connacht	79	88	80	90.8

Table A2 *Female farmers as %s of total farmers in Ireland 1861, 1891, 1911*

	1861	1891	1911
IRELAND	6.8	16	14.7
Leinster	9.3	18	16.9
Munster	6.5	15	13.3
Ulster	5.5	16	13.7
Connacht	4.5	16	14
Carlow		17.5	16.5
Co. Dublin		19.4	16.3
Kildare		19.3	19.8
Kilkenny		18.3	15.6
King's		15.3	15.8
Longford		14	15.8
Louth		20.8	20.2
Meath		19	13.7
Queen's		19.3	19.3
Westmeath		18.2	18
Wexford		19	17
Wicklow		20	15
Clare		13.2	11.9
Cork		15	12.3
Kerry		12.8	10.6
Limerick		17.3	14
Tipperary		17.5	16
Waterford		18	15
Antrim		14.3	12
Armagh		19.9	17
Cavan		17.8	14
Donegal		15.3	14
Down		16.4	13.7
Fermanagh		13.3	11.7
Londonderry		13.5	12.5
Monaghan		21	16.6
Tyrone		15	11.8
Galway		17	15
Leitrim		15	12.8
Mayo		16	12.5
Roscommon		16.8	16
Sligo		15.6	14.3
IRELAND	6.8	16	14.7

Table A3 *The principal occupations of males and females gainfully employed (GE) in Ireland (%s), in 1851 and 1911*

	1851	1911
MEN		
Total male population	3,190,630	2,192,048
Total males GE (all ages) as % total male population	1,903,443 (59.6)	1,387,198 (63)
Occupations as %s of males GE		
Farmers	383,931 (20)	328,473 (23.6)
Labourers, herds[a]	878,058 (46)	192,105 (13.8)
General labourers	56,969 (3)	147,519 (10.6)
Shopkeepers, dealers[b]	29,788 (1.5)	34,481 (2.5)
Prof., admin, WC[c]	51,479 (2.7)	69,886 (5)
Domestic servants	29,720 (1.6)	23,077 (1.6)
Tailor, boot and shoe	63,632 (3.3)	26,467 (1.9)
Weavers	75,513 (3.9)	
WOMEN		
Total female population	3,361,755	2,198,171
Total females GE[d] (all ages) as % total female population	938,185 (28)	430,002 (19.5)
Occupations as %s of females GE		
Farmers	19,707 (2)	54,694 (12.7)
Labourers, herds[a]	146,844 (15)	3,984 (0.9)
Shopkeepers[b]	15,795 (1.6)	20,931 (4.8)
Prof, admin, WC[c]	12,441 (1.3)	37,531 (8.7)
Dressmakers[e]	46,392 (4.9)	33,785 (7.8)
Spinners, weavers	146,428 (15.6)	46,799 (10.8)
Seamstresses[f]	45,150 (4.8)	30,633 (7.1)
Domestic servants	230,802 (24)	128,457 (29.8)

Notes:

[a] Labourers, herds 1911 includes indoor farm servants also.

[b] Shopkeepers, dealers includes grocers, mercers, drapers, hucksters, but not pedlars, fishmongers, victuallers or innkeepers.

[c] Prof, admin, WC: professions, teaching, nursing, white-collar government and private employment.

[d] Farmers' wives were not counted as GE, so female farmers are widows or single women. Women 'engaged in home duties' were not counted as GE either.

[e] Includes milliners.

[f] Includes shirtmakers.

Table A4 *Proportions of single (S), married (M) and widowed (W)
persons to 100 men and 100 women aged 20 years and upwards, 1881*

| | Men | | | Women | | |
	S	M	W	S	M	W
Ireland	40.8	52	7.2	34.3	48.4	17.3
Leinster	45.3	47.6	7.1	37.1	45	17.9
Munster	40.1	53.1	6.9	30.5	50.4	19.1
Ulster	39.6	52.9	7.5	37.9	46.6	15.5
Connacht	36.3	56.8	6.9	26.8	55.8	17.4
Carlow	44.7	48.7	6.6	36.1	46.3	17.6
Dublin city	40.7	52.2	7.1	33.0	46.8	20.2
Dublin Co.	44.9	48.7	6.4	45.1	38.5	16.4
Kildare	55.9	38.4	5.7	36.3	46.6	17.1
Kilkenny	43	48.8	8.2	35.9	45.4	18.7
King's	46.8	45.8	7.4	34.4	47.3	18.3
Longford	42.4	50.6	7	32.6	50.9	16.3
Louth[a]	44.1	48.3	7.6	37.2	45.1	17.7
Meath	50.6	41.8	7.6	38.7	43.5	17.8
Queen's	47.9	45	7.1	36.7	45.4	17.9
Westmeath	47.6	44.5	7.9	35.7	46.1	18.2
Wexford	44.2	48.5	7.3	39.1	44.8	16.1
Wicklow	45.9	47.2	6.9	36.2	46.6	17.2
Clare	39.9	53.6	6.5	27	52.8	20.2
Cork[a]	39.8	53.5	6.7	30.3	50.8	18.9
Kerry	36.1	57.4	6.5	24	57.2	18.8
Limerick[a]	40.1	52.2	7.7	32.2	48	19.7
Tipperary	44.2	48.5	7.3	34.8	46.5	18.7
Waterford[a]	40.3	52.3	7.4	34.6	46.7	18.7
Antrim	36.8	55.8	7.4	38.7	47	14.3
Armagh	38.1	54.0	7.9	36.4	47.3	16.3
Belfast	33.7	59.8	6.5	37.5	46.3	16.2
Cavan	41.2	51.3	7.5	31.6	51.8	16.6
Donegal	40.5	52	7.5	36.2	48.1	15.7
Down	37.7	54.5	7.8	39.3	45.5	15.2
Fermanagh	44	48.4	7.6	38.1	46.2	15.7
Londonderry[a]	41.1	51.1	7.8	40.1	45	14.9
Monaghan	43.7	48.8	7.5	38.4	45.7	15.9
Tyrone	44.4	47.8	7.8	39.8	44.8	15.4
Galway[a]	36.8	56.5	6.7	24.8	56	19.2
Leitrim	38.9	53.7	7.4	29.1	54.4	16.5
Mayo	32.2	61.5	6.3	25.5	58.3	16.5
Roscommon	39.5	52.9	7.6	29.4	53.8	16.8
Sligo	37.6	55.3	7.1	29.9	53.6	16.5
Ireland	40.8	52	7.2	34.3	48.4	17.3

Note: [a] Including city/town, unless otherwise counted.

Source: Adapted from *Census of Ireland*, 1881, General report, table 83.

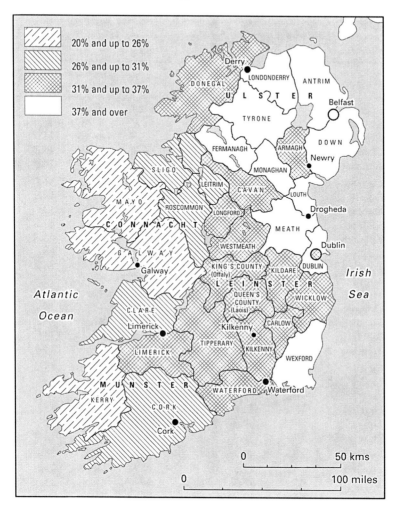

Map A1 *Proportions of single women
to 100 women aged 20 and above, 1881*

Table A5 *Proportions of single (S), married (M) and widowed (W) persons to 100 males and 100 females aged 20 and above, by provinces, counties, 1911*

| | Men | | | Women | | |
	S	M	W	S	M	W
IRELAND	48.3	44.8	6.9	40.4	44.4	15.2
Leinster	51.5	42.1	6.4	42.8	42.1	15.1
Munster	50.3	42.8	6.9	39.6	44.5	15.9
Ulster	44.7	48.0	7.3	41.1	44.7	14.2
Connacht	47.4	45.4	7.2	34.5	48.6	16.9
Carlow	53.2	40.0	7.2	41.4	42.6	16.0
Dublin city	45	48.4	6.6	39.6	44.3	16.1
Dublin Co.	48.3	46.2	5.5	51.5	35.5	13
Kildare	61.5	33.5	5	38.1	47.4	14.5
Kilkenny	52.8	40.1	7.1	41.9	42.3	15.8
King's	56.1	37.7	6.2	41.7	42.5	15.8
Longford	49.9	43.2	6.9	38.3	46.4	15.3
Louth	52.8	40.4	6.8	42.7	41.4	15.9
Meath	56.7	37.2	6.1	43.1	41.6	15.3
Queen's	56.3	37.7	6	41.4	42.5	16.1
Westmeath	57.3	36.5	6.2	41.9	42.4	15.7
Wexford	52.2	40.6	7.2	44.3	41.7	14
Wicklow	51.3	42.3	6.4	40.1	44.5	15.4
Clare	51.4	41.8	6.8	37.2	45.6	17.2
Cork[a]	49.9	43.2	6.9	40.2	44.1	15.7
Kerry	45.5	46.8	7.7	34.1	49.6	16.3
Limerick[a]	50.5	42.8	6.7	40.6	43.6	15.8
Tipperary	54.5	39.2	6.3	42.6	42.4	15
Waterford[a]	51.4	41.4	7.2	41.8	42.4	15.8
Antrim	42.8	49.7	7.5	42.1	44.5	13.4
Armagh	44.5	47.5	8	39.9	44.5	15.6
Belfast	35.6	57.8	6.6	38	48.6	13.4
Cavan	51.8	40.7	7.5	38.1	45.5	16.4
Donegal	51	41.8	7.2	43.1	42.2	14.7
Down	42.4	49.8	7.8	41.7	44.3	14
Fermanagh	51.5	41.7	6.8	41.3	43.7	15
Londonderry[a]	45.4	47.2	7.4	44.8	41.8	13.4
Monaghan	51.6	41	7.4	42.2	42.2	15.6
Tyrone	50.7	41.8	7.5	43.8	42.1	14.1
Galway[a]	50	43	7	34.7	47.9	17.4
Leitrim	45.8	46.7	7.5	33.9	49.1	17
Mayo	43.3	49.4	7.3	32.6	50.6	16.8
Roscommon	49.2	43.4	7.4	35.4	48.1	16.5
Sligo	49.3	43.5	7.2	38.2	45.4	16.4
IRELAND	48.3	44.8	6.9	40.4	44.4	15.2

Note: [a] Including city/large town, unless otherwise counted.

Source: Adapted from *Census of Ireland*, 1911, General report, table 67.

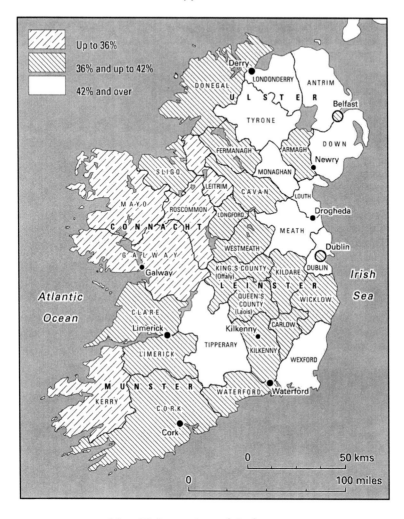

Map A2 *Proportions of single women
to 100 women aged 20 and above, 1911*

Table A6 *Percentages of women aged 35–44 who were single, in counties and cities, 1881 and 1911*

	1881	1911
Carlow	20.8	34.3
Dublin city	21.4	26
Co. Dublin	33	40.7
Kildare	25	29
Kilkenny	23.6	33
King's	21.6	35
Longford	16	32
Louth	25	33
Meath	26.7	35
Queen's	24	35
Westmeath	18	35.4
Wexford	28	38.6
Wicklow	23	31
LEINSTER	24.8	33
Clare	12.8	28
Cork	11.7	29
Kerry	9.2	20
Limerick	17.7	31
Tipperary	20.6	33
Waterford	22.2	33
MUNSTER	16	29
Antrim	33	34
Armagh	24.4	33
Belfast	21	25.7
Cavan	16	31.9
Donegal	24.5	37.8
Down	28.5	33
Fermanagh	27.4	34.9
Londonderry	29.7	36
Monaghan	28.5	36.5
Tyrone	29	36.7
ULSTER	26	32.4
Galway	11	26.6
Leitrim	13.5	27.8
Mayo	9.8	23.6
Roscommon	13	27.8
Sligo	13.5	31.3
CONNACHT	12	26.6
IRELAND	21.4	28.4

Sources: W. E. Vaughan & A. J. Fitzpatrick, *Irish Historical Statistics: population 1821–1971* (Dublin 1978), pp. 87–161; *Census of Ireland*, 1881 and 1911, General reports.

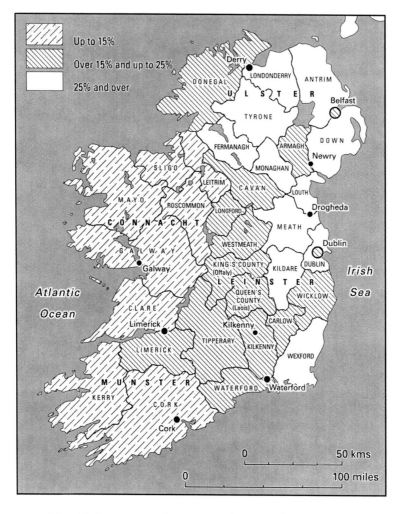

Map A3 *Percentages of women aged 35–44 who were single,
in counties and cities, 1881*

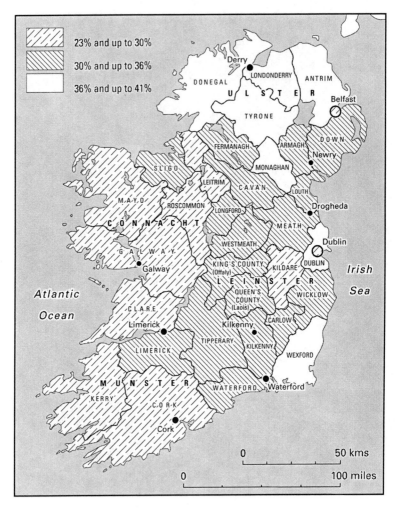

Map A4 *Percentages of women aged 35–44 who were single,*
in counties and cities, 1911

Table A7 *Rates (per 1,000 of the population) of temporary sickness in 1861, and on the nights the Census was taken, 5 April 1891 and 2 April 1911*

	1861	1891	1911
IRELAND	13	7.6	7
Leinster	16	9.6	8.7
Munster	14	9.1	7.5
Ulster	11	5.8	6.3
Connacht	11	5.9	4.9

Table A8a *Superintendent Registrars' districts in which the rates of sickness per 1,000 population were lowest (bottom 20 from lowest up) on the nights the Census was taken, 1891 and 1911*

1891	1911
Limavady, Co. Londonderry (3.4)	Stranorlar, Co. Londonderry (2.2)
Castleblayney, Co. Monaghan (3.5)	Limavady Co. Londonderry (2.4)
Baltinglass, Co. Wicklow (3.7)	Ballymahon, Co. Longford (2.5)
Claremorris, Co. Mayo (3.7)	Killala, Co. Mayo (2.8)
Ballymena, Co. Antrim (3.8)	Swinford, Co.Mayo (2.8)
Castlereagh, Co. Roscommon (4)	Inishowen, Co. Donegal (2.9)
Larne, Co. Antrim (4)	Castlederg, Co. Tyrone (3.3)
Magherafelt, Co. Londonderry (4)	Kilkeel, Co. Down (3.3)
Armagh, Co. Armagh (4.1)	Ballina, Co. Mayo (3.4)
Cootehill, Co. Cavan (4.1)	Bawnboy, Co. Cavan (3.6)
Mountbellew, Co. Galway (4.2)	Cahirciveen, Co. Kerry (3.6)
Coleraine, Co. Londonderry (4.3)	Irvinestown, Co.Tyrone (3.7)
Boyle, Co. Roscommon (4.4)	Thomastown, Co. Kilkenny (3.7)
Ballyshannon, Co. Donegal (4.5)	Belmullet, Co. Mayo (3.8)
Mitchelstown, Co. Cork (4.5)	Glenties, Co. Donegal (3.8)
Mohill, Co. Londonderry (4.5)	Mohill, Co. Londonderry (3.9)
Tuam, Co. Galway (4.5)	Oughterard, Co. Galway (3.9)
Castlederg, Co. Tyrone (4.7)	Tobercurry, Co. Sligo (3.9)
Drogheda, Co. Louth (4.8)	Castlereagh, Co. Roscommon (4)
Newry, Co. Armagh (4.8)	Cootehill, Co. Cavan (4)

Table A8b *Superintendent Registrars' districts in which sickness per 1,000 population was highest (top 15 from highest down) on nights Census was taken, 1891 and 1911*

1891	1911
Ballyvaughan, Co. Clare (26.4)	Cork city (13)
Dublin South (14.7)	Lisburn, Co. Antrim (12.7)
Corofin, Co. Clare (14.4)	Croom, Co. Limerick (11.4)
Tulla, Co. Clare (14.1)	Kilmacthomas, Co. Waterford (11.3)
Limerick city (13.6)	Ballyvaughan, Co. Clare (11.2)
Clonmel, Co. Tipperary (13.5)	Limerick city (10.9)
Ennis, Co. Clare (12.3)	Naas, Co. Kildare (10.5)
Kilkenny city (12.3)	Dublin South (10.4)
Kildysart, Co. Clare (12.2)	Dublin North (10.2)
Cork city (11.9)	Clonmel, Co. Tipperary (8.9)
Naas, Co. Kildare (11.8)	Dungarvan, Co. Waterford (8.6)
Kilmacthomas, Co. Waterford (11.5)	Kells, Co. Meath (8.6)
Ennistymon, Co. Clare (11.3)	Dingle, Co. Kerry (8.2)
Dingle, Co. Kerry (10.8)	Belfast (8)
Borrisokane, Co. Tipperary (10.6)	Carlow town (8)

Table A9a *Blind people per head of the population in Ireland by province, 1861, 1891 and 1911*

	1861	*1891*	*1911*
Leinster	1 in 870	1 in 1067	1 in 1097
Munster	1 in 590	1 in 588	1 in 741
Ulster	1 in 921	1 in 1112	1 in 1813
Connacht	1 in 1077	1 in 1093	1 in 1212

Note: People in institutions were assigned their counties of origin for Census purposes.

Source: *Census of Ireland*, 1861, 1891, and 1911.

Table A9b *Percentage of blind per 10,000 of population by province, 1891 only*

	1891
IRELAND	11.1
Leinster	9.4
Munster	17
Ulster	9
Connacht	9.1

Source: *Census of Ireland*, 1891, General report, diagram 9, p. 104.

Table A10 *Proportion of vagrancy (excluding prostitution) prosecutions to total non-indictable offences determined summary (i.e. petty crimes in police courts) 1866–1914 (actual numbers for selected years)*

	IRELAND	Leinster	Munster	Ulster	Connacht
1866	.77 (1,835)	1.05 (905)	.7 (523)	.5 (304)	.4 (103)
1867	.86	1.5	.7	.37	.32
1868	.87	1.5	.5	.5	.34
1869	.67	.79	.5	.55	.35
1870	.88	1.3	.7	.52	.35
1871	.68	1	.67	.47	.64
1872	.86	1.3	.87	.82	.38
1873	.7	1.2	.6	.7	.4
1874	.79	1	.8	.57	.46
1875	1.1	1.4	1	.94	1
1876	.9	1.2	.8	.79	.66
1877	.8 (2,383)	1 (1,015)	.8 (589)	.7 (591)	.5 (188)
1878	.99	1.3	.97	.77	.62
1879	1.3	1.6	1.3	.97	1
1880	1.3	1.7	1.1	.95	1.2
1881	1.3	1.6	1.1	1.3	.7
1882	1.4	1.7	1.3	1.5	1.1
1883	1.1 (2,648)	1.7 (1,362)	.7 (469)	1 (572)	.8 (245)
1884	1.2	1.8	.76	1.1	.5
1885	1.3	1.9	.9	1.2	.9
1886	1.7	2.4	1.1	1	1.4
1887	1.6	2.3	1.1	1.3	.9
1888	1.6	2.2	1.3	1.3	1
1889	1.78	2.3	1.5	1.3	1.7
1890	1.48	1.9	1	1	.8
1891	1.4	1.8	1	1.4	.75
1892	1.4	1.9	.86	1.6	.86
1893	1.5 (3,399)	2 (1,604)	1 (632)	1.6 (933)	.9 (230)
1894	1.6	2.2	.97	1.69	.78
1895	1.3	2.1	.9	1.2	.7
1896	1.48	2.3	.9	1.3	.88
1897	1.3 (3,042)	1.8 (1477)	1.1 (689)	1.1 (718)	.5 (158)
1898	1.2	1.9	.87	1.1	.49
1899	1.1	1.6	.75	1.2	.49
1900	1.2	1.9	.8	1.1	.4
1901	1.4	2.2	.9	1.1	.74
1902	1.3	2	.88	1.1	.6
1903	1.4 (3,829)	2.3 (1,446)	.8 (450)	1.4 (771)	.7 (162)

1904	1.7	2.6	1.1	1.7	.6
1905	1.79	2.7	1.3	1.6	.6
1906	1.7	2.7	1.3	1.5	.57
1907	1.6	2.6	1	1.4	.69
1908	1.5	2.5	.97	1.4	.4
1909	1.5 (3,164)	2.1 (1,391)	1.1 (631)	1.8 (999)	.5 (143)
1910	1.5	2.3	.92	1.8	.48
1911	1.4	2.2	.93	1.6	.34
1912	1.6	2.3	1.1	1.8	.45
1913	1.4	2	.9	1.7	.4
1914	1.5	2	.9	1.8	.5

Source: Judicial Statistics: persons proceeded against for offences determined summarily, 1866–1914.

Table A11 *Admissions of night-lodgers (i.e. very short-stay, non-Poor Law Union residents) to Irish workhouses: annual total of admissions for the first week of every month, every ten years from 1870–71 to 1910–11*

	Men	Women	Total
1870–71	11,610	3,222	14,832
1880–81	31,237	7,822	39,059
1890–91	27,261	7,057	34,318
1900–1	30,115	8,146	38,261
1910–11	49,595	10,800	60,395

Note: These figures refer to 'bed-nights': the same person could be counted numerous times.

Bibliography

MS sources and Parliamentary Papers

Irish Folklore Commission MSS, microfilm at James Hardiman Library, NUI, Galway.

Committal registers, prisons Clonmel, Galway, Cork, Castlebar, Carrick-on-Shannon, Athy, National Archives, Dublin.

Census MSS, 1901, National Archives, Dublin.

Thurles Union Indoor Relief Register 1849-1924, Thurles Library, Co. Tipperary.

Census of Ireland, 1851–1911, General reports and county books: occupational tables, tables relating to institutions, marriage, farm size.

Reports and Communications on Vagrancy 1847–8 (987), Vol. 53.

Reports of Inspector-Generals of State Prisons in Ireland, 1854–1914.

Reports of inspectors of reformatory and industrial schools in Ireland, 1858–1900.

Annual Reports of Registrar-General of Births, Marriages and Deaths, 1865–1920.

Judicial Statistics (Ireland), 1866–1914.

Correspondence with regard to epidemic of smallpox at Athenry 1875 (422), Vol. 60.

Return of infants born in Irish workhouses and attempted to be reared there 1872–4 (1878–79) (245), Vol. 61.

Reports from Poor Law Inspectors in Ireland in pursuance of instructions dated 9th May 1872 ... obtaining information on the subject of labourers' dwellings in that country 1873 (1873) [c.764], Vol. 22.

Report of the commissioners for National Education 1884 (1884–85) [c.4458], Vol. 24.

Report of the Intermediate Education Board for Ireland 1884 (1884–85) [c.4425], Vol. 24.

Report on migratory Irish agricultural labourers 1884–5 (1885) [c.4601], Vol. 85.

Special report on alleged increasing prevalence of lunacy in Ireland 1894 (1894) [c.7331], Vol. 43.
Report on migratory Irish agricultural labourers 1899 (1899) [c.9490], Vol. 106.
Return of names of Unions in which a third meal is not allowed daily to healthy inmates ... (1867–68) (322), Vol. 61, Reports and correspondence.
Report of the Special Commission on Vagrancy (1906) [cd.2852, 2891], Vol. 103 (Appendix 14 refers to Ireland).
Royal Commission on the Care and Control of the Feebleminded (1908) [cd 4215–21], Vols 1–7.

Secondary works

Akenson, D. H. *The Irish Education Experiment* (London 1970).
—— *The Irish Diaspora: a primer* (Belfast 1996).
Atkinson, S. *Mary Aikenhead, Her Life, Her Work, Her Friends* (Dublin 1878).
Barnes, J. *Irish Industrial Schools 1868–1908* (Dublin 1989).
Beckett, J. C. et al. (eds) *Belfast: the making of the city 1800–1914* (Belfast 1983).
—— and R. D. Glasscock (eds) *Belfast: the origins and growth of an industrial city* (London 1967).
Ballard, Linda M. *Forgetting Frolic: marriage traditions in Ireland* (Belfast 1998).
Barber, S. 'Irish migrant agricultural labourers in nineteenth-century Lincolnshire', *Saothar*, Vol. 8 (1982), pp. 10–23.
Barrington, R. *Health, Medicine and Politics in Ireland 1900–1970* (Dublin 1987).
Beale, J. *Women in Ireland: voices of change* (London 1986).
Beckett, J. C. et al. (eds) *Belfast: the making of the city* (Belfast 1983).
Bhreatnach, A. *Becoming Conspicuous: Irish travellers, society and the State* (Dublin 2006.)
Bielenberg, A. *Cork's Industrial Revolution 1780–1870: development or decline?* (Cork 1991).
Bock, G. & Thane, P. (eds) *Maternity and Gender Policies: women and the rise of European welfare states* (London 1991).
Bolger, P. (ed.) *And See Her Beauty Shining There: the story of the Irish countrywomen* (Dublin 1986).
Bourke, A. *The Burning of Bridget Cleary: a true story* (London 1999).
—— *Maeve Brennan: homesick at the New Yorker – an Irish writer in exile* (New York 2004).

Bourke, J. *Husbandry to Housewifery: women, housework and economic change 1890–1914* (Oxford 1993).

—— 'The health caravan: domestic education and female labor in rural Ireland', *Eire–Ireland*, Vol. 24, No. 4 (1989), pp. 21–38.

Bowen, D. *The Protestant Crusade in Ireland 1800–1870* (Dublin 1978).

Boyle, E. 'Linenopolis: the rise of the textile industry', in Beckett et al. (eds), *Belfast: the making of the city*, pp. 41–56.

Boyle, John W. 'A marginal figure: the Irish rural labourer', in Clark and Donnelly (eds), *Irish Peasants*, pp. 311–37.

Bradley, A. and Valiulis, M. (eds) *Gender and Sexuality in Modern Ireland* (Massachusetts 1997).

Bradley, D. *Farm Labourers: Irish struggle 1900–1976* (Belfast 1988).

Breathnach, C. *The Congested Districts Board of Ireland 1891–1923* (Dublin 2005).

Breathnach, E. 'Charting new waters: women's experience in higher education 1879–1908', in Cullen (ed.), *Girls Don't Do Honours*, pp. 55–78.

Breen, R. 'Farm servanthood in Ireland 1900–1940', *Economic History Review*, Vol. 36 (1983), pp. 87–102.

Brown, T. *Ireland: a social and cultural history 1922–1985* (London 1985 [1981]).

Browne, A. (ed.) *Masters, Midwives and Ladies-in-waiting: the Rotunda Hospital, Dublin 1745–1995* (Dublin 1995).

Brunton, D. 'The problems of implementation: the failures and success of public vaccination against smallpox in Ireland 1840–1873', in Jones and Malcolm (eds), *Medicine, Disease and the State*, pp. 138–57.

Bulfin, W. *Rambles in Eirinn* (Dublin 1907).

Burke, H. *The People and the Poor Law in Nineteenth-Century Ireland* (Dublin 1987).

C. J. M. 'The intermarriage of relatives and its consequences', *Irish Ecclesiastical Record*, Vol. 11 (February 1890), pp. 97–108.

Butler, M. *The Ring of Day* (London 1906).

Cameron, Charles A. *A Manual of Hygiene, Public and Private, and Compendium of Sanitary Laws* (Dublin 1874).

Campbell, J. 'The representation of everyday life in Irish painting of the nineteenth century: the European context', in Murray (ed.), *Whipping the Herring*, pp. 24–33.

Candon, G. *Headford 1840–1922* (Maynooth 2004).

Carbery, M. *The Farm by Lough Gur* (London 1937, Cork 1973).

Carey, T. *Mountjoy: the story of a prison* (Cork 2000).

Carroll, Mother A. *Leaves from the Annals of the Sisters of Mercy* (New York 1888).

Central Statistics Office *Farming Since the Famine: Irish farming statistics 1847–1996* (Cork 1997).

Clancy, M. 'The western outpost: local government and women's suffrage in Co. Galway 1898–1918', in Gillespie and Moran (eds), *Galway: history and society*, pp. 557–88.

Clark, S. *Social Origins of the Irish Land War* (Princeton, NJ 1979).

—— and Donnelly, J. S. Jr (eds) *Irish Peasants: violence and political unrest 1780–1914* (Manchester 1983).

Clarke, K. *Revolutionary Woman: autobiography of Kathleen Clarke 1878–1972*, ed. Helen Litton (Dublin 1991).

Clarkson, L. and Crawford, E. M. *Feast and Famine: a history of food and nutrition in Ireland 1500–1920* (Oxford 2001).

Clear, C. *Nuns in Nineteenth-Century Ireland* (Dublin 1987).

—— 'Homelessness, crime and poverty in Galway 1850–1914', *Journal of the Galway Archeological and Historical Society*, Vol. 50 (1998), pp. 117–34.

—— 'My mother taught me how to pray: the nine Murphys of Newmarket-on-Fergus', *The Other Clare*, Vol. 19 (1995), pp. 64–8.

—— *Women of the House: women's household work in Ireland 1921–1961* (Dublin 2000).

Clonown Community Centre *Clonown: the history, traditions and culture of a south Roscommon community* (Athlone 1989).

Coldrey, B. *Faith and Fatherland: the Christian Brothers 1838–1921* (London 1988).

Collins, B. 'The Edwardian city', in Beckett et al. (eds), *Belfast: the making of the city*, pp. 167–81.

Colum, M. *Life and the Dream* (New York 1928).

Conley, C. A. 'No pedestals: women and violence in late nineteenth-century Ireland', *Journal of Social History*, Vol. 28, No. 4 (summer 1995), pp. 801–18.

—— *Melancholy Accidents: the meaning of violence in post-Famine Ireland* (Lenham 1999).

Connolly, S. J. 'Illegitimacy and pre-nuptial pregnancy in Ireland before 1864', *Journal of the Irish Economic and Social History Society (IESH)*, Vol. 6 (1979), pp. 5–23.

—— 'The moving statue and the turtle dove: approaches to the history of Irish religion', *IESH*, Vol. 31 (2004), pp. 1–22.

Connell, K. H. *Irish Peasant Society: four historical essays* (Oxford 1968, Dublin 1996)

Conry, Michael J. *Dancing the Culm: burning culm as a domestic and industrial fuel in Ireland* (Carlow 2001).

Coolahan, J. *Irish Education: its history and structure* (Dublin 1982).

Corbin, A. *Women for Hire: prostitution and sexuality in France after 1850* (Cambridge, MA 1990).

Corkery, D. *The Hidden Ireland: a study of Gaelic Munster in the eighteenth century* (Dublin 1925).

Cosgrove, A. (ed.) *Marriage in Ireland* (Dublin 1985).

Coughlan, B. *Achill Island Tattie-Hokers in Scotland and the Kirkintilloch Tragedy 1937* (Maynooth 2006).

Court, Artelia, *Puck of the Droms: the lives and literature of the Irish tinkers* (Berkeley, CA 1985).

Cowley, U. *The Men Who Built Britain: a history of the Irish navvy* (Dublin 2001).

Crawford, E. M. 'Typhus in nineteenth-century Ireland', in Jones and Malcolm (eds), *Medicine, Disease and the State in Ireland*, pp. 121–37.

Cronin, Denis A. et al. (eds) *Irish Fairs and Markets: studies in local history* (Dublin 2001).

Cronin, M. 'Work and workers in Cork city and county', in O'Flanagan and Buttimer (eds), *Cork: history and society*, pp. 721–58.

—— *Country, Class or Craft? The politicisation of the skilled artisan in nineteenth-century Cork* (Cork 1994).

Cross, E. *The Tailor and Ansty* (London 1942).

Crossman, V. *Local Government in Nineteenth-Century Ireland* (Belfast 1994).

Crotty, R. D. *Irish Agricultural Production: volume and structure* (Cork 1966).

Cullen, B. *Thomas L. Synnott: the career of a Dublin Catholic 1830–1870* (Maynooth 1997).

Cullen, L. *Life in Ireland* (Dublin 1968).

—— (ed.) *The Formation of the Irish Economy* (Cork 1968).

—— *An Economic History of Ireland Since 1660* (London 1972).

Cullen, M. (ed.) *Girls Don't Do Honours: Irish women in education in the nineteenth and twentieth centuries* (Dublin 1987).

Cunningham, J. *Labour in the West of Ireland: working life and struggle, 1890–1914* (Belfast 1995).

—— *St Jarlath's College, Tuam 1800–2000* (Tuam 1999).

—— *A Town Tormented by the Sea: Galway 1790–1914* (Dublin 2004).

Curtin, G. *The Women of Galway Jail: female criminality in nineteenth-century Ireland* (Galway 2001).

Czira, S. G. *The Years Flew By: recollections of Madame Sidney Gifford Czira*, ed. Alan Hayes (Dublin 1974, Galway 2000).

Daly, Mary E. 'Late nineteenth- and early twentieth-century Dublin', in Harkness and O'Dowd (eds), *Town in Ireland*, pp. 221–52.

—— *Social and Economic History of Ireland since 1800* (Dublin 1981).

—— Hearn, M. and Pearson, P. *Dublin's Victorian Houses* (Dublin 1998).

Danaher, K. *In Ireland Long Ago* (Cork 1964).

D'Arcy, F. 'Wages of labourers in the Dublin building industry', *Saothar: Journal of the Irish Labour History Society*, Vols 14 (1989), pp. 17–34, and 15 (1990), pp. 21–38.

De Cléir, S. 'Bhí Bród As Sin I gConaí: cruthaitheacht agus cultúr na mban in dtraidisiúin fheisteas Oileáin Arainn', *Béascna: Iris Céaloideasa agus Eitneolaíochta*, Vol. 1 (2002), pp. 85–100.

Delaney, T. (comp.) *Castlecomer, Co. Kilkenny Census 1901* (Baile Atha Cliath 2000).

Dillon, C. and Jefferies, H. (eds) *Tyrone: history and society* (Dublin 2000).

Diner, H. *Erin's Daughters in America: Irish immigrant women in the nineteenth century* (Baltimore 1983).

Doherty, L. 'The folklore of cattle diseases: a veterinary perspective', *Béaloideas: Journal of the Irish Folklore Society*, Vol. 69 (2001), pp. 41–75.

Donnelly, J. S. Jr *The Land and People of Nineteenth-century Cork* (London 1975).

—— 'The Irish agricultural depression 1859–64', *IESH*, Vol. 3 (1976), pp. 33–54.

Doran, J. S. *Turn Up The Lamp: tales of a Mourne childhood* (Belfast 1980).

Dunlevy, M. *Dress in Ireland* (Cork 1999).

Drudy, P. J. (ed.) *Irish Studies*, Vol. 2: *Land, politics and people* (Cambridge 1982).

Durcan, T. *A History of Irish Education Since 1800* (Bala, Wales 1971).

Dwork, D. *War Is Good for Babies and Young Children: a history of the infant and child welfare movement in England 1891–1918* (London 1987).

Evans, R. J. 'Prostitution, state and society in imperial Germany', *Past & Present*, Vol. 70 (1976), pp. 106–28.

Fahey, T., 'Nuns in the Catholic Church in Ireland in the nineteenth century', in Cullen (ed.), *Girls Don't Do Honours*, pp. 7–30.

Fallon, R. *A County Roscommon Wedding, 1892: the marriage of John Hughes and Mary Gavin* (Dublin 2004).

Farmar, T. *Holles Street 1894–1994: the National Maternity Hospital – a centenary history* (Dublin 1994).

—— *Patients, Potions and Physicians: a social history of medicine in Ireland* (Dublin 2004).

Fealy, Gerard M. (ed.) *Care to Remember: nursing and midwifery in Ireland* (Cork 2005).

Feehan, J. *Farming in Ireland: history, heritage and environment* (Dublin 2003).

Ferguson, K. *Lessons in Cookery and Housewifery: leabhairíní na seamróige* (Dublin 1900).

—— *Sickroom Cookery with Notes on Sick Nursing* (Athlone 1903).

Ferriter, D. *The Transformation of Ireland 1900–2000* (London 2004).

Finegan, J. *The Story of Monto: an account of Dublin's notorious red-light district* (Cork 1978).

Fingall, E. *Seventy Years' Young: memories of Elizabeth, Countess of Fingall* (Dublin 1992 [1937]).

Finnane, M. *Insanity and the Insane in Post-Famine Ireland* (London 1982).

Finnegan, F. *Do Penance or Perish: a study of Magdalen asylums in Ireland* (Kilkenny 2001, Oxford 2005).

Fitzgerald, S. *Mackerel and the Making of Baltimore, Co. Cork, 1879–1913* (Maynooth 1999).

Fitzpatrick, D. 'The disappearance of the Irish agricultural labourer', *IESH*, Vol. 7 (1980), pp. 66–92.

—— *Irish Emigration 1801–1921: studies in Irish economic and social history* (Dundalk 1984).

—— 'The modernisation of the Irish female', in O'Flanagan et al. (eds), *Rural Ireland 1600–1800*, pp. 162–80.

—— 'Divorce and separation in modern Irish history', *Past & Present*, No. 114 (1987), pp. 172–96.

—— *Oceans of Consolation: personal accounts of Irish migration to Australia* (Cork 1994).

Fitzpatrick, J. *Three Brass Balls: the story of the Irish pawnshop* (Cork 2001).

Flanders, J. *The Victorian House* (London 2003).

Fleming, D. 'Public attitudes to prostitution in eighteenth-century Ireland', *IESH*, Vol. 32 (2005), pp. 1–18.

Foley, P. 'The Carlow Workhouse', *Carloviana: Journal of the Old Carlow Society*, Vol. 47 (December 1999), pp. 7–13.

Fraser, M. *John Bull's Other Homes: state housing and British policy in Ireland 1883–1922* (Liverpool 1996).

French, P. *Prose, Poems and Parodies of Percy French (1854–1920)* (Dublin 1941), pp. 5–6.

Gailey, A. 'Changes in Irish rural housing 1600–1900', in O'Flanagan et al. (eds), *Rural Ireland 1600–1900*, pp. 86–103.

—— *Rural Houses of the North of Ireland* (Edinburgh 1984).

—— *Ireland and the Death of Kindness: the experience of Constructive Unionism 1885–1903* (Cork 1987).

Galway Labour History Group, *The Emigrant Experience* (Galway 1991).

Geary, Laurence M. *The Plan of Campaign* (Cork 1988).

—— '"The whole country was in motion": mendicancy and vagrancy in pre-Famine Ireland', in Hill and Lennon (eds), *Luxury and Austerity*, pp. 121–36.

—— *Medicine and Charity in Ireland 1718–1851* (Dublin 2004).

Gillespie, R. and Moran, G. (eds) *Galway: history and society* (Dublin 1996).

Gilligan, Jim, 'Murrays of Dunshaughlin 1896–1910', in Cronin et al. (eds), *Irish Fairs and Markets*, pp. 224–47.

Gillis, J. *A World of Their Own Making: myth and ritual in family life* (Oxford 1997).

Glassie, H. *Passing the Time in Ballymenone: culture and history of an Ulster community* (Indiana, IN 1982).

Gittins, D. *Madness in its Place: narratives of Severalls Hospital 1913–1997* (London 1998).

Goldstrom, J. M. *The Social Content of Education 1808–1870* (London 1972).

Gow, J. 'The Irish tinkers', *Ulster Folklife*, Vol. 17 (1971), pp. 76–89.

Gribbon, S. 'An Irish city: Belfast 1911', in Harkness and O'Dowd (eds), *The Town in Ireland*, pp. 204–20.

Green, E. R. R. 'Early industrial Belfast', in Beckett and Glasscock (eds), *Belfast*, pp. 78–87.

Grieff, M. '"Marching through the streets singing and shouting": industrial struggle and trade unionism among female linen workers in Belfast and Lurgan 1872–1910', *Saothar*, Vol. 22 (1997), pp. 29–46.

Griffin, B. 'The Irish police: love, sex and marriage in the nineteenth and early twentieth centuries', in Kelleher and Murphy (eds), *Gender Perspectives in Nineteenth-Century Ireland*, pp. 168–78.

Guinnane, T. *The Vanishing Irish: households, migration and the rural economy in Ireland 1850–1914* (Princeton, NJ 1997).

Hackett, W. 'The Irish *bacach*, or professional beggar, viewed archeologically', *Ulster Journal of Archeology*, Vol. 9 (1861–2), pp. 255–71.

Hamell, M. 'Something of Cloughjordan: looking back from 1987 to 1918–27', *Cloughjordan Heritage*, Vol. 2 (1987), pp. 28–33.

Hamill, J. 'Childcare arrangements within the Belfast linen community', in Whelan (ed.), *Women and Paid Work in Ireland*, pp. 120–32.

Handley, James E. *The Navvy in Scotland* (Cork 1970).

Harkness, D. and O'Dowd, M. (eds) *The Town in Ireland: historical studies, Volume 13* (Belfast 1981).

Harris, R. A. *The Search for Missing Friends: Irish immigrant advertisments placed in the Boston Pilot* (Boston 1989).

Healy, M. *For the Poor and for the Gentry* (Dublin 1989).

Healy, J. *Nineteen Acres* (Achill 1978).

Hearn, M. *Below Stairs: domestic service remembered, in Dublin and beyond, 1880–1922* (Dublin 1993).

Helleiner, J. *Irish Travellers: racism and the politics of culture* (Toronto 2000).

Henry, B. *Dublin Hanged* (Dublin 1994).

Hepburn, A. C. *A Past Apart: studies in the history of Catholic Belfast 1850–1950* (Belfast 1996).

Hill, J. and Lennon, C. (eds) *Luxury and Austerity: historical studies, Volume 21* (Dublin 1999).

Holloway, P. and Cradden, T. 'The Irish Trades Union Congress and working women 1894–1914', *Saothar*, Vol. 23 (1998), pp. 47–60.

Holmes, H. 'Organizing the Irish migratory potato workers: the efforts in the early twentieth century', *Rural History*, Vol. 11 (2001), pp. 207–29.

Holmes, J. and Urquhart, D. (eds) *Coming into the Light: the work, politics and religion of women in Ulster 1840–1940* (Belfast 1994).

Hoppen, K. T. *Ireland Since 1800: conflict and conformity* (London 1989).

Horgan, D. *The Victorian Visitor to Ireland: Irish tourism 1840–1910* (Cork 2002).

Hoy, S. 'The journey out: the recruitment and emigration of Irish religious women to the United States 1812–1914', *Journal of Women's History* (Indiana), Vol. 6, No. 4 and Vol. 7, No. 1 (winter–spring 1994–95), pp. 65–98.

—— and MacCurtain, Margaret (eds) *From Dublin to New Orleans: the journey of Nora and Alice to America 1889* (Dublin 1994).

Hufton, O. *The Poor of Eighteenth-Century France 1750–1789* (Oxford 1974).

—— *The Prospect Before Her: a history of women in Western Europe 1500–1800* (London 1995).

Hughes, T. Jones 'Landholding and settlement in Co.Tipperary in the nineteenth century', in Nolan and McGrath (eds), *Tipperary: history and society*, pp. 339–66.

—— 'Continuity and change in rural Wexford', in Whelan (ed.), *Wexford: history and society*, pp. 342–72.

Humphreys, A. *New Dubliners: urbanisation and the Irish family* (London 1966).

Hunt, T. *Portlaw, Co. Waterford 1825–1876: portrait of an industrial village* (Maynooth 2000).

Hyman, L. *Jews in Ireland: from earliest times to the year 1910* (Shannon 1972).

Hynes, C. 'District nursing in Ireland 1880–1939', M.Phil thesis, NUI, Galway, 1999.

Ignatieff, M. *A Just Measure of Pain: the penitentiary in the industrial revolution* (London 1978).

Irwin, F. *The Cookin' Woman: Irish country recipes* (Belfast 1948, 1986).

Jackson, M. *The Borderland of Imbecility: medicine, society and the fabrication of the feeble mind in late Victorian and Edwardian England* (Manchester 2000).

Jackson, S. 'Gender, crime and punishment in late nineteenth-century Ireland: Mayo and Galway examined', MA thesis, NUI, Galway, 1999.

Jacobs, D. 'Limerick clothing manufacturers and retailers', in Jacobs and Lee (eds), *Made in Limerick*, pp. 23–36.

—— and Lee, D. (eds) *Made in Limerick: history of industries, trade and commerce* (Limerick 2003).

Johnston, J. 'Society in the Clogher Valley c. 1750–1900', in Dillon and Jefferies (eds), *Tyrone: history and society*, pp. 543–65.

Jones, D. J. V. *Crime, Protest, Community and Police in Nineteenth-Century Britain* (London 1982).

Jones, David S. 'The cleavage between graziers and peasants in the land struggle', in Clark and Donnelly (eds), *Irish Peasants*, pp. 374–417.

Jones, G. *'Captain of All These Men of Death': the history of tubercolosis in nineteenth- and twentieth-century Ireland* (Amsterdam 2001).

—— and Malcolm, E. (eds) *Medicine, Disease and the State in Ireland 1650–1930* (Cork 1999).

Jones, E. 'Late Victorian Belfast', in Beckett and Glasscock (eds), *Belfast*, pp. 109–19.

Jordan, Thomas E. *Ireland and the Quality of Life 1841–1861* (New York and Lampeter 1997).

Joyce, N. with Farmar, A. *Traveller* (Dublin 1985).

Kearns, K. *Dublin Tenement Life: an oral history* (Dublin 1995).

Kelleher, M. and Murphy, J. (eds) *Gender Perspectives in Nineteenth-Century Ireland* (Dublin 1997).

Kelly, M. 'Down memory lane: the tea travellers', *Cathair na Mart: Journal of the Westport Historical Society*, Vol. 15 (1995), pp. 66–9.

Kelly, Patricia Sr 'From workhouse to hospital: the role of the Irish workhouse in medical relief to 1921', MA thesis, University College, Galway 1972.

Kennedy, L. 'Retail markets in rural Ireland at the end of the nineteenth century', *IESH*, Vol. 5 (1978), pp. 46–63.

—— and Ollerenshaw, P. (eds) *An Economic History of Ulster 1820–1939* (Manchester University Press 1985).

Kennedy, Robert E. *The Irish: emigration, marriage and fertility* (Berkeley 1973).

Keogh, D. *Jews in Twentieth-century Ireland* (Cork 1998).

Keogh, D., O'Shea, F. and Quinlan, C. (eds) *Ireland in the 1950s: the lost decade* (Cork 2004).

Kickham, Charles *Knocknagow, or the homes of Tipperary* (London 1870).

Kinealy, Christine 'The workhouse system in Co. Waterford 1838–1923', in Nolan and Power (eds), *Waterford: history and society*, pp. 541–78.

Kinmonth, Claudia *Irish Country Furniture 1700–1950* (Yale 1993).

Lacy, Brian *Siege City: the story of Derry and Londonderry* (Belfast 1990).

Lambe, Miriam 'At the cross: a shop in rural Ireland 1880–1911', in Cronin et al. (eds), *Irish Fairs and Markets*, pp. 206–23.

Lane, Fintan 'Music and violence in working-class Cork: the "band nuisance" 1879–82', *Saothar*, Vol. 24 (1999), pp. 17–31.

Lane, P. 'The organization of rural labourers 1870–1890', *Cork Historical and Archeological Society Journal*, Vol. 100 (1995), pp. 149–60.

Langan-Egan, M. *Galway women in the nineteenth century* (Dublin 1999).

Laverty, M. *Never No More: the story of a lost village* (London 1942).

—— *Kind Cooking* (Tralee 1946).

Leckey, J. 'The railway servants' strike in Cork 1898', *Saothar*, Vol. 2 (1975–76), pp. 39–44.

Lee, David 'The Munster Soviets and the fall of the house of Cleeve', in Jacobs and Lee (eds), *Limerick*, pp. 287–306.

Lee, J. J. 'The railways in the Irish economy', in Cullen (ed.), *The Formation of the Irish Economy*, pp. 77–88.

—— *The Modernisation of Irish Society 1848–1918* (Dublin 1973).

—— *Ireland 1912–1985: politics and society* (Cambridge 1989)

Levistone Cooney, D. A. 'Switzers of Grafton Street', *Dublin Historical Record*, Vol. 55, No. 2 (autumn 2002), pp. 154–6.

Lewis, J. *The Politics of Motherhood: child and maternal welfare in England 1900–1939* (London 1980).

Light, Alison 'The word made flesh', *History Workshop Journal*, Vol. 46 (autumn 1998), pp. 177–86.

Logan, John 'The dimensions of gender in nineteenth-century schooling', in Kelleher and Murphy (eds), *Gender Perspectives in Nineteenth-Century Ireland*, pp. 36–49.

Lohan, R. 'Women in Mountjoy Convict Female Prison 1858–63', in Whelan (ed.), *Women and Paid Work*, pp. 86–101.

Loudon, I. *Death in Childbirth: an international study of maternal care and maternal mortality 1800–1950* (Oxford 1992).

Lowe, W. J. 'Irish Constabulary officers 1837–1922: profile of a professional elite', *IESH*, Vol. 32 (2005), pp. 19–46.

Luddy, M. *Women and Philanthropy in Nineteenth-Century Ireland* (Cambridge 1995).

—— 'Nuns as workhouse nurses 1861–1898', in Malcolm and Jones (eds), *Medicine, Disease and the State in Ireland*, pp. 102–13.

—— 'Prostitution and rescue work in nineteenth-century Ireland', in Luddy and Murphy (eds), *Women Surviving*, pp. 51–84.

Luddy, M. and Murphy, C. (eds) *Women Surviving: studies in Irish women's history in the nineteenth and twentieth centuries* (Dublin 1990).

Madden, Gerard 'Upstairs, downstairs: some East Clare servants and farm workers 1869–1940', *Sliabh Aughty: East Clare Heritage*, No. 9 (2000), pp. 17–21.

McCarthy, A. 'Personal letters and the organization of Irish migration to and from New Zealand 1848–1925', *IHS*, Vol. 33, No. 131 (2000), pp. 297–319.

McCarthy, M. J. F. *Priests and People in Ireland* (London 1902).

McCrum, E. *Fabric and Form: Irish fashion since 1950* (Ulster 1996).

McDowell, Florence M. *Other Days Around Me* (Belfast 1966).

MacEinrí, S. 'Ceant agus Saol na dTincéirí', *Béaloideas*, Vol. 9 (1939), pp. 219–39.

McElligott, T. J. *Secondary Education in Ireland 1870–1921* (Dublin 1981).

McEvoy, Dan 'My years in the monster house', *Old Kilkenny Review*, No. 49 (1997), pp. 131–8.

McGay, B. 'Emigrant's letter 19th March 1899', *The Glynns: Journal of the Glens of Antrim Historical Society*, Vol. 25 (1997).

McGill, P. *Children of the Dead End* (London 1985 edition).

McGlinchey, C. *The Last of the Name*, ed. Brian Friel (Belfast 1986).

McGoff-McCann, Michelle *Melancholy Madness: a coroner's casebook* (Cork 2003).

MacGréine, P. 'Irish "tinkers" or "travellers"', *Béaloideas*, Vol. 3 (1931–32), pp. 170–86.

McKay, E. 'The housing of the rural labourer 1883–1916', *Saothar*, Vol. 17 (1992), pp. 27–39.

McLoughlin, D. 'Workhouses and Irish female paupers 1840–1870', in Luddy and Murphy (eds), *Women Surviving*, pp. 117–47.

—— 'Superfluous and unwanted deadweight: the emigration of Irish pauper women', in O'Sullivan (ed.), *Irish Women, Irish Migration*, pp. 66–88.

McNamara, S. *Those Intrepid United Irishwomen: pioneers of the Irish Countrywomen's Association* (Parteen 1995).

Maher, S. *The Road to God Knows Where* (Dublin 1972).

Mahon, B. *Land of Milk and Honey: the story of Irish traditional food and drink* (Cork 1991).

Mahood, L. *The Magdalenes: prostitution in the nineteenth century* (London 1990).

Malcolm, E. 'Troops of largely diseased women: VD, the Contagious Diseases Acts and moral policing in late nineteenth-century Ireland', *IESH*, Vol. 26 (1999), pp. 1–14.

—— 'The House of Strident Shadows: the asylum, the family and emigration in post-Famine rural Ireland', in Jones and Malcolm (eds), *Medicine, Disease and the State in Ireland*, pp. 177–93.

Marnane, D. 'Tipperary town 100 years ago: the evidence of the 1901 Census', *Tipperary Historical Journal* (2001), pp. 1–26.

Matson, L. *Méiní: the Blasket Nurse* (Cork 1996).

Melling, J. and Forsythe, W. (eds) *Insanity, Institutions and Society 1800–1914: a social history of madness in comparative perspective* (London 1999).

Messenger, Betty *Picking Up the Linen Threads* (Belfast 1980).

Miller, Kerby A. *Emigrants and Exiles: Ireland and the Irish exodus to North America* (Oxford 1985).

Moore, G. *A Drama in Muslin* (London 1886).

—— *Parnell and His Island* (London 1887).

Moran, G. 'A passage to Britain: seasonal migration and social change in the west of Ireland 1870–1890', *Saothar*, Vol. 13 (1987), pp. 22–31.

—— *Sending Out Ireland's Poor: assisted emigration to North America in the nineteenth century* (Dublin 2004).

Murphy, M. 'The Fionnuala factor: Irish sibling emigration at the turn of the century', in Bradley and Valiulis (eds), *Gender and Sexuality in Modern Ireland*, pp. 85–101.

Murnane, B. 'The recreation of the urban historical landscape: Mountjoy Ward, Dublin, c.1901', in Smyth et al. (eds), *Common Ground*, pp. 189–207.

Murphy, G. 'Bacaigh Baile Mhúirne', *Eigse*, Vol. 3 (1941), pp. 101–2.

Murphy, M. 'The economic and social structure of nineteenth-century Cork', in Harkness and O'Dowd (eds), *The Town in Ireland*, pp. 125–54.

Murray, P. 'A militant among the Magdalens?', *Saothar*, Vol. 20 (1995), pp. 41–54.

Murray, Peter (ed.) *Whipping the Herring: survival and celebration in nineteenth-century Irish art* (Cork 2006).

Murray, James P. *Galway: a medico-social history* (Galway 1993).

National Co-operative Council *Plunkett: a symposium on co-operation* (Dublin 1954).

Neill, M. 'Homeworkers in Ulster 1850–1911', in Holmes and Urquhart (eds), *Coming into the Light*, pp. 2–32.

Ní Chinnéide, M. *Maire de Buitléir: bean athbheochana* (Baile Atha Cliath 1993).

Ní Ghuithín, M. *Bean an Oileáin* (Baile Atha Cliath 1985).

Nolan, F. 'Aspects of social life in County Wexford in 1885', *Journal of the Wexford Historical Society*, No. 9 (1983–84), pp. 55–65 .

Nolan, J. *Ourselves Alone: women's emigration from Ireland 1885–1920* (Kentucky 1989).

Nolan, W. and McGrath, T. (eds) *Tipperary: history and society* (Dublin 1985).

Nolan, W. and Power, T. (eds) *Waterford: history and society* (Dublin 1992).

Nowlan, Kevin B. *Travel and Transport in Ireland* (Dublin 1983).

O Baoill, M. and Og, S. *Ceolta Gael* (Cork 1975).

O'Beirne, M. *Mister: a Dublin childhood* (Belfast 1979).

O'Brien, G. 'The New Poor Law in pre-Famine Ireland: a case history', *IESH*, Vol. 12 (1985), pp. 33–49.

O'Brien, K. *The Land of Spices* (London 1941).

—— *Presentation Parlour* (London 1963).

O'Brien, Joseph V. *Dear, Dirty Dublin: a city in distress 1899–1914* (Berkeley, CA 1982).

O Catháin, S. *Irish Life and Lore* (Cork 1982).

O Cathaoir, E. 'The Poor Law in Co. Wicklow', in Hannigan and Nolan (eds), *Wicklow – History and Society: interdisciplinary essays on the history of an Irish county* (Dublin 1994), pp. 503–80.

O'Connell, T. J. *100 Years of Progress: a history of the INTO 1868–1968* (Dublin 1969).

O'Connor, Anne V. 'The revolution in girls' secondary education in Ireland 1860–1910', in Cullen (ed.), *Girls Don't Do Honours*, pp. 31–54.

—— and Parkes, S. (eds) *Gladly Learn and Gladly Teach: Alexandra College and School, Dublin 1866–1966* (Dublin 1983).

O'Connor, E. *A Labour History of Ireland 1824–1960* (Dublin 1992).

O Cróinín, S. *Seanchas Amhlaoibh Uí Luínse* (Baile Atha Cliath 1980).

O Dálaigh, B. (ed.) *The Stranger's Gaze: travels in Co. Clare 1534–1950* (Ennis 1998).

O Domhnaill, E. *Scéal Hiúdaí Sheáin* (Baile Atha Cliath 1940).

O'Donnell, L. *The Days of the Servant Boy* (Cork 1997).

O'Dowd, A. *Spalpeens and Tattie Hokers: the history and folklore of the Irish migratory agricultural worker in Ireland and Britain* (Dublin 1991).

O'Farrell, P. *The Irish in Australia* (Sydney 1986).

O'Flanagan, P. and Buttimer, C. (eds) *Cork: history and society* (Dublin 1993).

—— et al. (eds) *Rural Ireland 1600–1900: modernisation and change* (Cork 1987).

O Gaoithín, M. *Is Trua ná Fannan an Oige* (Baile Atha Cliath 1953).

O Glaisne, R. *Modhaigh: scéal Pobail, scéal Eaglaise* (Baile Atha Cliath 1998).

O Gráda, C. *Ireland: a new economic history 1780–1939* (Oxford 1994).

—— 'Seasonal migration and post-Famine adjustment in the West of Ireland', *Studia Hibernica*, Vol. 13 (1973), pp. 48–76.

—— 'Of bullocks and men: agricultural change after the Famine', in C. O Gráda, *Ireland Before and After the Famine* (Manchester 1988), pp. 128–52.

O Guithín, M. *Bean an Oileáin* (Baile Atha Cliath 1985).

O hEidhin, M. *Cas Amhrán 1* (Inreabhán 1975).

Okely, J. *Traveller–Gypsies* (Cambridge 1983).

O Laoghaire, P. *Mo Scéal Féin* (Baile Atha Cliath 1900), trans. S. O'Sullivan as *My Own Story* (Dublin 1973).

O'Mahony, C. and Thompson, V. *Poverty to Promise: the Monteagle emigrants 1838–1858* (Darlinghurst, NSW 1994).

O Murchadha, C. 'Paphian nymphs and worshippers of the Idalian goddess: prostitution in Ennis in the mid-nineteenth century', *The Other Clare*, Vol. 27 (2000), pp. 32–6.

O Muirithe, D. and Nuttall, D. (eds) *Folklore of County Wexford* (Dublin 1999).

O'Neill, Timothy P. 'Tools and things: machinery on Irish farms 1700–1981', in Trefor Owen (ed.), *From Corrib to Cultra: folklife essays in honour of Alan Gailey*, pp. 101–14.

O Riain, D. and O Cinnéide, S. *Stair agus Béaloideas Páirtín agus Míliuc/Meelick and Parteen History and folklore* (Limerick 1994).

O'Sullivan, P. (ed.) *Irish Women and Irish Migration* (Leicester 1995).

O'Toole, E. *Whist for Your Life, That's Treason: recollections of a long life* (Dublin 2003).

O Tuathaigh, G. 'The historical pattern of Irish emigration: some labour aspects', in Galway Labour History Group, *The Emigrant Experience*, pp. 9–28.

Owen, T. (ed.) *From Corrib to Cultra: folklife essays in honour of Alan Gailey* (Belfast 2000).

Phelan, M. and Cantwell, A. 'Katie O'Neill, weaver and millworker', *Old Kilkenny Review*, Vol. 4, No. 4 (1992), pp. 1057–64.

Prendergast, F. 'The decline of traditional Limerick industries', in Lee and Jacobs (eds), *Made in Limerick*, pp. 2–22.

Pauline, Mary, Sr *God Wills It: the centenary story of the Sisters of St Louis* (Dublin 1959).

Pyle, H. (ed.) *The Sligo–Leitrim World of Kate Cullen* (1832–1913) (Dublin 1997).

Quane, M. 'Primary education in Kerry one hundred years ago', *Journal of the Kerry Archeological and Historical Society*, No. 5 (1972), pp. 133–59.

Raftery, D. 'The nineteenth-century governess: image and reality', in Whelan (ed.), *Women and Paid Work*, pp. 57–68.

Redington, J. *Economic Cookery Book* (Dublin 1905).

Rees, J. *Surplus People: the Fitzwilliam clearances 1847–1856* (Cork 2000).

Reynolds, J. *Grangegorman: psychiatric care in Dublin since 1815* (Dublin 1992).

Robins, J. *The Lost Children: a study of charity children in Ireland 1700–1900* (Dublin 1980).

—— *Fools and Mad: a history of the insane in Ireland* (Dublin 1986).

—— *The Miasma: epidemic and panic in nineteenth-century Ireland* (Dublin 1995).

—— *From Reflection to Integration: a centenary of service by the Daughters of Charity to Persons with a Mental Handicap* (Dublin 1992).

—— *Nursing and Midwifery in Ireland in the Twentieth Century* (Dublin 2000).

Rose, L. *Rogues and Vagabonds: the vagrancy underworld in England 1815–1945* (London 1988).

Rossiter, N. 'The life of a Wexford gentleman 100 years ago: based on the diaries of Edward Solly-Flood, J.P.', *Journal of the Wexford Historical Society*, Vol. 13 (1990–91), pp. 117–29.

Rowlands, D. and McGrath, W. 'The Dingle train in the life and lore of Corkaguiney', *Journal of the Kerry Archeological and Historical Society*, No. 11 (1978), pp. 85–133.

Ryan, M. *Fenian Memories* (Dublin 1946).

Rynne, S. *Fr John Hayes, Founder of Muintir na Tire* (Dublin 1960).

Sandford, J. (ed.) *Mary Carbery's West Cork Journal 1898–1901* (Dublin 1998)

Sarti, R. *Europe at Home 1500–1800* (Yale, CT 2002).

Sayers, P. *Peig* (Baile Atha Cliath 1936).

Scanlan, P. *The Irish Nurse: a study of nursing in Ireland* (Leitrim 1991).

Schrier, A. *Ireland and the American Emigration 1850–1900* (Minneapolis 1958).

Segalen, M. *Love and Power in the Peasant Family* (London 1991).

Sexton, R. *A Little History of Irish Food* (Dublin 1998).

Shanklin, E. '"Sure and what did we ever do but knit?" Women's lives and work in south-west Donegal', *Donegal Annual*, Vol. 40 (1988), pp. 40–54.

Simon Community of Ireland, *Closing Down the County Homes* (Dublin 1980).

Simonton, D. *A History of European Women's Work 1700 to the Present* (London 1998).

Sheehan, P. A. *My New Curate* (USA 1893).

—— *Glenanaar* (London 1916).

Smith, F. B. *The People's Health 1830–1910* (Canberra 1979, London 1990).

Smithson, Annie M. P. *Myself – and Others* (Dublin 1944).

Smyth, W., Whelan, K. and Jones Hughes, T. (eds) *Common Ground: essays on the historical geography of Ireland* (Cork 1988).

Snell, K. *Annals of the Labouring Poor* (Cambridge 1985).

Somerville-Large, P. *The Irish Country House: a social history* (London 1995).

Swanton, D. L. *Emerging from the Shadow: the lives of Sarah Anne Lawrenson and Lucy Olive Kingston based on personal diaries 1883–1969* (Dublin 1994).

Sweeney, F. *The Murder of Connell Boyle, Co. Donegal 1898* (Dublin 2002).

Sweetnam, R. 'The Development of the Port', in Beckett et al. (eds), *Belfast: the making of the city*, pp. 57–60.

Swift, R. and Gilley, S. (eds) *The Irish in Britain 1815–1939* (London 1989).

Taylor, L. *The Study of Dress History* (Manchester 2002).

Turner, M. *After the Famine: Irish Agriculture 1850–1914* (Cambridge 1996).

University of Limerick, *Historical Resources for Research into the Social, Economic and Cultural History of the Irish Travelling Community* (Limerick 2005).

Uttley, A. *The Country Child* (London 1931, 1963).

Vaughan, W. E. *Landlord and Tenant in Ireland 1850–1914* (Dublin 1984).

—— *Sin, Sheep and Scotsmen: John George Adair and the Derryveagh evictions 1861* (Belfast 1983).

—— and Fitzpatrick, A. J. *Irish Historical Statistics: population 1921–1971* (Dublin 1978).

Walkowitz, J. *Prostitution and Victorian Society: women, class and the state* (Cambridge 1980).

Walsh, O. 'The designs of providence: race, religion and Irish insanity', in Melling and Forsythe (eds), *Insanity*, pp. 323–41.

—— '"Tales from the big house': the Connacht District Lunatic Asylum in the late nineteenth century', *History Ireland*, Vol. 13, No. 6 (2005), pp. 21–6.

Walsh, T. J. *Nano Nagle and the Presentation Sisters* (Dublin 1959).

Waters, D. and Williams, T. 'Taghmon village: the 1901 Census', *Journal of the Taghmon Historical Society*, 4 (2001), pp. 150–94.

Ward, Inspector J. *Instruction Book for the Dublin Metropolitan Police* (Dublin 1865).

Watson, M. 'The role of the horse on Irish farms', in Owen (ed.), *From Corrib to Cultra: folklife essays in honour of Alan Gailey*, pp. 122–35.

Whelan, B. (ed.) *Women and Paid Work in Ireland 1500–1930* (Dublin 2000).

Whelan, K. (ed.) *Wexford: history and society* (Dublin 1987).

Wickham, A, '"She must be content to be their servant as well as their teacher": the early years of district nursing in Ireland', in Fealy (ed.), *Care to Remember: nursing and midwifery in Ireland*, pp. 102–37.

White, A. *Frost in May* (London 1978 [1933]).

Index

Note: historians are not listed in the index; however, contemporary writers or those whose autobiographies, memoirs or memories are used as evidence are listed. The four provinces of Ireland – Leinster, Munster, Ulster and Connacht – are not listed separately but are listed through other entries.

There is no specific heading for women: references to females and males can be found in sub-headings under work, education, marriage, agriculture, poverty and so on.

CPSIA information can be obtained at www.ICGtesting.com
Printed in the USA
LVOW081116100812

293710LV00003B/8/P